BABY'S FIRST PICTURE
ULTRASOUND AND THE POLITICS OF FETAL SUBJECTS

Appearing through developments in medicine, in volatile debates over abortion rights, in popular guides to pregnancy, and in advertisements for cars and long-distance telephone plans, the fetus has become an increasingly familiar part of our social landscape in Canada. Lisa Mitchell provides a critical anthropological perspective on the fetal subject, particularly as it emerges through the practice of ultrasound imaging.

'Seeing the baby' is now a routine and expected part of pregnancy and prenatal care in Canada. Conventionally understood as a neutral and passive technology, ultrasound appears to be a 'window' through which to observe fetal sex, age, size, physical normality, and behaviour. However, Mitchell argues, what is seen through ultrasound is neither self-evident nor natural, but historically and culturally contingent and subject to a wide range of interpretation.

Drawing upon fieldwork conducted over the past ten years, the author includes observations at ultrasound clinics, interviews with pregnant women and their partners, and a discussion on how ultrasound's echoes become meaningful as 'baby's first picture' – a snapshot of the fetus *in utero*.

Throughout, Mitchell probes our acceptance of this technology, our willingness to take fetal imaging for granted, and illuminates the links between this technologically mediated 'fetal reality' and the politics of gender and reproduction in Canada.

LISA M. MITCHELL is an assistant professor in the Department of Anthropology at the University of Victoria in British Columbia.

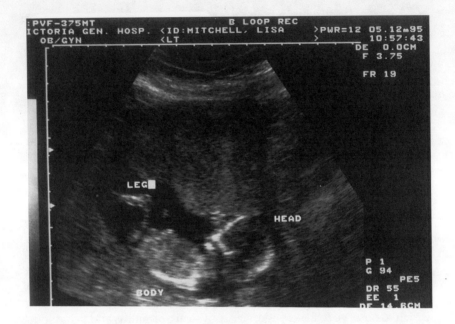

Photograph courtesy of the author

Baby's First Picture

Ultrasound and the Politics of Fetal Subjects

LISA M. MITCHELL

UNIVERSITY OF TORONTO PRESS
Toronto Buffalo London

© University of Toronto Press Incorporated 2001
Toronto Buffalo London
Printed in Canada

ISBN 0-8020-4810-2 (cloth)
ISBN 0-8020-8349-8 (paper)

Printed on acid-free paper

National Library of Canada Cataloguing in Publication Data

Mitchell, Lisa Meryn
Baby's first picture : ultrasound and the politics of fetal subjects

Includes bibliographical references and index.
ISBN 0-8020-4810-2 (bound)   ISBN 0-8020-8349-8 (pbk.)

1. Fetus – Ultrasonic imaging – Social aspects.   2. Fetus – Ultrasonic imaging – Québec (Province) – Montréal – Case studies.
3. Pregnant women – Québec (Province) – Montréal – Attitudes.
4. Medical personnel – Québec (Province) – Montréal – Attitudes.
I. Title.

RG527.5.U48M57 2001   618.3'207543   C2001-930695-4

This book has been published with the help of a grant from the Humanities
and Social Sciences Federation of Canada, using funds provided by the Social
Sciences and Humanities Research Council of Canada.

The University of Toronto Press acknowledges the financial assistance to its
publishing program of the Canada Council for the Arts and the Ontario Arts
Council.

University of Toronto Press acknowledges the financial support for its
publishing activities of the Government of Canada through the Book Publishing Industry Development Program (BPIDP).

'Ultrasound Sold as Baby's First Picture'

(Vancouver, Canada) Ultrasound videos of fetuses are being marketed as 'family entertainment' by an ultrasound technician. At any stage in their pregnancies, expectant mothers pay Derek Kirkham, president of First Moments Video Productions, $49.95 to 'capture baby's first pictures on video.' The setting for the 10-minute shoot can be anywhere – a hotel room or the customer's kitchen. Kirkham narrates and lets parents participate by talking to the baby, playing music or reading.

Toronto Star, 12 January 1993: C1

To: 'Lisa M. Mitchell'
Subject: Woman Breaks all Bladder Retention Records! News at 11:00!

Well, I could not simply walk in there 'unawares' – so despite the intense agony (my bladder was 'ready' for 10:40, I was only seen at 11:30), I kept looking for signs of the meaning of our communication. I was so tense though (I mean this was too much for me!), that she had a hard time seeing anything (also the bladder was too full!). Anyway, it was always 'the baby': 'see how the baby is moving about', 'look at what the baby is doing now'. I cried. Well, what else could I do? That first image is overwhelming. But it was still hard to imagine that this was happening inside of me (oh, quit looking at me like fodder now). Seeing that I was nervous, she engaged me more and more with the experience: 'come on, scoot down a bit on the table so you can see the screen better. Oh, good, here is a good picture, let me capture that one for you.' Then, thankfully after being able to relieve myself, she did a transvaginal, which gives much better images anyway. Then, with the pictures so clear, I really got into looking at the images. Weird, weird, weird. She kept talking about the limbs and organs that she could see (she then said, 'look here's the heart, let me turn on the audio.' I cried again.) I took all that chit-chat as a very good sign. So, how did I do?

Love,
N.

Contents

Acknowledgments

As I was writing this book, an American woman ovulated. What made this event worthy of international media coverage was that the woman, Margaret Lloyd-Hart, who had gone through premature menopause, produced the egg from her recently defrosted and reimplanted ovary. A few days later, a second woman had ovarian tissue transplanted into her forearm – apparently to make egg retrieval easier for *in vitro* fertilization. Stories, like this one, about the technological mastery over fetal production, or what used to be called 'having a baby,' are proliferating. But the fetus is becoming public in more common, everyday sites within our landscape – in advertisements for cars, telephone companies, and television programming, in posters warning of the dangers of smoking during pregnancy, in violent confrontations over the issue of abortion, in proudly displayed ultrasound photos, in movies, in the tiny pink plastic wombs of Mummy-to-Be dolls, and elsewhere.

In this book I focus on one of the most widely used, but no less fascinating, sites of fetal production – ultrasound imaging. The core of the material grew out of my doctoral research conducted at an ultrasound clinic in Montreal. When I came back to the dissertation some time later with a book in mind, it was clear to me that my thinking about the intersections of gender, reproduction, and technology had changed. I went back to the original interview transcripts and field notes, spread them out on the floor, and started again. What resulted is this book.

Many people have contributed to the conception, gestation, and birth of this book. I am particularly grateful to the many women and men who have talked so openly with me about both the intimate and the public aspects of pregnancy and ultrasound. I extend a sincere thank you to the sonographers, physicians, and others at the hospital where I conducted the primary fieldwork and at other sites where I have observed ultrasound. For stimulating discussion, frankly worded commentary, and unwavering encouragement, as well as child care, shelter, and diversions over the years, I am particularly indebted to Naomi Adelson, Marjorie Mitchell, Donald Mitchell, Eugenia Georges, Joel Minion, and my colleagues at the University of Victoria. The initial research and the writing of the dissertation on which this book is based benefited greatly from the tutelage of Allan Young, Atwood Gaines, and Jill Korbin. For assistance with the transition from dissertation to book, I am grateful for the assistance and comments given by the editors at University of Toronto Press and by anonymous reviewers. The research assistance provided by Renae Satterly, Louise Coté, and Theresa Ford in tracking down documents and odd bits of information and the formatting help provided by Karen-Marie Woods is much appreciated.

I wish to thank the Medical Research Council of Canada and the Wenner-Gren Foundation for Anthropological Research for providing financial support for graduate study and doctoral fieldwork. My continuing research has been generously supported by the Vancouver Foundation and National Science Foundation.

This book is for my family, my kids, and my companion.

BABY'S FIRST PICTURE

Chapter One

Introducing Ultrasound Fetal Imaging

The beginning of life – the time when new flesh must be interpreted, shaped, and transformed into socially meaningful forms – is especially revealing of how competing views of personhood are 'worked through the body.'

Conklin and Morgan (1996: 663)

One of the most common rituals of pregnancy in late twentieth-century urban North America begins when a woman and her partner are ushered into a small room by a white-coated person known as 'the sonographer.' The room is dark, illuminated only by the glowing screen of a machine. The sonographer asks the woman to lie down on a table, then squirts her belly with a cool blue gel, moves a device over her abdomen, and taps at a keyboard. Suddenly, a greyish blur appears on a luminescent screen. Customarily during this ritual, the couple smile, laugh, and point at the screen, even though they often do not recognize anything in the blur. The sonographer taps at the keyboard again and looks closely at the grey-and-white blur. She measures parts of it and calculates its age, weight, and expected date of delivery. She observes the couple closely to see if they like the blur and show signs of 'bonding' with it. The couple also look closely at the sonographer, anxious in case she finds something wrong with the blur. Sometimes, when the blur seems really pleasing, the sonographer talks to it, strokes it, and congratulates the couple. After about fifteen minutes, the blur is turned off, and the gel wiped away, and the couple are given a copy of the greyish blur to take home. This copy is known as 'Baby's First Picture,' or as 'Baby's First Video' if they get the moving version. It is often shown to other people, who are also expected to smile at it.

This book offers a critical anthropological perspective on these blurs, or, as they are more widely called, sonograms or ultrasound fetal images. In particular, I investigate what these blurs mean to sonographers and pregnant women at one hospital in Montreal, Canada. I look at ultrasound images not as neutral windows onto the fetus but rather as artefacts emerging out of particular historical, social, and cultural contexts. I explain in detail how ultrasound's patterns of echoes become culturally meaningful as 'Baby's First Picture,' a snapshot of the individual *in utero*. If we are to understand this process, we must also consider the extent to which fetal images may engage, contest, and transform other meanings, for example, about nature, technology, identity, normality, gender, and motherhood. I examine several of the many semiotic and material practices through which fetal images are produced, interpreted, and experienced; for this purpose, I discuss changes in ultrasound technology, contemporary sonographic practice, contests over abortion rights, and the embodied ideas and practices of pregnant women. Throughout this book, my concerns are two: *first*, to show how these collections of echoes have become taken for granted as windows onto fetal reality, and *second*, to illuminate the links between this technologically mediated reality and the politics of gender and reproduction. Talk about the fetus and ultrasound is inseparable from talk about women and power.

For several decades, ultrasound imaging has been widely regarded by medical professionals as 'the most important antepartum diagnostic technique available' (Gabbe 1988: 1).[1] Popular because it is considered to be a 'non-invasive' technique, ultrasound is said to open 'a window of unsurpassed clarity into the gravid uterus ... capable of providing exquisite detail regarding the fetus and the intrauterine environment' (Pretorius and Mahony 1990: 1). Claims about what can be seen through this window are numerous: the state of fetal anatomy, fetal growth and development, hundreds of fetal pathologies, fetal sex as early as eleven weeks, and fetal sleep, rest, and activity patterns (Graham 1983; Pretorius and Mahony 1990). There are even claims of witnessing fetal masturbation (Meizner 1987). Finally, as Lisa Cartwright (1993) has pointed out, enough fetal behaviour has been observed for one psychiatrist to begin the practice of fetal psychoanalysis (Piontelli 1992). Ultrasound is thought to reduce maternal anxiety and to stimulate the parents' emotional 'bond' to the fetus; in this regard, it offers a means for influencing women into complying with prenatal care recommendations about food, cigarette, alcohol and/or drug intake.[2]

Since the technology was first adopted in the late 1950s, ultrasound fetal imaging has become both an expected and a routine part of pregnancy for millions of women around the world. One, two, and sometimes four or five ultrasounds during pregnancy are now common in many European nations, in urban Australia, and in the United States. The technology is no longer restricted to women in the industrialized 'West,' and is becoming part of the 'modern' obstetrical repertoire in many countries around the world. Wherever it is used, it is adapted to fit with social imperatives and cultural meanings; for example, it is used for sex determination in India and China (Hartmann 1995; Patel 1989). In Quebec, where I conducted the research for this book, ultrasound is widely seen as an 'essential' part of prenatal care, and around 97 per cent of all pregnant women undergo at least one scan (Royal Commission on New Reproductive Technologies 1993: 816). Yet clinical studies have not clearly demonstrated that the routine use of ultrasound in early or late pregnancy is without risk, or that it improves maternal or fetal outcomes. Even so, its use is covered by all of this country's provincial health insurance plans, and remarkably, physicians do not have to request a woman's consent for ultrasound.[3]

Looking through the Window of Ultrasound

Most people – which includes practitioners, pregnant women, and the wider public – perceive ultrasound as a neutral and passive technology, as a 'window' through which the viewer can observe the fetus. Actually, ultrasound images are highly ambiguous and must be interpreted. Sonographers need special training to see the grey reflected echoes as a pattern of 'landmarks' – the distinctive uterine and fetal structures that are used to assess the fetus's physical growth and development. Several studies, including my own, have found that most expectant couples have difficulty recognizing fetal shape, anatomy, and movement in the ultrasound image without the sonographer's assistance (Kohn et al. 1980; Villeneuve et al. 1988). Paradoxically, although many parents recognize little or nothing in the fetal image, they take considerable pleasure in regarding it and are eager to have and willing to pay for a paper or video copy of the ultrasound image (Berwick and Weinstein 1985). Ultrasound, then, is firmly lodged in North American cultural discourses as a 'normal part of pregnancy' that allows prospective parents a sneak preview of their infant's sex, age, size, physical normality, and personality. So convincing is the ultrasound fetus that millions of North American women experience a

'technological quickening' several weeks before they sense fetal movement in their own bodies (Duden 1992). The ultrasound fetus is so
emotionally compelling that it has become a source of cultural entertainment. It appears in movies (Kaplan 1994), television shows, and
comic strips, as well as in print and electronic advertisements – for
example, for computers, cars (Taylor 1992), telephone companies, and
sports cable networks.

Ultrasound's 'facts' are not simply a technical matter requiring expert decoding; they are also culturally and socially constructed and
are subject to multiple interpretations. The most controversial aspect
of ultrasound imaging is what this 'window' says about the fetus as a
person. In clinical practice, ultrasound's fetal images are taken as observations of natural processes that allow physicians to assess fetal
age, development, and normality. These assessments made through
ultrasound are then translated into statements about fetal viability,
diagnoses of normality or abnormality, and recommendations for treatment. What is seen through ultrasound is conditioned as well by legal
statutes and institutional practices regarding birth and death. In
Canada, the delivery of a fetus older than twenty weeks is a 'register-
able' event, and a birth certificate must be issued. In contrast, younger
fetuses are 'products of conception' and not registered as persons.[4]

For some parents, the ability to see fetal parts – especially the beating heart – and to see the fetus sucking its thumb, kicking, excreting,
and responding to external stimuli may demonstrate that the fetus is
aware of its surroundings and has the potential for or actually pos-
sesses distinctive human consciousness and personhood. Alternatively,
they may regard ultrasound simply as a diagnostic tool, that offers
information about the progress of the pregnancy; but says little or
nothing about the fetus as a person. Parents may also interpret in
multiple ways ultrasound images in which fetal anomalies are detected. Some couples I have interviewed decide that their fetus does
not have the potential to become a full person, and thus do not feel
morally obligated to carry that fetus to term (see also Drugan et al.
1990). Conversely, they may believe that all fetuses, regardless of development stage or abnormality, are persons with the right to life and
to fulfil their distinctive potential as humans. In this latter case, parents may view these rights as imposing certain obligations to nurture
and protect the fetus – obligations that extend to the physician. Some
American lawmakers have attempted to legislate mandatory viewing
of ultrasound fetal images as a means of dissuading pregnant women

from having an abortion (Lippman 1986: 442). Pro-choice groups generally argue that decisions related to when fetal 'selfhood' begins are part of a pregnant woman's right to self-determination over her own body and involve ultrasound and other 'evidence' only if she so chooses (Petchesky 1990). A growing number of feminist perspectives on this issue assert 'a woman's right to choose,' yet also reveal how the very existence of technologies such as ultrasound tend to structure 'choice' in ways that 'have increased the potential for others to exercise an even greater control over women's lives' and to discriminate in particular against low-income and minority women and people with disabilities (Stanworth 1987: 4; see also Arditte et al. 1984, Corea 1985, Corea et al. 1987, Himmelweit 1988, Overall 1989, Spallone 1989, among others). In short, although ultrasound is perceived to be a 'window,' it is a 'window' through which different groups see different things.[5]

The implications of what is 'seen' through ultrasound extend far beyond the clinic, reaching deep into the lived worlds of women, their partners, and sonographers, and into some of the most volatile cultural struggles in Canada and the United States. In Canada at present, the fetus is not legally a person and is not specifically included in the Canadian Charter of Rights and Freedoms (1982). Abortion was decriminalized in 1969 and is regarded by Health Canada as 'a medically necessary procedure that must receive full funding through provincial health care plans' (Anderson 1999: 4). Nonetheless, Canadian women are facing increasingly restrictive policies on reproductive rights. A woman's right to determine what will happen to her body during pregnancy, or to terminate a pregnancy, or to refuse a medically indicated procedure, is under scrutiny in Canada (Gee 1996; Ginn 1999). Societal confidence about women's reproductive decisions appears to be wavering, and conflict between fetal and women's rights is increasing, at the expense of women's control over both their own and fetal bodies. Several widely publicized court cases have kept the question of fetal rights and the rights of pregnant women in the Canadian news. In particular, access to safe abortions is being eroded in the name of family values, right-wing and Christian politics, and budget cuts. In the face of ongoing harassment, threats, and physical violence, physicians and hospitals are becoming less and less willing to provide abortions. Canadian women's access to safe, legal abortions is tenuous.

In the United States, anti-choice violence has resulted in the deaths of at least six abortion clinic physicians and workers, and more than double that number have been injured (National Abortion Federation 1997). Access to abortion in the United States has decreased dramatically over the past ten years. Medicaid funding for low-income women is restricted, with over half of all states now enforcing 'parental notification laws' and mandatory waiting periods, and fully 84 per cent of American counties do not have a provider for legal abortions (National Abortion Federation 1997). In the latest well-publicized flare-up in the abortion rights controversy, the U.S. Supreme Court is preparing to rule on the legality of late-term abortions, or what anti-choice groups call 'partial birth abortions' (Thomas 1999).

In both Canada and the United States, abortion debates have revolved around competing constructions of personhood. Specifically, the chasm has formed between anti-choice claims, which are primarily about fetal personhood, and pro-choice claims, which have tended to focus on women's personhood. Thus, in North America the debate over abortion has evolved into a fierce struggle between two sets of rights: those of fetuses to life, and those of women to choose. Within these Canadian and American debates, despite often sharply divergent positions on abortion and on who should be considered a person, there is a shared set of assumptions about 'personhood.'

One of these assumptions is that the debate over who is a person and who/what is not can be resolved from a physical, time-based perspective. Thus, arguments about fetal rights in North America tend to focus on physical features such as the number of cells, morphological completeness, chromosomal composition, and bodily functioning, as well as on temporal events such as conception, first trimester, 20 weeks, and birth. Implicit in this search for the onset of personhood is the assumption that personhood is an either/or state. A further significant element in the debates surrounding personhood – especially those which converge on the terrain of abortion rights – is that the most compelling evidence brought to bear on this question comes from the practices, technologies, and discourses of medical science. While many sources of evidence – ethics, religion, feminism, humanism, among others – have been marshalled in debates over personhood, the 'facts' of science and medicine are seen as especially salient and powerful.

Canadian and American arguments about personhood tend to coalesce around individualism, biology, and technology; in other places, different configurations have emerged. For example, Beth Conklin and Lynn Morgan have observed that among the Wari' of Amazonian

Brazil, pregnancy does not necessarily produce a human, and person-hood is 'processual' rather than fixed in time and in biology:

> In Western biomedical models of conception, once one sperm meets one egg, the fetal body begins to develop through more or less automatic biological processes. The Wari', in contrast, see the making of the fetus as a process that requires the ongoing participation of people other than the mother. Flesh and bones – the solid parts of the fetal body – are literally created out of semen and nourished by it ... The idea that semen builds fetal bodies means that couples should have sex often during pregnancy; failure to do so is believed to endanger the fetus. (1996: 671)

Being human, then, as far as the Wari' are concerned, is not an innate state of being; rather, humans are socially created 'through exchanges of substance between individual bodies' (669). Where fetuses are concerned, repeated acts of sex between the mother and a man (not necessarily the biological father) have only the *potential* to produce a human. Awareness is central to North American notions of fetal personhood; yet as Conklin and Morgan explain it (678), even though the Wari' consider fetuses to be aware and 'endowed with relational capacities, this does not automatically confer personhood on either the fetus or the newborn.' Significantly, neither does the biological event of birth. Newborns who do not live long enough to be nursed are not persons and are not publicly mourned (679). Wari' personhood is constituted not through that single act of nursing; rather, it 'is acquired gradually and incrementally as a individual interacts with other people and incorporates their bodily fluids' (1996: 674). Similarly, a woman's fertility is a social achievement. A young Wari' girl does not 'naturally' become a fertile woman once she begins to bleed vaginally. Instead, her status as an adult female person is created socially when the semen introduced into her body during sexual intercourse makes her 'fatter, taller, and stronger – able to do women's work' – and stimulates her true menstruation (1996: 674).

In contrast, many Japanese regard the fetus as sentient and aware, labelling it *mizuko*, or a newborn baby (Oaks 1994: 515, 516). For this reason, Japanese women may regard abortion as 'killing a baby.' Moreover, the social status of Japanese women is deeply invested with their role as mothers and caregivers, and with the notion of *ameru* or emotional dependence, which is particularly strong between mother and child (Lock 1980: 77). As Oaks observes, 'Motherhood allows a Japanese woman to become an adult for the first time, to attain *ichininmae*, full adulthood, and to be recognized by society as a whole being (Lebra, 1984, p. 165; Tananka, 1984, p. 233). The mother-child relationship is privileged over that of wife-husband in the structure of many Japanese families' (518).

Yet Japan has one of the highest abortion rates in the world (Oaks 1994). Furthermore, there is only a small public debate over abortion, and that debate is not constructed in terms of either individual rights or the opposition of maternal and fetal interests. As Oaks points out, those who are familiar with North American notions of personhood and debates about abortion perceive the Japanese situation as 'paradoxical' and 'contradictory.' Her analysis suggests that what is at stake in Japan engages quite different meanings of fetality, abortion, motherhood.

Abortion has been decriminalized in Japan since 1948, and is 'the chief means of birth control' there (LaFleur 1992: 136). Condoms are widely available but generally disliked by Japanese men, and oral contraceptives were illegal until early 1999 (LaFleur 1992: 136; Parker 1999). In Canada, abortion is construed primarily in terms of maternal–fetal rights; in contrast, the issues in Japan are the welfare of the fetal spirit and the welfare of the woman. As Oaks writes (516), in Japan 'there is less concern for the fetus in the womb as a person than there is for the spirit of the aborted fetus as an active agent.' Specifically, 'the spirit of an aborted fetus has the power to cause misfortune and illness to the woman who terminated the pregnancy and her family members.' That spirit can be appeased and put to rest through a series of rituals, most of them Buddhist in origin and nature, referred to as *mizuko kuyo* (516; see also LaFleur 1992). These rituals vary in cost and complexity, and may entail making offerings in the home to a *jizo* icon who guards unborn children; placing toys, hand-made clothes, or food on the *jizo* at local temples; or performing elaborate and expensive rites involving priests and the recitation of prayers (LaFleur 1992; Oaks 1994). Drawing from his extensive historical study, LaFleur sees the *mizuko kuyo* as a 'ritual apology' to the aborted fetus (155). This apology, he claims, affirms the 'bond of emotional intimacy between the parent and the deceased child' (158) and provides 'concrete evidence that she still remains a person who cares and who has human feelings' (155).

This book does not attempt to answer the ontological question of whether the fetus is a person (either in Canada or more universally);

nor does it suggest how one might go about resolving that issue. Instead, my analysis of ultrasound fetal imaging is directed at three concerns. *First*, against the broader goal of showing how fetality is contingent – that is, embedded in and constituted through particular histories, meanings, and struggles that vary from place to place and over time – I use my research in Montreal to examine fetality in the Canadian context. I do not claim to be offering an ethnographic account of 'the Canadian fetus' or of what fetality means to all Canadians; even so, the women and sonographers I interviewed articulated ideas and engaged in practices about the fetus that need to be positioned as both cultural (i.e., emerging out of particular dynamic configurations of meaning) and culturally specific (i.e., Canadian rather than Wari', or Japanese, or even American). Moreover, there are variations in the interpretations by the Canadians I interviewed that can be analysed and traced to differing views relating to medical knowledge, reproductive pasts, the technology of ultrasound, and cultural frameworks of meaning.

Second, I am concerned with making problematic the 'naturalness' of the fetus and its personhood. As the examples of the Wari' and the Japanese suggest, people everywhere assume that their particular way of deciding what constitutes a person is 'natural,' true, and free from cultural influence. Drawing from my research, I explore in detail how fetality is a cultural product, the result of material and semiotic practices enacted in particular historical, social, and cultural contexts. Here I am particularly interested in the meanings and practices of ultrasound as this technology is used to 'reveal' and know the fetus. Ultrasound appears to many of us to supply a culture-free and correct understanding of nature and, hence, of the 'true' nature of fetuses; I counter that vision with an analysis of how the naturalness of fetal persons is constituted through the very technology said to locate it objectively. In particular, my own work focuses on how collections of ultrasound echoes become meaningful for sonographers and women. In this book I acknowledge, as Petchesky (1987: 78) and others have, that 'images by themselves lack "objective" meanings,' and attempt to establish empirically how images become meaningful. Based on my observations of ultrasound imaging and interviews with sonographers and pregnant women, I describe how particular aspects of personhood are used by sonographers and by women to interpret the fetal image. In sonographers' interpretations, what precisely communicates the idea of the fetus as a person? What parts of the fetal image are selected to demonstrate personhood? How do women respond to and participate in or resist these interpretations?

Third, I examine the implications of fetality as it is variously constructed, mobilized, and resisted among a group of Canadian women and sonographers. Struggles over the meanings of personhood have implications for other persons, and I am interested in the ramifications of 'seeing' into women and 'seeing' particular fetuses. I examine how women experience, narrate, and act upon the 'facts' of ultrasound. To what extent and under what circumstances is this technology empowering for women, allowing them to become 'agents of their [own] reproductive destinies' (Petchesky 1987: 72)? To what extent is it disempowering, subjecting women, fetuses, men, and sonographers to a normalizing gaze? How have sonographers used these images to support particular claims to expert knowledge and professionalism? What has been the evidentiary status of fetal images in the struggle over abortion rights?

Theorizing Persons, Bodies, and Technology

The theoretical approach I take toward the analysis of ultrasound fetal imaging in Canada is forged from my reading of feminist and anthropological writings on self and person, the body, and the politics of reproduction. Anthropologists have argued that ideas about 'person' vary greatly from culture to culture, and over time within cultures. Until recently, in arguing that ideas about the 'person' vary cross-culturally[6] we have tended to describe the 'Western' self as 'a bounded, unique, more or less integrated motivational and cognitive universe, a dynamic center of awareness, emotion, judgement, and action organized into a distinctive whole and set contrastively both against other such wholes and against its social and natural background' (Geertz 1983: 59).

Western constructs of self and person, it is argued, reflect the cultural emphasis placed on the autonomous *individual* – one who is distinct from others and from society and is perceived as free from the ties of social relationships. This construction of the 'Western' or 'ego-centric' self is often contrasted with the 'relational' or 'sociocentric' self found in other cultures, such as the Wari' (Conklin and Morgan 1996; see also Mageo 1995; Schweder and Bourne 1984; and others). Illustrative of the many critiques of these static and conventionalized representations,[7] Dorinne Kondo suggests that anthropologists should be 'asking how selves *in the plural* are constructed variously in various situations, how these constructions can be complicated and enlivened by multiplicity and ambiguity, and how they shape, and are shaped by, relationships of power' (1990: 43; author's emphasis).

There is now a wealth of data showing how concepts of self, and of social action based upon those concepts, are constituted differently among different collectivities within particular societies. Besides cultural differences, gender (Kondo 1990), class (Bourdieu 1984), religion (Gaines 1982), ethnicity (Blu 1980), illness (Kapferer 1979), and disability (Murphy 1990) have all been described as important determinants of how individuals experience themselves and others.

Within this recent proliferation of anthropological writings, the terms 'self' and 'person' are used in multiple ways, sometimes differentiated, often not (see Spiro 1993 for a review). Mageo (1995: 283) for example, uses 'self' to refer to the experience, in the phenomenological sense of the term, of being a person' – that is, of being part of a social group. Grace Harris (1989: 599) differentiates 'individual as member of the human kind, self as locus of experience, and person as agent-in-society.' My interest lies primarily in representations of female and fetal personhood as they are variously constructed, negotiated, and resisted in and around pregnancy, fetal imaging, and abortion politics. I am also concerned with female selves – that is, with understanding how women experience fetality, pregnancy, and ultrasound. Among the women I interviewed, the embodied experience (self) of being in the world – was inseparable both from the transformation in their own personhood from woman to mother, and from producing another human who at some (contested) point(s) in time would become both self and person. As Sarah Franklin (1991: 202) argues, 'the very term "individual", *meaning one who cannot be divided,* can only represent the male.' Pregnant women, in contrast, are divisible: simultaneously one and two, self and other (Rothman 1989: 89). That pregnant women are 'the exact anti-thesis of in-dividuality,' as Franklin (203) maintains, does more than simply call into question our assumptions about the uniform and unitary being; it leads directly to the links between person, gender, and power. 'This is ... why women have had so much trouble counting as individuals in modern western discourses. Their personal, bounded individuality is compromised by their bodies' troubling talent for making other bodies, whose individuality can take precedence over their own' (Haraway 1988: 39, cited in Franklin 1991: 203).

It might be argued that we cannot analyse fetal selves since the fetus has no voice, and that to theorize fetal selfhood is to accept that fetuses are subjects. Yet many groups claim to speak for the fetus (women, sonographers, anti-choice groups), and fetal subjectivity is a key element in contemporary representations of fetality in North America. The issue then becomes less a matter of definition and more a matter of vested interests: Of what use is the idea of a distinctive fetal person and fetal subjectivity to individuals and particular groups in Canadian society? Fetal versus maternal personhood and fetal subjectivity are more than cultural constructs: they are political issues. Understanding them as such involves intentionally troubling the culturally and historically specific binary of self–other and subject–object on which the distinction between self and person is prefaced.

My interest in notions of subjectivity and personhood operating at the beginning of human life focuses on their intersection with the technology of ultrasound fetal imaging. I assume that ultrasound, like any other technology, is not simply a utilitarian apparatus, nor is it a neutral tool, nor is it a stable entity.[8] Rather, ultrasound images are 'cultural objects' (Petchesky 1987: 66) whose meanings are determined by historically variable assumptions about the nature of society and individuals and by relationships among certain groups in society. The technology and practice of ultrasound can be understood further as the site of multiple, often competing discourses. As I discuss in more detail later in this book, the ultrasound machines that are used to 'see' into the interior of pregnant women, and the resulting images of that interior, are conditioned by medical definitions of obstetrical problems; research and design issues; market forces; assumptions about nature, bodies, and persons; political policies; economic priorities; legal constraints; and local traditions of scanning. At the same time, ultrasound is an instrument through which multiple, overlapping, and changing discourses about the body, gender, disability, health economics, and sexuality operate on and construct women, fetuses, sonographers, and others.

Along with the person and the self, the body has become the site of intense popular and scholarly interest. Deconstructed in social scientific theories, bypassed and fragmented by the technologies of work, medicine, and communication, and commodified as the measure of both social identity and individual worth, the body can no longer be taken for granted as a universal, stable, organic entity. Rather, the body is malleable and fluid, a construct that takes different forms and shapes across time and across different cultures.[9] The 'body,' then, like 'self' and the 'person,' is a historical and cultural product that is enacted through social practices in specific configurations of power.

Anthropological theories of the body have produced different representations of the body (see reviews by Lock 1993; Csordas 1994; and others). By some accounts there are two (Douglas 1973), three (Scheper-Hughes and Lock 1987), or even five 'bodies' (O'Neill 1985) that can be delineated in theoretical terms. My engagement with this literature is motivated by the desire to understand the technologically mediated body as a locus of experience, a cultural construct, and a site of control through which issues of personhood are raised and contested. As I discuss in more detail below, I approach the technologically mediated bodies of ultrasound from three perspectives – embodied perception, the social body, and the politics of embodiment.

Embodied Perception

'Embodiment,' or the idea of 'the body as an experiencing agent,' has been taken up by Csordas (1990; 1994: 3) as a key category of anthropological analyses. Others among the growing number of anthropologists who have explored the notion of 'embodiment' in their work include Gordon (1990), Kirmayer (1988), Pandolfi (1990), and Scheper-Hughes and Lock (1987). A central assumption of this approach is that 'our bodies are not objects to us ... [rather] they are an integral part of the perceiving subject' (Csordas 1990: 36). Even though we are often unaware of our bodies, we all live through them – seeing, tasting, touching, hearing, smelling, thinking, moving. Yet embodiment, as Csordas means it, is not about the body as a symbol of society, or as a surface on which social relations are inscribed, or as a discursive effect. Rather, his perspective gives centre stage to the idea of embodiment as 'the existential condition of possibility for culture and self' (1994: 6). Thus, body is defined as 'a biological, material entity,' while embodiment is 'defined by perceptual experience and mode of presence and engagement in the world' (12). This grounding of experience in the body has been closely studied with respect to chronic pain and to life-threatening illnesses (e.g., Scarry 1985; Good 1984), but not as of yet to pregnancy. Iris Young's article (1984) on pregnancy as a process of becoming, of being 'de-centered,' and of being other is a notable exception.

What does it mean to incorporate embodied perception in a critical perspective on pregnancy and fetality? The concept of embodiment opens a window onto women's lives, highlighting the sensory and engaged aspects of being pregnant in the world. This reading attends to the materiality of pregnancy, and to the sense of enlargement, sensuality, reflection, and growth, as well as to perceptions of discomfort, unfamiliarity, and anxiety. Called for here is a description not only of 'what it feels like to be pregnant,' or 'to have ultrasound,' but also of the consequences of those sensations for perception, meaning, and action. Of particular interest in this book is the intersection of technology and embodiment. For example, what does it mean for a woman to see the fetus on an external monitor in an image produced by a machine, sometimes weeks before that fetus is felt by her body? How does the technology of ultrasound intervene in intersubjectivity and in the ways that pregnancy 'flows out from the body into the social world' (Good 1984: 123). What is the embodied experience of ultrasound imaging for its practitioners – for the sonographers who employ this technology to scrutinize fetal bodies inside female bodies?

In engaging the idea of embodiment, I am not suggesting that the female body be privileged as a ground of common sense, intuitive, or 'natural' understandings of pregnancy. Embodiment is not about essentialized, biologized Woman. It is about understanding what difference one's body makes to the experience of being in the world, and – specific to the project of this book – what difference a technologically mediated pregnancy makes to being in the world. Put somewhat differently, the task is not to view women only as pregnant bodies (and then to 'read' or deconstruct their bodies as symbols of the dominant moral and social order and as sites for control), but rather to include women's sensations and experiences of being pregnant and having ultrasound.

Social Bodies

Besides being the 'existential ground' for the self, for perception and subjectivity, the body provides what Comaroff (1985: 6) describes as 'a constellation of physical signs with the potential for signifying the relation of persons to their contexts.' The body's relationship to society has been explored in great depth in anthropology. Several decades ago, influenced by the writings of Durkheim and Mauss, Douglas (1970) argued that the body is a 'natural symbol' that is classified, regulated, and decorated in ways that reproduce the dominant social and moral order. As Lock has pointed out (1993), Douglas's work has spawned innumerable examinations of how the human body has been recruited by various groups as a metaphor of society, of the relationship between individuals and society, and of personhood. More recently, anthropologists have been influenced by Bourdieu's (1977, 1984) writings on how culture is embodied – that is, reproduced in the material world (tools, houses, organization of physical space) and in the everyday bodily practices of people (ways of walking, eating, talking, and being in physical space). Douglas and Bourdieu draw attention to the body-mediated relationship of the individual to society; however, both assumed a natural, precultural body – a notion that has been thoroughly critiqued by many feminists and postmodern theorists. The body is not merely a reflection of, or a surface for the inscription of, or a vehicle for, the enculturation of the social and moral order. Nor is it necessarily – as Douglas and Bourdieu assumed – the stable, impermeable, and bounded body of Cartesian thinking. Notions of the body, forms of embodiment, and meanings of the person are culturally constituted; they are also interwoven. In North America, for example, notions of autonomous actors, rational inner subjects, and mind–body dualism are concretized, reproduced, and enacted in assumptions and practices that value and privilege 'disciplined, controlled, restrained and autonomous bodies' (Conklin and Morgan 1996: 664) and other triumphs of 'mind over matter' and of 'will power.' In contrast, 'Fijians closely monitor changes in body shape [as] an intersubjective somatic mode of attending to others' (Becker in Csordas 1994: 15), rather than as an expression of self.

Perhaps the earliest critical attention to the fetus as a semiotic object was Rosalind Petchesky's premise that the fetal image is a symbol, 'a kind of empty signifier that condenses within it many different meanings at once' (Petchesky 1990: xvi). Thus, she argues, ultrasound fetal images are meaningful for physicians as a form of diagnostic evidence (1987: 66), as a means of monitoring maternal and fetal behaviour (69), and as a fantasy of scientific control over the human (female and fetal) body (68–71). From this perspective, too, Petchesky (1990) maintains that fetal images are used by anti-choice groups not only as evidence of fetal personhood, but also for their symbolic function in affirming the values of religious fundamentalism, neoconservative politics, and other 'New Right' movements in the United States. What is evoked, then, for the viewer in anti-abortion representations of fetality is a particular social and moral order – a 'mythic secure past,' a time of sexual innocence, of 'good' mothers, of the 'traditional' family (xiv).

This book examines how one particular form of reproductive technology – ultrasound imaging – is implicated in the construction in Canada of particular meanings of both fetus and of pregnant woman.

I examine the conditions under which fetal bodies become both others and subjects, and I interrogate the role of ultrasound technology in that process, asking how collections of echoes come to be narrated as fetal persons and maternal persons in particular, morally weighted relationships. In addition, I try to show how the persons objectified through ultrasound are felt, interpreted, and experienced within the diverse social conditions of women's lives. How do women's readings of their bodies and of their fetal images conflict? How do they converge? How are fetal images used to dis/prove, negotiate, and resist personhood and other social claims such as professionalism, kinship, love, and maternalism? To what extent do anti-abortion readings of fetal and female bodies such as those Petchesky (1990) describes condition the experience of women and sonographers? What alternative representations of fetality and maternity are offered by pro-choice women and groups?

The Politics of Embodiment

What is often absent from discussions of 'embodiment and experience' is an accounting of the ways in which bodies and power intersect and reconfigure one another. The goal is not simply to identify how the body reflects or reproduces the social order (e.g., Douglas 1970), nor is it to use the body as a window onto the workings (power relations, social inequities) of Canadian society and culture. Rather the experience of one's body and of being a subject is conditioned by relationships of power, inequality, and domination. Foucault's (1979) notion of 'biopower,' as it has been interpreted and theorized by Sawicki (1991) and Lock and Kaufert (1998) among others, offers a means to analyse the lived experiences of these operations of power, including the ways in which they are desired and resisted.

Sawicki (1991: 67) describes 'biopower' as the 'set of discourses and practices governing both the individual's body and the health, education and welfare of the population.' The technologies and practices of biopower are deeply routinized in society and are widely taken as benevolent, even empowering. As Kaufert and Lock (1998: 7) write, biopower has two forms: first, '"anatomo-politics," focused on the manipulation of individual bodies and, [second,] the manipulation and control of populations.' The first draws attention to the minutiae of power operating on bodily routines, gestures, capacities, and de-

sires; the second operates through the policies and regulation of populations (Sawicki 1991: 67–8; Armstrong 1983; Foucault 1979). Ultrasound clearly has this dual quality: it is deeply enmeshed in how
women experience pregnancy (as a way of monitoring 'risks,' as a
source of knowledge superior to their own sensations), and it is routinized in clinical practice and hospital and health care policies (as a
means to screen for anomalies, improve population health, and encourage 'bonding').

Foucault (1975) rejected the notion of a natural body, arguing that
medical science among other discourses does not merely observe and
report on bodies; it constructs bodies through particular strategies of
investigation and surveillance. Central to understanding both ultrasound as a technique of biopower and the lived experiences of biopower
is the notion of the fetal patient. During the 1980s, several authors
argued that the use of reproductive technologies such as prenatal diagnosis, fetal heart monitors, and ultrasound imaging was fetocentric,
that is, premised on the idea of the fetus as a particular sort of person
– a patient – with rights distinct and different from those of the pregnant woman. William Arney (1982) and Anne Oakley (1986a), for example, linked the historical emergence of the fetus as a patient to
medicine's claims to authority over the management of pregnancy.
Techniques such as ultrasound, which enable physicians 'to dispense
with mothers as ... necessary informants on fetal status and life style'
(Oakley 1986a: 155), and which define the fetus as the primary patient,
have been a fundamental element in obstetrical 'claims to expertise'
(183).

Others see the issue of fetal personhood more broadly, not as a self-
interested discursive creation of obstetrics or medicine, but rather as
reflecting more widespread, deeply rooted ideologies of gender and
individualism. Barbara Katz Rothman (1989: 114, 59) for example, con-
tends that ultrasound's view of the fetus, 'not as part of its mother, but
as separate, a little person lying in the womb,' has deep historical
roots in the American tradition of viewing individuals as 'autonomous, atomistic, isolated beings.' The fetus as person is created from,
and perpetuated in, what she calls the American ideologies of patriarchy, technology, and capitalism (1989). Biopower, then, is inseparable
from other regimes of power, control, and discipline.

In my research, I have paid close attention to the role of ultrasound
in the emergence of the fetal patient, and to the implications of this for

women. Arney, Oakley, and I (1994), and others, have argued that ultrasound transforms pregnant women from embodied, thinking, and knowledgeable individuals into 'maternal environments,' or tissue that may or may not yield a clear ultrasound image. How are discourses and relations of fetal personhood lived and embodied by women during pregnancy? Any answer to this will require careful analysis of how women are disciplined to be certain kinds of patients and mothers and, through their perceptions, actions, and bodies, come to be those patients and mothers. Here I resist the tendency to talk about biopower only in terms of broad ideologies and passive or docile bodies. Several anthropologists (Georges 1997; Morgan 1994; Morton 1993; Rapp 1997, 1999; Saetnan 1996, 2000; Taylor 1998), including myself, have turned our attention to the local and situated meanings of ultrasound fetal images at the varied sites where men and women are creating, using, advocating, and criticizing fetal images. The newer approach deals not in terms of hegemonic ideologies and passive or naturalized women, but rather in terms of negotiated meanings, competing discourses, and partial perspectives (Rapp 1991). While ultrasound is clearly a key element in the extension of medical-scientific control over the reproductive lives and ideas of Canadians, my analysis also examines the complexities of women's participation in their own medicalization. In addition, I discuss other kinds of practices and discourses – law and media – that have contributed to constructing the fetus as a patient.

In summary, in this book I try to show what it means for individual women and for Canadian society to have ultrasound fetal imaging as a routine part of the experience of pregnancy.

In chapter 2, I offer a historical and social context for ultrasound fetal imaging by examining the development and routinization of this technology, as well as the controversies surrounding its efficacy and safety. In chapter 3, I situate the technology and practice of routine fetal imaging in the increasingly more local and detailed contexts of Quebec's health care system, the city of Montreal, and my fieldwork among sonographers and women at one hospital. In chapter 4, I explore women's embodied experiences and interpretations of being pregnant and of fetality prior to their first routine ultrasound. In chapter 5, I elaborate on the local tradition of routine ultrasound with a detailed ethnographic account of how sonographers translate and narrate fetal imaging at the research hospital. In chapter 6, I discuss women's interpretations of ultrasound imaging over the course of their pregnancy and post-partum. In chapter 7, I re-examine questions about the co-construction of personhood, bodies, and technology raised in this first chapter. In the concluding chapter, I suggest interventions that might make ultrasound less feto-centric.

Chapter Two

Opening the Black Box: The Ontology of Fetal Ultrasound Images

The sonogram does not simply map the terrain of the body; it maps geopolitical, economic, and historical factors as well.

Barad (1998: 93)

The eyes made available in modern technological sciences shatter any idea of passive vision; these prosthetic devices show us that all eyes, including our own organic ones, are active perceptual systems, building in translations and specific ways of seeing, that is ways of life.

Haraway (1999: 193)

In ultrasound fetal imaging, high-energy sound waves enter the woman's body, reflect off internal structures, and are converted into an electric signal displayed as dots on a screen. This chapter examines several of the historical processes through which those dots have materialized as a fetal subject on the ultrasound screen. I do not claim to offer a 'complete' history, nor even a particularly detailed ontology, of the fetal image in Montreal, in Canada, or in general. My intent is to examine some of the technical changes, organizational politics, and social meanings that have converged at particular times and places to produce what is widely taken for granted in Canada today as 'baby's first picture.'

The connections between ultrasound's development and the emergence of fetal subjectivity are neither random nor logical nor coincidental. Those connections cannot be fully understood if we conceptualize ultrasound as an instrument of male, 'techno-doc' domination over women's passive bodies and minds. As Karen Barad (1998: 101–

2) writes, 'apparatuses are not preexisting or fixed entities; they are themselves constituted through particular practices that are perpetually open to rearrangements, rearticulations, and other reworkings.' The dots that many of us now read as 'baby's first picture' are the product of particular possibilities heavily invested with the efforts, desires, and limitations of heterogeneous individuals, groups, and domains. Viewed from this perspective, ultrasound is not simply a rapidly changing piece of complex equipment; rather, it materializes through

> a multitude of practices, including those that involve: medical needs; design constraints (including the legal, economic, biomedical, physics and engineering ones); market factors; political issues; other R&D projects using similar materials; the educational background of the engineers and scientists designing the ... [technology] and the workplace environment of the engineering firm or lab; particular hospital or clinic environments where the technology is used; receptivity of the medical community and the patient community to the technology; legal, economic, cultural, religious, political, and spatial constraints on its uses; positioning of patients during examination; and the nature of training of technicians and physicians who use the technology. (Barad 1998: 102)

From these multiple strands in ultrasound's past, I draw out a few for examination – namely, the medicalization and technologization of prenatal care in Canada, changes in the technology of ultrasound, the institutionalization of ultrasound as standard practice, and the emergence of the fetal patient within medicine. In chapter 3, I will situate the changing technology and practice of prenatal ultrasound within the social history of Quebec and Montreal.

The Fetus Within and the Physician Without

The desire to visualize the interior of pregnant women long predates ultrasound. For centuries, theological, artistic, and scientific images of female interiors and fetal bodies have offered evidence in debates about bodily essences, sexual differences, personhood, and the role of the divine in conception (see Bynum 1991; Duden 1993; Jordanova 1989; Newman 1996). In Canada, the biomedical community's yearning to see the fetus is rooted in early twentieth-century concerns about maternal mortality, medical authority, and national identity.

In the early 1900s, pregnant women in Canada faced the very real possibility that they might die during childbirth and that their infants would not live to see their first birthday. When the first national statistics became available in the 1920s, infant mortality was 92 per thousand live births and the maternal mortality rate was 5.6 per thousand (Buckley 1979: 134–5). Yet even several decades before these statistics were published, the collective deaths of women and infants evoked multiple meanings in the minds of Canadian physicians, reformers, and government officials. Physicians in Canada, organized since 1869, continued to stake their claims to professional status on the bodies of pregnant women. Ignoring the fact that many urban and rural Canadians lived in poverty without adequate housing, food, or clean water, numbers of physicians blamed 'meddlesome' midwives, 'ignorant' mothers, and 'backward' doctors for the alarmingly high mortality (Arnup 1994; Plummer 2000). The solutions then seemed straightforward: educate mothers about infant care, and establish greater control – that is, physician's and nurse's control – over labour and delivery. Canadian physicians were highly successful in persuading the various governments that they and professionally trained nurses, rather than midwives, were the appropriate practitioners for childbirth, and that the hospital rather than the home was the safest place for labour and delivery (Arnup et al. 1990; Benoit 1991). Midwives found themselves socially and legislatively pushed to the nation's symbolic peripheries, attending women in the North, in remote rural areas, and in Newfoundland and Labrador (Benoit 1991; Laforce 1990; Plummer 2000). Canada's first maternity hospital was established in 1842 in Montreal. Even so, as of the 1920s less than one-quarter of Canadian women were giving birth in hospital, and many of those women were impoverished (Abbott 1931: 83; James-Chetelat 1990: 304). Although the statistics did not always support physicians' claims that hospitalization was safer than home births,[1] by 1950 the majority of women in Quebec and other Canadian provinces were giving birth in hospital attended by physicians (Laurendeau 1987: 129; Mitchison 1991a, 1991b).

Women's bodies were also a site for political concerns about the future of Canada as a nation.[2] High rates of infant and maternal mortality threatened Canada's claims to be an 'advanced' nation and – perhaps more importantly for the mainly Anglophone politicians and upper class – threatened its status as a 'civilized' member of the British Commonwealth (Buckley 1979: 134–5). In 1910 the author of the first Canadian Government Special Report on Infant Mortality laid bare the link between babies and nationhood: 'We are only now discovering that Empires and States are built up of babies. Cities are dependent for their continuance on babies. Armies are recruited only if and when we have cared for our babies' (MacMurchy 1910: 3, cited in Arnup 1994: 21).

The author of that report, Dr Helen MacMurchy, like many eugenics-minded reformers of the day, was alarmed not only by the problem of dwindling numbers of surviving infants but also by the growing numbers of immigrants who were not Anglo-Saxons (Buckley 1979: 135). Reproduction, particularly by citizens of 'good stock,' was seen as the key to nation building; as one result, reducing the scourge of maternal and infant mortality became a national priority.

Although some cities instituted milk banks, well baby clinics, and home visits to new mothers by nurses, the fate of Canada's babies, it was argued, fell largely on the shoulders of mothers. A contradictory message went out to Canadian women – one that continues to shape the experience of pregnancy today. Physicians and government bureaucrats claimed that 'the mother is the only one who can save the baby' (MacMurchy 1911, cited in Arnup 1994: 23). At the same time they insisted that if mothers were 'to safeguard the babies of the Nation ... they needed expert advice' (Arnup 1994: 31). Faced with both the national statistics showing high infant and maternal mortality and reports which found that maternal death rates were higher in hospitals than at home, physicians and reformers argued that hospitalization during delivery was not enough: women should also be in the care of physicians for the duration of their pregnancies (Mitchison 1991b; Oppenheimer 1990: 67).

Medical wisdom shifted, and by 1924 the prenatal period became 'the most critical period in one's life' (Ontario government pamphlet entitled *The Baby* 1924: 3, cited in Arnup 1994: 63). Prior to this time, a woman might be examined by a physician once during pregnancy and then not again until the hours of childbirth. Attentive to the reformers' calls for expanded prenatal care, a few Canadian provinces began offering one free medical visit per pregnancy. Yet before universal health insurance was introduced in the 1960s and 1970s, relatively few women could afford regular and frequent prenatal care (Arnup 1994: 72). If pregnant women could not afford to come to the expert, perhaps expert advice could be brought to them by other means.

Beginning in the 1920s, booklets on prenatal and infant care were published by federal, provincial, and municipal governments and widely distributed free of charge to Canadian women. In these early advice books on pregnancy, women were urged to get plenty of rest, exercise through housework, avoid 'excessive passions,' be cheerful, and, above all, 'Do what the doctor tells you' (Arnup 1994: 68). As Arnup (63) notes: 'These recommendations were largely for the woman's comfort, rather than the well-being of the fetus. In that regard, the authors of advice literature and members of the medical profession adopted an attitude that amounted to letting nature take its course. Nineteenth-century faith in the naturalness of pregnancy underscored a belief that nature would ensure that all went well. Maternal and infant deaths were viewed as unfortunate but unavoidable, part of God's will and His mysterious ways.'

Prenatal care slowly became an organized part of clinical practice in Canada. In the early decades of the 1900s, physicians relied mainly on auscultation, palpation, the woman's own accounts of the pregnancy, and analyses of maternal blood and urine to gauge *in utero* developments (Eastman and Hellman 1961; Oakley 1986a). These methods conveyed little information about any obstetrical 'disasters' that might be happening within the womb: malformation, developmental delay, placental anomalies. Decades later, one of the first specialists in fetal medicine reflected on the pre-ultrasound era in obstetrics: 'We knew virtually nothing of what was happening in the uterus until it was emptied at delivery. I thought of the uterus as being a black box' (Berkowitz, cited in Kolata 1990: 136).

With the discovery of X-rays, physicians thought they might finally have their window into this black box. As early as 1898, only two years after Röntgen publicized his discovery, X-rays were being used in difficult obstetric cases to establish fetal head size (Leavitt 1986: 267). By the 1930s, X-rays were in general obstetrical use in North America and Great Britain as a means of confirming pregnancy, determining the cephalopelvic index (the ratio of fetal head size to maternal pelvic diameter) prior to labour, and searching for fetal skeletal anomalies (Hiddinga and Blume 1992; Oakley 1986a). The first concerns about the effects of irradiation on human health were published in the 1920s, but hospitals did not begin to limit obstetrical radiological exams until after 1956, when Alice Stewart published a study that clearly linked childhood cancer and exposure to X-rays *in utero* (Oakley 1986a). The existence of research that seemed to refute Stewart's findings, and reluctance to close this window onto the fetus, kept X-rays in prenatal practice for another twenty years (Greene 2000).

At about the same time that Alice Stewart published her study, interest in the obstetrical applications of ultrasound began to grow (Oakley 1986a).

Sonar, Submarines, and the Fetus

In the mid-1950s, Ian Donald, an obstetrician-gynecologist in Glasgow, found himself faced with what he later called the 'clinical frustration [of the] ... problematical female abdomen' (Donald 1980: 8). While searching for a way to distinguish abdominal, uterine, and ovarian tumours among his patients, Donald borrowed ultrasound equipment from a Glasgow foundry, where it was used for detecting metal flaws, and began to experiment. The first representation of the fetus through ultrasound appears to have been accidental, made while Donald and two of his colleagues were trying to determine the cause of uterine enlargement in one woman (McNay and Fleming 1999: 8). Often erased from the origin stories is that ultrasound fetal imaging's own 'mother' was a young midwife: 'In pregnancy the only echoes of which we could be reasonably sure ... were those provided by the fetal head, a fact which enabled my staff nurse, Miss Marjorie Marr (later promoted to matron at the Queen Mother's Hospital), to be certain of the [fetal] presentation in obese or difficult cases by the secret use of the apparatus in advance of our staff rounds on Friday mornings' (Donald 1980: 9–10).

Upon learning of Marjorie Marr's work, Donald began to concentrate on applying ultrasound to obstetrical patients. Recalling ultrasound's early ties to the military, Donald explained that the use of reflected echoes in SONAR 'had been developed in the 1914–1918 war for the detection of German U-boats lurking within the depths of the ocean ... There is not so much difference after all between a fetus in utero and a submarine at sea. It is simply a question of refinement' (Donald 1969: 610, 618).

The fetal ultrasound images produced by Marr and Donald in 1957 used what is called A-mode ultrasound. A beam of sound waves directed into the woman's uterus was reflected back onto a cathode ray tube and converted into a single line signal.[3] Marr and then Donald were able to use these spikes and dips in a limited fashion to locate the fetal head and the full maternal bladder. However, most of the blips and valleys were, as Donald referred to them, 'meaningless' (1976: 560).

Ian Donald and his male colleagues soon moved on to what is known as compound B-mode scanning. In B-mode, a beam of ultrasound energy is swept across a woman's abdomen from a number of angles, and the reflected echoes appear as dots of light in a two-dimensional cross-section or 'slice' of her body's interior. Representing the interior of the body as a series of reflections from the interfaces of anatomical structures may have been, as its proponents claimed, more 'dramatically direct' or 'pictorial' than A-mode (Wild and Reid 1954: 281–2). Yet when obstetrical ultrasound images were first produced, there was no consensus among physicians that these images held any useful information, or even that human tissue could be reliably and consistently differentiated with reflected echoes.

When one looks today at ultrasound images – particularly if one has been studying similar images for a year or two – a process of attributing meaning to echoes is not suggested. Once the viewer has become familiar with the circle that is always labelled as the fetal head or cranium, it is impossible to see that particular configuration of echoes as anything else: it becomes a 'fact.' The historical process of assigning meaning to those echoes has been masked. Yet Bernike Pasveer (1989: 369) notes that in the early days of X-ray imaging, 'the act of visualizing [the interior of the body] itself, and not merely diagnosing, was at stake.' In order for X-rays 'to become "true" – to [have them] represent health and disease in a knowledgeable and useful way – they needed a context and an intelligible content' (362). Experimenters with ultrasound first had to show that echoes could be produced from within the interior of the living human body. Then they had to find a way to transform those echoes into a meaningful representation of that interior. Significantly, producing ultrasound images has not always been a matter of getting ultrasound machines to produce anatomical pictures.

One of the key unresolved issues at the time Marr and Donald first began to conduct fetal ultrasounds was whether the technology's diagnostic potential lay in its ability to map the interior of the body, or whether it lay in its capacity to differentiate normal from abnormal tissue. In other words, were the blips and blurs of ultrasound going to be a reflected 'picture' of anatomy, akin to an X-ray or photograph, or were they going to be registers of normality and abnormality, like the spikes and dips of an electrocardiogram (ECG)?

The tension between these two representational possibilities for ultrasound is discussed by Ellen Koch (1993) in her analysis of the work of Douglas Howry and John Wild in the United States during the early 1950s. Working separately and 'unaware of each other's work for several years,' Howry and Wild both developed cross-sectional ultrasound images. Howry had been trained as a radiologist and was conversant in physics and engineering, and his goal was 'to produce images comparable in detail and clarity to the photographs of fixed and stained cross sections appearing in Gray's Anatomy, the standard anatomy reference' (Koch 1993: 864). Howry struggled to eliminate echoes that did not conform to the 'true' picture of the body's interior – an approach that emphasized 'standardized, reproducible results' (873). This was a difficult task with early B-mode cross-sectional ultrasounds, since within the complex interior of the body there was virtually no way to know which surfaces were being reflected. Thus, ultrasounds were reliable only when used on organ specimens or on a patient's extremities. Not only did one still need to know beforehand what was being visualized, but 'one [needed] to be able to visualize how any given slice [of the body's interior would] appear' (Yoxen 1987: 293–4). Of course, the structural interior of the human body was relatively well known by this time, and cross-sectional diagrams were available for comparison with ultrasound images. However, most physicians (the exceptions being surgeons and pathologists) were unaccustomed to seeing the interior of the body in cross-section, as a series of planes (Leopold 1990: 24).

Howry was seeking to eliminate reflected echoes and 'noise,' which could not be consistently reproduced. Meanwhile, Wild was turning to ultrasound's variable echoes as means of identifying pathology. For Wild, a surgeon, ultrasound's potential lay in differentiating 'the relative acoustic behavior of ... tissue, not any direct visualization of abnormal lumps' (Koch 1993: 876). Wild was influenced by the individualistic, try-it-and-see approach of surgery, and was relatively unconcerned with reproducibility. Instead, he 'used each patient as his or her own norm, comparing one side of the body against the other' (878) in an effort to distinguish cancerous from non-cancerous tissue. This individualistic method of producing the images severely limited their diagnostic potential: 'Inherent in the experimental biological method is the concept of controlling systems in such a manner that all variables except one are held constant. Thus a second echogram ... is recorded through normal breast tissue *without alteration of the controls of the echograph* [the apparatus]. Since there is a case to case alteration of the controls, *it is not valid to compare echograms from case to case'* (Wild and Reid 1954: 280, my emphasis).

Koch's analysis makes it clear that what was at stake in debates about methods – Howry's versus Wild's – was not the 'best' means of exploiting ultrasound. Appraisals of their work were strongly influenced by institutional agendas and local research traditions. And of course, prestige and grant money hinged on those appraisals. For example, in 1957, NIH reviewers – most of them physicists – criticized Wild's methods as 'subjective' and 'tinkering,' and supported Howry's application because it fit the current dominant model of basic research. 'In providing quantifiable measurements of ... ultrasound in biological tissues, Howry fit the physicist's model of research; in studying the patterns of acoustic behavior in normal tissue prior to working on the abnormal, he paralleled the physiologist's approach to understanding the human body; in producing recognizable images of the outlines of soft tissue structure, he subscribed to diagnostic mores current in radiology' (Koch 1993: 888).

Five years later, although his approach had not changed, Wild's 'tinkering' was regarded by NIH reviewers as commendable and worthy of considerable financial support. Why? The composition of the review panel had changed (i.e., it included more physicians); also, support was growing for cross-disciplinary methodologies, and there was pressure on the NIH to fund clinical care studies rather than just basic research (Koch 1993).

Donald's initial approach to ultrasound was closer to Wild's, in that he was concerned with distinguishing different types of abdominal tumours.[4] But as his gaze turned to the fetus, his desire grew to 'see' the fetus pictorially.

In 1958, shortly after switching to compound B-mode scanning, Donald and his colleagues published their initial ultrasound findings in *The Lancet* in a paper titled 'Investigation of Abdominal Masses by Pulsed Ultrasound.' The many photographs in this article presented 2-D ultrasound images of ovarian cysts, uterine fibroids, and the healthy abdomen of one of the authors, as well as an image of a 'foetal skull in utero at 34 weeks' gestation,' 'twins,' 'hydramnios' and a 'uterus at 14-weeks' gestation, showing echoes from foetus' (Donald, McVicar, and Brown 1958). The article concluded:

Our experience of 78 cases in which diagnosis was quickly verified by laparotomy and subsequent histology indicates that ultrasonic diagnosis is still very crude, and that the preoperative diagnosis of histological structure is still far off, although such a possibility in the future is an exciting prospect. The fact that recordable echoes can be obtained at all has both surprised and encouraged us, but our findings are still of more academic interest than practical importance and we do not feel that our clinical judgement should be influenced by our ultrasound findings ... It is only fair to point out that the illustrations shown herewith are among the very best we have been able to produce out of about 450. They do however, encourage great efforts to refine our technique. (1190)

While in this passage Donald and his colleagues were talking about cysts and tumours rather than fetuses, their desire to use ultrasound to see the fetus was evident. As they explained, 'the pregnant uterus offers considerable scope for [ultrasound] because it is a cystic cavity containing a solid foetus' (1192).

Donald admitted his surprise at being able to produce an image. At the same time, however, he assumed that ultrasound was capable of providing diagnostic information: all he had to do was improve the technology and learn how to read the images so as to release their diagnostic significance. By the time Ian Donald began publishing his fetal images, much of the cultural groundwork for visually representing the interior of the living body had been laid. A variety of techniques, including X-rays (by then in medical use for sixty years), for visually depicting structures and activities inside the human body had already become routinized in medicine (Pasveer 1989). In addition, since the 1930s researchers in Europe, Japan, the United States, and elsewhere had been experimenting with ultrasound as a diagnostic tool for the brain, abdomen, breast, and heart (Woo 1998). Also by the early 1960s black-and-white visual representations from photography and from television had been accepted as part of the taken-for-granted world. Donald did not feel it necessary to provide reference diagrams in his first articles; he assumed that his ultrasound images would be understood with only descriptive headings and the occasional indicating arrow. In Pasveer's terms, ultrasound images, like X-rays, quickly came to be equated with photographs, which 'suggest hardly any interference, hardly any constructive activities' (1990: 1).

After the publication of Donald's article in 1958, a number of obstetricians in Great Britain, Sweden, Australia, Japan, and the United States began to experiment with ultrasound and to publish their results (McNay and Fleming 1999). In looking over the obstetrical images published in medical journals from 1958 through the 1960s, I was especially struck by how few show anything of the fetus except the head. Some images depict the uterine wall, the early gestational sac, and the placenta, but most show the outline of the fetal cranium, the side-by-side crania of twins, and cranial anomalies, such as microcephaly (very small) and hydrocephaly (grossly enlarged). Many of the images labelled 'normal fetus' in fact show only the fetal head. In the B-mode ultrasound used in these early images, the fetal cranium appears as a white oval, in sharp contrast to the dark, 'echo-free spaces' of the watery brain and amniotic fluid. The masses of reflections from the rest of the fetal body are hidden in another plane or appear as undifferentiated, unlabelled dots. In effect, prior to grey-scaled and higher-resolution images, the fetal body was presented as 'noise' in the ultrasound image. For example, the fetal spine – one of the most recognizable parts of the fetal image today – 'was not demonstrated echographically until 1962 and then it was only as a white blob on a black background' (Garrett 1988, cited in McNay and Fleming 1999: 15).

By the mid-1960s, 'seeing' the fetus through ultrasound was mainly about determining pregnancy (through an enlarged gestational sac), which could be done as early as six weeks (Woo 1998); or locating the position of the fetal head; or determining the number of fetuses based on the number of heads. Ultrasound played only a small role in obstetric care, and physicians relied heavily on other tests, other senses, and other forms of knowledge – including the mother's knowledge – to guide that care. The 1966 edition of *Williams Obstetrics*, a widely used textbook in Canada and the United States, acknowledged the use of ultrasound to locate the head, but instructed that the reliable diagnosis of pregnancy depended on hearing the fetal heart, feeling fetal movement, or seeing the skull by means of an X-ray (Eastman, Hellman, and Pritchard 1966: 260). A significant barrier to 'seeing' the fetus routinely through ultrasound and using the image as a clinical tool was noted in the 1966 *Yearbook of Obstetrics and Gynecology*. As the yearbook editor explained, ultrasound still required the 'presence not only of the physician performing the *experiment* but also of a physicist or at least a physician who knows a great deal about physics' (Greenhill 1966: 49; my emphasis). As a consequence, until the early 1970s articles on ultrasound contained calculations, diagrams, and technical explanations intended to familiarize physicians with the technical principles of producing images from within the human body so that they would be able to interpret those images.

As the production of images became standardized and less a matter of calculations and equations, measuring the fetus became increasingly important. After the Second World War, clinical practice and bioengineering converged on the terrain of patients' bodies; and statistically based measures of normality, made with increasingly complex and precisely calibrated equipment, came to be regarded as the only objective means for assessing patient health. Physicians once used the terms 'normal' and 'abnormal' with reference to a specific context – an individual's overall health, life stage, and experience, for example. As statistical representations of the world gained credibility and power, the terms 'normal' and 'pathological' shifted in meaning to refer, respectively, to a statistically derived 'unenthusiastic objective average' and to specific degrees of variation from that average or normal range (Hacking 1990: 169). Since the mid-1700s, the measured female pelvis had been used as a gauge of whether a birth was likely to be 'abnormal' or 'uncomplicated' (Hiddinga and Blume 1992: 159). With the advent of X-rays, fetal cephalometry began to shift the assessment of pregnancy from the maternal pelvis to the fetal head (Hiddinga and Blume 1992: 165).

Ultrasound measurements began with the ear-to-ear, or biparietal, diameter of the cranium, and were made initially on photographs of the ultrasound image rather than 'on-screen.' These measurements were rendered diagnostically significant by comparing them throughout pregnancy to the results of existing hormonal tests of fetal maturity (Donald 1968b: 251), and to post-partum measurements and examinations (Campbell 1971). In this fashion, 'standardized growth charts' were developed for various fetal dimensions, including biparietal diameter (BPD), crown–rump length (CRL), abdominal circumference (AC), and femoral length (FL) (McNay and Fleming 1999). These measures, along with many others, are used to describe the prenatal growth profile; and provide values against which images are interpreted as 'normal' or 'abnormal' (Dubose 1996; Jaffe and Bui 1999).

Fetal Pathology

In the early B-mode scans, different types of body tissue were poorly distinguished (Leopold 1990). In the early 1970s, two techniques borrowed from photography and television were applied to ultrasound – a standard film grey-scale, and scan converters. With a scan converter, the fetal image can be seen on a TV monitor rather than through a camera positioned above a capture tube. With grey-scaling, different types of tissues appear in varying shades of black, grey, and white (Donald 1980; McNay and Fleming 1999; Woo 1998). Dense surfaces, such as bone and the lens of the eye, which reflect rather than absorb most of the ultrasound energy, are translated into white or light-grey dots. Gases and fluids are highly absorbent, so urine-filled bladders and full stomachs appear nearly black. Soft tissues such as the liver and the kidneys appear in varying shades of grey. At first, some practitioners resisted the more complex grey-scaled images, having come to regard the black-and-white images as normal (MacKay 1984: 235). This resistance was short-lived, however, and the grey-scaled images were rapidly accepted as both more 'pictorial' and more accurate. As the fetus materialized on screen, the technical details about the equipment, and the physical principles of ultrasound and how echoes were produced and reflected within the body, receded from physicians' knowledge. Differentiating among anatomical structures became a matter of memorizing what 'normal' looked like in terms of shades of grey.

Rendered visible as differentiated tissues and organs – as multiple sites awaiting signification through observation and measurement – the fetal body began to appear in published ultrasound images. Clinical significance for these increasingly differentiated images was built up slowly and reflexively over many years. Variations in fetal anatomy were noted, tentative diagnoses were made, and then, after delivery or autopsy, these diagnoses were confirmed, or the ultrasound images were reviewed to see what should have been seen (Pasveer 1989: 370). This was the reflexive process implicit in Donald's (1976b: 559) statement that 'diagnostic expertise ... has been built up quickly by the instruction afforded by mistakes and the declared outcome of the case.'

What made ultrasound especially compelling was the idea that it would allow physicians to follow the natural course of fetal pathologies from *early* in the pregnancy, even before a woman knew she was pregnant: 'I will never forget the excitement which attended the first recording of an early gestational sac ... At first we did not recognize the significance of the white ring which is now such a commonplace finding, but when we did, and observed its growth at repeated examination, our excitement became boundless' (Donald 1969: 623).

As late as 1976, the only fetal pathologies that could be 'diagnosed with certainty' by ultrasound, according to Ian Donald (1976: 568), were two anomalies in the size and appearance of the cranium (i.e., hydrocephaly and anencephaly). The first report of termination of pregnancy following ultrasonic diagnosis of anencephaly was in 1972 (McNay and Fleming 1999: 42). The construction of a natural history of fetal pathology, beginning with variations in the shape, location, and development of that 'white ring,' rapidly extended the grids of normality and abnormality against which the fetus was evaluated. Today the fetus is understood to be 'at risk' for hundreds of anomalies (see, for example, Keeling 1994; Woo 1998), which are described in countless articles and volumes on 'sonopathology' (Nimrod and Ash 1993). Michael Harrison (cited in Kolata 1990:87), one of the leaders of fetal medicine, talks about pathologizing the fetus in this way: 'No one had any idea when we started out what the natural history of a urinary tract obstruction in a fetus was. Or hydrocephalus. All the diseases. I mean, just think about this. In this last decade and a half or so, we ... were able to define diseases that no one had seen before because you couldn't see the fetus. It's like medicine started all over again.'

With ultrasound, as had happened with X-rays several decades earlier, 'the tables gradually turned: the relation between the unknown and the known world partly reversed' (Pasveer 1990: 2). Patterns of echoes had become the means of creating a new reality – the fetus as a complex, acting, sentient, diagnosable, and treatable individual. In short, ultrasound imaging has been fundamental to the creation of the fetus as a patient: 'The concept that the fetus may be a patient ... is alarmingly modern. The fetus could not be taken seriously as long as he remained a medical recluse in an opaque womb; and it was not until the last half of this century that the prying eye of the ultrasono- gram rendered the once opaque womb transparent, stripping the veil of mystery from the dark inner sanctum, and letting the light of scien- tific observation fall on the shy and secretive fetus' (Harrison 1982: 19).

At the same time that grey-scaled fetal images were appearing on monitors, 'real time' ultrasound was extending the pathologization of the fetus to include fetal movement. In real-time ultrasound, dozens of complete images are displayed per second, much faster than the hu- man eye can distinguish among them (MacKay 1984: 117). The result- ing image seems to be moving. 'Seeing' fetal movement has done much to authenticate ultrasound's 'window' onto the fetus. Conse- quently, the notion of fetal well-being has evolved to include func- tional and behavioural indices as well as morphological and biochemi- cal ones. Fetal breathing, gross body movements (e.g., rolling from side to side), fetal tone (flexion of arms, legs, head, hand), heart rate, and amniotic fluid volume have been rated and standardized as indices of developmental normality and fetal well-being. For this, the tool is the Fetal Biophysical Profile, which was developed by a Manitoba obstetrician, Frank Manning (Manning et al. 1980; American College of Obstetricians and Gynecologists 1987). Fetal swallowing and excreting are now monitored as an indicator of fetal digestive and renal function; and fetal eye and body movements are now monitored as indicators of sleep and rest periods, which are considered to measure immediate well-being and to predict post-partum behavioural normality (Birnholz 1988; Krasnegor 1988; Manning 1995).

Prior to the mid-1970s, most of the echoes in the ultrasound image were 'noise' that prevented the viewer from 'seeing' the fetus. With the addition of grey-scaling and real-time fetal images, and with the development of a normalizing clinical discourse on fetal development, risk, and behaviour, these echoes have been redefined as evidence of ultrasound's unique ability to 'see' the real fetus.[5] The sense that one is looking directly at the fetus, rather than at an image of the fetus, continues to be reinforced with recent technological changes. In the 1990s, high-resolution images were introduced, made possible by changes in the technology of transducers and in how the resulting signals were converted on their way to the monitor (Woo 1998). The images today, relative to those I saw when I began my research in 1989, are much less grainy and blurry. Many of the machines used in Canadian hospitals today are specifically tailored for fetal imaging. That is, they include software that enables the operator to 'click and point' to pull-down menus listing fetal biometry measures (head circumference, femoral length etc.), standardized growth charts, and annotations such as 'AC' and 'FL' to speed the process of labelling images.

Although not widely used, 3-D ultrasound may further authenticate ultrasound's vision of the fetus. Ironically, although 3-D ultrasound would seem to offer a 'more natural' view of the fetus, not all sonographers are convinced that it is a significant improvement over the 2-D images. As one technician recently commented to me, 'It's another toy and not all that easy to understand.'

The Institutionalization of Obstetrical Ultrasound

During the 1970s, as the technology of ultrasound became an increasingly familiar feature in the clinical landscape, scientific meetings and journals devoted to diagnostic ultrasound imaging flourished (White 1990). More than simply forums where sonographers could 'exchange information about their practices' (White 1990: 342), these sites of knowledge production and distribution facilitated the normalization of ultrasound images as a way of representing fetal and maternal bodies. Ultrasound images began to seem familiar, readily understandable, and compelling, and their production soon seemed commonplace. A rapidly expanding literature on what had been seen by ultrasound – fetal position, number, and size, and in particular fetal anomalies – contributed to the growing sense that ultrasound was indispensable to obstetrical practice. 'Medline,' a computerized indexing of medical literature, contains fewer than 250 listings on fetal ultrasound imaging for the entire decade of the 1960s. By the mid-1980s there were over 250 entries each year.

Conferences and journals were also sites for negotiating the norms for ultrasound practice. As Pasveer (1989: 365) describes for X-rays, 'rules, which initially were formulated to urge individual workers to work along the same lines, later became part of the tacit knowledge and practices possessed by competent Röntgenologists.' Canadian and American guidelines for obstetrical ultrasounds have been in existence since the early 1980s (American College of Obstetricians and Gynecologists 1981; Society of Obstetricians and Gynaecologists of Canada 1981). These recommendations, along with later revisions, reflect the development and recognition of standardized procedures and measurements in obstetrical scanning. Norms for doing a scan by producing a series of images (of the fetal head, fetal spine, and so on) helped transform ultrasound imaging from an experimental procedure into a reproducible method of acquiring diagnostic information about the fetus (Pasveer 1989: 365).

Standardized practices and norms of imaging also meant that the production of ultrasound fetal images became increasingly task-oriented – a 'prescriptive technology' in the words of Ursula Franklin (1999: 24ff). Each ultrasound scan followed a general pattern. The diagnostic information was produced through a series of measurements and images. The information recorded in measurements, and in photographic reproductions of the images, could then be compared to growth charts and to the viewer's knowledge of normal fetal appearance. In ambiguous cases, the ultrasound images could be compared directly with photographs or with other ultrasound images. Once norms of ultrasound practice were established, the processes of producing the images and interpreting them could be separated slightly.[6] A physician could look at a photograph or radiographic film of the image and determine whether the fetus was normal without having been involved in the production of that image, or meeting the woman in whose body the fetus lay.

As obstetrical ultrasound became routinized, and as the process of making the images became increasingly separate from the process of interpreting them, two main types of sonographers emerged. There are now physician-sonographers, usually radiologists or obstetricians, who supervise routine ultrasounds and carry out many of the lengthy, 'detailed' scans involving a suspected fetal anomaly.[7] There are also technician-sonographers (often licensed radiology technicians, some of whom have taken certification courses in ultrasound), who carry out the routine procedures of conducting fetal measurements, localizing the placenta, and screening for anomalies. This division of diagnostic responsibility means that technician-sonographers are expected to conduct ultrasound examinations without diagnosing problems. Nonetheless, technicians must be able to assess the fetus's appearance, size, position, development, and behaviour, and must know when it is necessary to call an obstetrician.

The 1980s and 1990s: Becoming Standard Practice Amidst Controversy

Ultrasound's role in opening the black box of pregnancy has not been without controversy. In the late 1970s, reflecting concerns from a variety of medical, scientific, and public interest groups, the U.S. Food and Drug Administration cautioned that 'it is much too early to assume that ultrasound is perfectly safe in pregnancy' (Thompson 1983: 11). An American news report, 'Fetal Effects of Ultrasound,' aired a few years later, highlighted evidence of *in vitro* chromosomal damage and anomalies in animals exposed to ultrasound. The reporter summarized this evidence as 'the signs of danger, warning signs that in the past predicted medical disaster' (CNN Transcript 1982: 2).

Is Ultrasound Safe?

Concerns about ultrasound's safety derive from *in vitro* and animal studies indicating that ultrasound's non-ionizing radiation causes cellular and chromosomal changes (Bolsen 1982; Stratmeyer and Christman 1983), and from recognition that there is no agreed upon method of quantifying ultrasound exposure (Gonzalez 1984; Neilson and Grant

1989). In light of the well-established dangers of prenatal X-ray, there is concern about the possible risk of harm to the fetus or the mother from diagnostic ultrasound. Also, research has not demonstrated that ultrasound imaging is safe; rather, a 'lack of risk has been assumed because no adverse effects have been demonstrated clearly in humans' (National Institutes of Health 1984: 1). Several studies have investigated the possibility of adverse effects on nonhuman tissue (e.g., Abdulla et al. 1971; Angles et al. 1990; O'Brien 1983; Pizzarrello et al. 1978; Tarnatal and Hendrickx 1989; Tarnatal, O'Brien, and Hendrickx 1993). In monkeys, there was significant mean birth weight reduction following frequent prenatal ultrasound exposure (Tarnatal and Hendrickx 1989; Tarnatal, O'Brien, and Hendrickx 1993). More recently, the media have reported that Irish researchers have shown that ultrasound imaging can create changes in the cells of mice, specifically, a significant reduction in the rate of cell division and a doubling of cell death (Jimenez 1999: A1).

Unfortunately, there have been few studies investigating the potential harmful effects of human prenatal exposure to ultrasound, and most were not conducted until years after routine ultrasound was in place (Brent et al. 1991; Lyons et al. 1988; Newnham et al. 1993; Salvesen et al. 1992). Several adverse effects have been suggested, including learning disorders, low birth weight, and miscarriage.

The issue of learning disorders was raised by an American follow-up study of 7- to 12-year-old children. Children who had been exposed to ultrasound prenatally had a higher incidence of dyslexia (Stark et al. 1984). A Canadian study compared the antenatal records of 72 children with delayed speech to 142 controls, matched/similar for sex, date of birth, birth order, class, birth weight, and length of pregnancy. The children with speech problems were twice as likely to have had ultrasound before birth (Campbell, Elford, and Brant 1993). A much larger Norwegian study followed the children of women who had been part of earlier, randomized trials of ultrasound between 1979 and 1981. Based on teachers' evaluations, school performance was not diminished, nor was dyslexia more likely, among the children whose mothers had routine ultrasound (Salvesen et al. 1993: 87).

Concerns about low birthweight are derived from a randomized controlled trial from Australia. The study was conducted to test the hypothesis that intensive use of Doppler flow and imaging ultrasound would improve pregnancy outcomes by reducing both pre-term birth rates and hospital stays for newborns (Newnham et al. 1993). In fact, the only significant finding was an increase in the number of low birthweight babies among women who received intensive ultrasound. The authors concluded: 'Our findings suggest that five or more ultrasound imaging and Doppler flow studies between 18 and 38 weeks gestation, when compared with a single imaging study at 18 weeks gestation, increases the proportion of growth restricted fetuses by about one third'[8] (Newnham et al. 1993: 890).

Surprisingly few studies have investigated the effect of ultrasound on fetal loss or miscarriage. While some individual studies have found higher rates of miscarriage among women having ultrasound (e.g., Saari-Kemppainen et al. 1990), two meta-analyses have not found spontaneous early fetal loss to be higher among women having routine ultrasound (Bucher and Schmidt 1993). A study from Helsinki found higher rates of miscarriage among women using ultrasound equipment in their work as physiotherapists (Taskinen et al. 1990).

Unfortunately, there is no consensus within the scientific community as to whether prenatal ultrasound exposure is safe for either woman or fetus. So far, there is no strong evidence of harm, but neither is there proof that ultrasound is harmless.

Does Ultrasound Improve the Outcome of Pregnancy?

Some clinical trials have found routine ultrasound examination of low-risk women associated with lower rates of labour induction, higher infant birthweights (e.g., Waldenstrom et al. 1988; Eik-Nes et al. 1984), and reduced perinatal mortality (Saari-Kemppainen et al. 1990). Others have found no benefit to routine prenatal scans (Bennett et al. 1982; Neilson et al. 1989; Bakketeig et al. 1984; Ewigman et al. 1993).

Motivated by growing concerns about ultrasound's efficacy and cost, in the 1980s several national and international bodies published statements on obstetrical ultrasound imaging. Most but not all of these statements concluded that routine fetal imaging was not warranted based on the evidence concerning its safety and clinical benefit.[8] One of the most widely cited of those reviews of ultrasound, and the one to which I was usually directed by the sonographers I interviewed in Montreal, was the 1984 report of the NIH Consensus Development Conference.[9] The NIH panel reached the following general conclusion about ultrasound: 'The data on clinical efficacy and safety do not allow a recommendation for routine screening at this time' (NIH 1984: 238). They concluded further that their information 'allowed no consensus that routine ultrasound examinations for all pregnancies improved perinatal outcome or decreased morbidity or mortality' (237). Similarly, the Society of Obstetricians and Gynaecologists of Canada issued guidelines in 1981 concluding that routine ultrasounds 'cannot be recommended.' Such statements appear to have had little impact on the routinization of obstetrical imaging. In Canada, as elsewhere, the use of fetal imaging continued to rise during the 1980s. By the end of that decade, there were an average of 2.1 ultrasound examinations per delivery in Canada.[10]

Five randomized controlled trials (Bakketeig et al. 1984; Ewigman et al. 1990, 1993; Saari-Kemppainen et al. 1990; Waldenstrom et al. 1988) provide the current best available evidence as to whether, and in what circumstances, routine ultrasound imaging makes a difference to the outcome of pregnancy. These studies examined pregnancy outcomes for over 30,000 low-risk women, who were randomized into two groups – those having a routine scan, and those having a 'selective' scan if an indication arose during the course of the pregnancy. The outcomes under investigation included maternal and perinatal mortality, and maternal and perinatal morbidity. Maternal morbidity included outcomes such as induction of labour, caesarean section, infection requiring antibiotics, and days in hospital. Perinatal morbidity included outcomes such as hospitalization, mechanical ventilation, seizures, intracranial hemorrhage, and spinal cord or nerve injury. The clinical trials generally also examined the impact of routine versus selective scanning on dating the fetus, multiple fetuses, intrauterine growth restriction (IUGR), birthweight, placental localization, induction of labour, and fetal anomalies.

These clinical trials, and other studies on the efficacy of ultrasound imaging, have garnered the attention of many review panels in Canada and around the world. In Canada and the United States the focus of these reviews has not been on questions of safety. Rather, in the context of diminished health care resources and pressure to rationalize services, the reviews have sought to determine whether the current practice of routine ultrasound is worth the costs and is 'evidence-based' (Acheson and Mitchell 1993). For example, in its 1993 final report Canada's Royal Commission on New Reproductive Technologies concluded: 'It is essential to control this rapid proliferation of routine ultrasound and to determine whether the substantial funds [$100 million per year] now being devoted to it are justified ... [An] important aspect is that a program framework must be developed that will serve to contain both utilization rates and total costs for routine ultrasound' (1993, vol. 2: 817).

In one of the most comprehensive and systematic reviews to date, the British Columbia Office of Health Technology Assessment (BCOHTA) evaluated six of the recent documents that incorporated evidence-based recommendations about routine ultrasound.[11] Based on their assessment and extensive appraisal criteria, the BCOHTA report (Green et al. 1996) concluded that 'research evidence shows that RUIP [routine ultrasound imaging in pregnancy] has no impact on final health outcomes, although some intermediate outcomes have been shown to change' (66). Specifically, the Green report reiterated that the review panels have 'consistently documented that evidence from randomized controlled trials does *not* demonstrate a reduction in perinatal or maternal morbidity or mortality in patients provided with routine ultrasound.'

Claims that the routine use of ultrasound improves pregnancy outcomes by allowing the monitoring of fetal age, fetal growth, multiple fetuses, placental position, and amniotic fluid levels were rejected by the report as 'untenable' (59). This report is only one of several in Canada; others have reviewed the same evidence and reached different recommendations. In 1994 a federal and provincial task force concluded that repeated ultrasounds did not show 'any statistically significant effect on perinatal mortality, morbidity, or birth weights,' yet felt there was 'fair evidence' (lower rates of induction, earlier detection of twins) to recommend a single ultrasound as part of routine prenatal care (Anderson 1994: 9).

Recent changes in policy statements from the Society of Obstetricians and Gynaecologists of Canada (SOGC) reflect the ongoing controversy over the value of routine scanning. In 1981 the SOGC concluded that routine ultrasounds 'cannot be recommended.' By 1994, the SOGC's policy was that 'a second trimester [16–20 week] ultrasound scan should be offered to all women' (1994: 2). This recommendation was in line with the findings of a survey which reported that 63 per cent of Canadian physicians felt that pregnant women should have at least one ultrasound (Renaud et al. 1993: 278). By 1999, in its most recent set of guidelines, the SOCG's recommendation was as follows: 'After appropriate discussion about the potential benefits, limitations and safety of the examination, women should be offered an ultrasound centered at 18 to 19 weeks gestation' (1999: 2).

That document, 'Guidelines for Ultrasound as Part of Routine Prenatal Care,' underscores the contradiction between how ultrasound is
being used and the evidence that it is useful. For example, 'sonographic
measurement at 18 to 19 weeks can establish gestational age to +/-
seven days ... None of the randomized controlled trials has shown that
dating with routine ultrasound reduces perinatal morbidity or mortality, unless associated with early termination of pregnancy for detected
anomalies' (3). Also, 'second trimester ultrasound leads to earlier detection of multiple gestations. Large randomized controlled trials indicate that early knowledge of twins does not lead to a significant reduction in perinatal morbidity and mortality' (4).

Regarding safety, the SOCG concludes that 'there is no scientific
evidence of a deleterious effect from diagnostic ultrasound on the
developing human fetus ... [Rather,] the biggest risk of ultrasound is
over-interpretation or missed diagnosis' (4–5). This point is particularly interesting for two reasons. *First*, calls for routine scanning are
increasingly being tied to claims about ultrasound's ability to detect
fetal anomalies. Several review committees have suggested, as does
the Green report, that 'the only benefit of ultrasound substantiated by
RCT [randomized clinical trial] evidence is early termination of pregnancy in fetuses with major malformation.' *Second*, routine ultrasound
can detect at best 50 per cent of fetal anomalies (Health Services Utilization and Research Commission 1996: 3). In practice, detection rates
vary with the type of anomaly, the skill of the operator, equipment
quality, and fetal age. According to one reviewer, the ability of routine
ultrasound to detect fetuses with anomalies ranges from 17 to 85 per
cent; its ability to identify those without anomalies ranges from 93 to
100 per cent (Chitty 1995: 1242; Health Services Utilization and Research Commission 1996, cited in Green et al. 1996: 83). Unfortunately,
these figures mean that some women are unnecessarily alarmed by
the incorrect finding that their babies will have anomalies, and that
some women are falsely reassured that their babies will be normal.[12]

What is especially noteworthy about the recent guidelines is how
women are co-opted to justify routine scanning. For example, the current SOGC policy, which recommends that ultrasound 'should be offered to all women' implies that at some given point in time, the
physician discusses with the woman whether she wants to have ultrasound. Of the nearly one hundred women I interviewed formally in
two studies, and of the dozens more I have talked to informally, only

a handful have ever had that kind of discussion with their physician. The truth is that most women in Canada are never asked if they want to have ultrasound, and there is no informed consent or informed choice for this form of prenatal diagnosis. The absence of informed choice around this technology is particularly worrisome, given the good possibility that through ultrasound, women may be either unnecessarily worried or falsely reassured.

Fetal Patients and the New Social Relationships of Pregnancy Care

Ultrasound fetal imaging is not the only prenatal procedure to have become routine amid controversy, nor is it the first (Oakley 1986b). Electronic fetal heart monitoring and caesarean section are two other examples.[13] There are a number of reasons why the use of ultrasound has continued to grow and become routine during this period of controversy. *First*, even when organizations and reports do not endorse a policy of routine ultrasound, the range of specific medical indications for ultrasound is very wide – wide enough to include most or all pregnancies.[14] The sonographers I interviewed in Montreal generally identified determining fetal age, screening for maternal or fetal risk factors, screening for fetal anomalies, and psychological benefits as the benefits of routine ultrasound. Thus, they explained, 'ultrasound has something for everyone.' *Second*, the lack of studies showing that scanning has clear benefits has not been perceived as implying that there is no benefit, but rather that adequate studies have not yet been undertaken. Today, older studies may be dismissed because of changes in ultrasound technology that make the image much clearer. *Third*, the absence of clear evidence of physical harm to women or to the fetus from ultrasound has been very important in the routinization of this technology. The sonographers I interviewed saw no convincing reasons not to use ultrasound routinely. The clinic staff maintained that ultrasound was safe, and that there was 'no good evidence' of harm, and argued that it was cost-effective. As one obstetrician remarked during my research:

> It cost under $50,000 to run the [ultrasound] clinic last year. That's nothing! You know, and this really bothers me, you could scan all women five times during pregnancy for the cost of three heart transplants ... So we find out that it's $10,000 to scan and intervene in a [fetal] growth retardation. That's just off the top of my head. Okay, so that $10,000

seems like a lot. But, I mean, here's the life of some poor little guy in there and what's that in comparison to the million dollars it costs to prolong the life of someone with heart disease for three months!

This comment was not unique. Another obstetrician told me:

Let's say for Quebec, at $100 a scan we're talking about $10 million dollars just to do a sixteen to eighteen week scan for all pregnant women. And, I'm being conservative. Is it preventing malformed, handicapped, and bad babies from being born? What is the saving to health care if it is preventing all malformed, handicapped, and bad babies from being born? It's not just a matter of the here and now, it's the future savings as well. And we can't project that.

Fourth, and perhaps most importantly, by the time ultrasound came under scrutiny in the early 1980s, there had been significant changes in the social organization of pregnancy care in Canada and the United States. Diane Eyers (1992: 146) described this change: 'There was a shift in focus from the management of childbirth procedures to monitoring and surveillance, and a shift from the woman as patient to the fetus.' Ultrasound fetal imaging was pivotal to that shift and to its permanence.

Although ultrasound's echoes now easily stand in for the 'real' fetus, when ultrasound was first used in obstetrics the fetus was not a focus of attention. For example, there were virtually no references to the fetus in the chapter headings of textbooks or in annuals such as the *Yearbook of Obstetrics and Gynecology*. The 1971 edition of *Williams Obstetrics* had a paragraph on the fetus; five years later the fetus had a chapter to itself (discussed in Renaud et al. 1987). By the 1981 edition, as Hahn (1987: 231) points out, that textbook was referring to the fetus as 'the second patient.' By 1989, in the eighteenth edition of *Williams Obstetrics*, 'the fetus emerge[d] as the most powerful force in childbirth':

The authors [of that edition] describe 'the fetal-maternal communication system,' in which information is exchanged through biomolecular nutrients and hormones. 'The physiological and metabolic accommodations in the maternal organism that contribute to successful pregnancy are orchestrated by fetal-directed biomolecular initiatives' ... The authors conclude 'unambiguously that the fetus ... [directs] the orchestration of the

physiological events of pregnancy. The maternal organism passively re-
sponds – even to the point of her own detriment.' (Hahn 1995: 220–1)

The 'fetocentric' trend in obstetrics is evident as well in the growing
number of journals, conferences, and subspecialty training programs
devoted to the fetus. In many ways, the field of obstetrics seems to be
redefining itself as 'maternal and fetal medicine' or 'perinatal medicine' (Mohide 1990). Parallel to this change in the status of the fetus
are changes in how ultrasound imaging is viewed. At first, ultrasound
was discussed as a means of distinguishing pregnancy from other
'abdominal masses' (Donald, MacVicar, and Brown 1958: 1188). Within
a few years, reviewers were talking about ultrasound's potential for
measuring the fetus and expressing hope 'that all the echoes visualized on any one somagram eventually would become significant'
(Greenhill et al. 1966). By the early 1990s, ultrasound had become as it
is today, a form of 'prenatal diagnosis' and a means of 'fetal surveillance' (Cunningham et al. 1989; Morrison 1990). The authors of a text
on fetal well-being note that ultrasound and other 'developments [have]
changed the role of an obstetrician from being primarily the mother's
doctor to a fetal physician as well' (Katz et al. 1990: np). Pregnancy
has thus been reconceptualized as an interaction among the health
provider, the woman, and the fetus.

In this new order of things, the new fetus is not merely an individual, but an individual at risk and in need of technological surveillance (Arney 1982). Claims of expertise in managing pregnancy have
come to depend on the ability to discover, monitor, and interpret fetal
signs. Accordingly, obstetrics has developed a wide range of technologies (ultrasound, fetal heart monitors, amniocentesis, chorionic villus
sampling, maternal serum screening) to monitor 'normal' pregnancies, on the assumption that 'something might go wrong.' Ultrasound's
ability to 'see' the fetus, in grey-scale detail and real-time movement,
has quickly rendered secondary, knowledge of the fetus gained through
palpation, history-taking, blood tests, and external measurement
(through fundal height). The reliability of some other methods of knowing the fetus, and the credibility of physicians who do not refer women
for routine ultrasounds, are called into question. Pregnancy indicated
by a hormonal test or a woman's own bodily changes must now be
'confirmed by ultrasound.' Fetal life, although indicated by auscultation and doptone monitoring, must be 'reliably confirm[ed]' with real-

time imaging of the fetal heart, respiration, and movement (AIUM guidelines, cited in Pretorius and Mahoney 1990: 14). As the pregnancy progresses, it cannot be considered 'normal' until placental and fetal anomalies in morphology, function, and development have been ruled out by ultrasound. Ultrasound fetal imaging is now widely viewed as an essential tool and as inseparable from the biomedical management of pregnancy, labour, and delivery.

These shifts in meaning and practice have not depended solely on the apparatus and utilization of ultrasound. Other technologies, most notably electronic fetal heart monitoring during labour, the use of Doppler ultrasound to hear the fetal heart beat, maternal serum screening, and prenatal genetic diagnostic procedures such as amniocentesis and chorionic villus sampling, have emerged alongside fetal imaging and have been equally important to this process (see for example, Kunisch 1989; Renaud et al 1993: 247). As they became routine methods for screening, monitoring, and diagnosing the fetus, the conditions were created for attempts to intervene in and solve problematic fetal conditions. As Monica Casper points out (1998: 87), fetal intrauterine transfusions and open fetal surgery were 'partners' with ultrasound and genetic diagnostic technologies in creating the unborn patient.

The 'need to see' the fetal patient inside the 'black box' of pregnancy rapidly became both compelling and entrenched within obstetrical practice, so much so that it has hampered efforts to evaluate ultrasound's safety and benefits (Meire 1987: 1122). For example, in a randomized blind study in England on the efficacy of ultrasound, '30 percent of clinicians were so uncertain of their own judgements they broke the code to obtain the information provided by ultrasound for women in the control group' (Neilson 1986: 15). Dependence on ultrasound is now so great that withholding it is considered unethical; for this reason, recent studies have compared the impact of serial to single ultrasound. The following passage, from a letter written by a group of British obstetricians to The Lancet, suggests just how routine this procedure had become by the late 1980s: 'We continue ultrasound screening in our unit, despite its marginal benefits, and believe that mother and physician expect ultrasound as essential in the antenatal care package' (Shafi et al. 1988).

Transformations in the meanings of fetality are not simply the product of technology, scientific knowledge, and biomedical agendas. The political, legal, and emotional debate around abortion in Canada has profoundly shaped both ideas about the fetus and the desire to 'see' into a pregnant woman's uterus.

In 1969, then prime minister Pierre Trudeau heralded a series of changes to the Criminal Code by saying: 'The state has no business in the bedrooms of the nation' (McLaren and McLaren 1986: 9). The amendments made divorce easier to obtain, decriminalized homosexual relations between consenting adults, and legalized contraception and medically approved abortions performed in hospital. Progressive as it seemed, that reform of abortion laws arose primarily because physicians – mostly men – were concerned about the criminality of the procedure they were carrying out (Jenson 1992). Neither women nor fetuses figured prominently in the debates. Women were victims needing legislation to protect them from backstreet abortionists, and fetuses were part of the biology of pregnancy – 'embryos.' Abortions were cast as medical matters, and were to be conducted in hospital when pregnancy threatened a woman's 'health,' but only when permitted by a hospital committee.

By the early 1980s, around the same time that real-time grey-scaled ultrasound was coming into wider use, the terms of the abortion debate had changed significantly. Pro-life groups mobilized in Canada shortly after the 1969 reform, with a campaign that represented 'abortion as murder, as the first line of attack on family values, and as the source of much social instability' (Jenson 1992: 53). Hospitals succumbed to this pressure and began to close down their abortion services. Increasingly aware that access to legal abortions was precariously dependent on the availability of physicians and the permission of hospital committees, feminists and pro-choice groups began to lobby for expanded access to abortion and for free-standing abortion clinics. 'By the mid-1980s, two groups faced off. One represented the issue as being about life, babies and rights. The other represented it as about women, freedom of choice, and rights' (Jenson 1992: 55).

In January 1988 the Supreme Court ruled that the 1969 reform, which established institutional and medical control over abortion, violated women's rights as persons. That decision was a central victory for pro-choice forces and for Canadian women's control over their reproduction. By then, this question – when does the fetus become a person? – had become central in the debates, especially for anti-choice groups. Aware of its enormously persuasive power, anti-choice groups turned to science – to its language, its experts, and its technology, including ultrasound – for support for their claims about the fetus (Petchesky 1987, 1990). In Canadian courtrooms, various experts in fetology and obstetrical ultrasonography, bearing slide and video images of 'fetal gymnastics and development,' have sought to prove that humans are legal persons from the moment of conception (Collins 1985: 68). In 1983, Canadian antichoice activist Joseph Borowski began his much publicized 'Trial for Life' (Persky 1988: 5) in Saskatchewan. Borowski recruited scientists, fetal medicine specialists, and ultrasonographers in his attempt to prove that the fetus was a human and therefore a person and entitled to full protection under the newly promulgated Canadian Charter of Rights and Freedoms (Collins 1985: 209).[15] Borowski and the anti-choice movement were unsuccessful in having fetal personhood made law. Nonetheless, by the end of the 1980s the abortion debate had been remade in the language of competing fetal and maternal interests. The January 1988 decision to strike down the federal abortion law was supported by five of the seven Supreme Court judges. 'Only one [of the five], however, Madam Justice Bertha Wilson, declared that women had a *right* to an abortion in the early stages of pregnancy. Moreover, all of the majority decisions conceded the state's interest in protecting the foetus' (Brodie 1992: 59).

In sum, our perceptions of the fetus have changed, and these changes are a result of the interplay between biomedicine, reproductive and gender politics, ethics, law, health care economics and even commercial and entertainment interests. I return to the content and implications of these broad semiotic and social changes in the final part of the book. In the next chapter, I situate ultrasound fetal imaging within the context of Quebec's health care system and my research in Montreal.

Chapter Three

The View from the Field

Feminist objectivity is about limited location and situated knowledge.

Haraway (1991: 188)

In this chapter, I begin to locate prenatal ultrasound and fetuses within the lives of the sonographers and expectant couples I interviewed. Much of this involves explaining what ultrasound and fetality *mean* in the ethnographic fabric of Montreal. The uses and meanings of ultrasound fetal imaging are not universal; rather, they are locally shaped and directed. I also discuss what my own role was in the production of those meanings.

I first saw ultrasound fetal imaging during the summer of 1986, when my own pregnancy dragged on past the 'normal' forty weeks. After listening to my midwife and my physician talk about 'placental insufficiency,' I agreed to have an ultrasound. I knew nothing about this technology. Not only was I having my first child, but as a woman planning to have a midwife-attended home birth in 1986, I was firmly on the fringe of biomedical ideas about childbirth. My advice book on pregnancy discussed ultrasound in two separate chapters – 'Before You Get Pregnant' and 'Complications in Pregnancy and Birth' – neither of which seemed especially relevant to my unplanned but healthy pregnancy (Hotchner 1984). The only pregnant women I knew were those attending the midwife-run prenatal class. None of us had had a routine ultrasound.

What I recall most vividly during my first ultrasound was the technician's concern when I didn't seem interested in the swirling grey mass on the screen. From my perspective, lying on my back with an enormous belly and a full bladder, I just wanted the scan to be over. I now understand that the technician incorrectly read my reaction to the ultrasound as a sign that I was ambivalent about or possibly even rejecting the baby.

Two years later, emerging from under a pile of diapers, I was searching for a doctoral research topic. Although I wanted to concentrate on women's experiences with and understandings of reproductive technology, I had dismissed ultrasound as too routine, everyday, and mundane. As I eventually came to understand, this taken-for-granted quality is precisely why ultrasound deserves our critical attention.

The Place

I chose Montreal as a research site mainly because I had been told that multiple or serial ultrasounds were routine there. Montreal is more widely associated with cosmopolitanism – great shopping, wonderful restaurants, distinctive architecture, the French language, and cultural diversity – and with extreme weather. 'Our New York,' was how one Canadian described it to me.

It is impossible to live in Montreal and not be aware of and affected by the 'language issue.' Although the majority of Canadians (60 per cent) are native English speakers, about 82 per cent of Quebeckers speak French as their first language, compared to only 9 per cent for English (Statistics Canada 1997). The distinctive linguistic make-up of Quebec has fuelled tremendous social and political tensions throughout the province's history. Francophone politicians and intellectuals have wrested economic power away from the minority English population, and moral authority from the Catholic Church, and have spawned an influential separatist movement mobilized around the idea that Quebec is a 'distinct society.' In this milieu, 'the collective self-conception changed from French-Canadians – a minority situation – to Québécois' (Breton 1987: 56), a shift congruent with Quebec's aspirations to be recognized as a distinct society. Since 1976, when the first separatist government was elected, Quebec governments have adopted an increasingly protectionist attitude toward the French language and francophone rights. Governments now closely monitor the cultural and linguistic character of the province's public institutions, including its medical ones (Trofimenkoff 1983). The most recent manifestation of this trend was the October 1995 referendum, in which just under 50 per cent of Quebec voters voted yes in a referendum on whether Quebec should become sovereign, and came close to toppling the 120-year-old federation of provinces (Wilson-Smith 1995).

In Montreal, Quebec's largest city, the intersection of language, identity, and authority is complicated by the fact that it is also Canada's most culturally diverse and ethnically segregated city (Balakrishnan and Kralt 1987). According to 1991 census data, 68 per cent of metropolitan Montreal's 3.3 million people are native French speakers and 15 per cent are native English speakers (Statistics Canada 1992). The remainder (nearly 17 per cent) are referred to as 'allophones,' individuals whose first language is neither French nor English. The city has large communities of people from southern Europe, the Middle East and North Africa, Southeast Asia, Central America, and the Caribbean.

The politics of language and ethnicity have seeped into everyday life in Montreal. Many of the women I interviewed had family or friends who moved out of Quebec during the 1970s, when over 100,000 English-speakers left in the wake of the growing separatist movement. Public signs in Quebec must conform to strict regulations for ensuring that French is more prominent than other languages, the children of immigrants must attend school in French, and businesses and public offices must answer the phone in French. Despite the protectionist approach to French in Quebec, in Montreal it is surprisingly easy to live one's life in another language. As I learned the districts and neighbourhoods of Montreal, I learned their cultural and linguistic valences – 'p'tit Haiti,' 'Little Italy,' 'Park Extension – the Greek area,' 'the Hasidic Jews of Outremont,' 'the Anglo West Island,' and so on. Linguistic choices permeate work, shopping, entertainment, and raising children in this multilingual city; in addition, language shapes one's choice of health care provider. Many of the anglophone women I interviewed were bilingual, but they still wanted an 'English doctor' and an 'English hospital.' 'I don't mind working and shopping in French, but I want to go through labour in English,' exclaimed one woman.

The Women

The forty-nine pregnant women I interviewed in Montreal did not form an easily identifiable 'community' or distinct ethnic group. The majority were born in Canada, in Quebec, between 1956 and 1967, and thus shared a place and a period of history in which they grew up, went to school, and were now working and having children. Most of the women referred to themselves as 'typical' or 'ordinary Canadian' women. Several prefaced their willingness to join the study by saying that they weren't sure what they could contribute since they weren't 'very different' or didn't lead 'very interesting lives.' At the same time, they constructed their identities along diverse cultural lines, including, by their own terms, 'Armenian,' 'Lebanese,' 'anglophone,' 'Italian-Canadian,' Québécoise,' 'Jewish,' 'WASP,' and 'just Canadian.' In linguistic terms, they were broadly similar to the general Canadian population: 60 per cent were native English speakers, 20 per cent were native French speakers, and 20 per cent were allophones. These linguistic labels lose some of their meaning when one considers that over 80 per cent of the women spoke more than one language in their daily lives, and nearly 40 per cent spoke a third language with their parents. Over half of the women indicated that they were 'Catholic,' and about one-quarter that they were 'Jewish,' yet nearly all described themselves as 'non-practising' or 'not very religious.'

Like the wider city, provincial, and national populations, the women had a rich diversity of histories, languages, social positions, and cultural identities, and could not be neatly characterized in terms of two or three 'cultural traditions' or 'ethnic groups.' Assigning the women to particular cultural and linguistic groups would have made their identities static and prioritized one source of meaning over all others, as if being Jewish, or having French as a first language, or being of Italian or Moroccan descent, was sufficient to explain their thinking and behaviour. What lumping and splitting I did along linguistic lines did not correlate particularly well with their ideas about the fetus, thoughts about pregnancy, or particular life circumstances.

For this study of ultrasound imaging, I needed a different approach to understanding how identities and histories influence women's experiences – one that didn't search for a single explanatory source of meaning, but acknowledged that Canadian women draw on a multitude of shifting, contradictory, and overlapping cultures and interpretive frameworks as they live their lives. David Hess suggests such an approach when he writes that anthropologists need to acknowledge that

> there are all sorts of intersecting and nested cultures: transcontinental, continental, national, urban, regional, occupational, class, organizational, neighbourhood, ethnic, gender and so on. Some occupational cultures,

such as physicists, have many similarities even in different national cultures, whereas other cultures are bound to local settings. Some cultures
can be thought of as contained within others the way that regional cultures are contained within a national culture. Some cultures are more or
less coterminous with societies and states, whereas others extend in significant ways beyond national borders (e.g., American Hollywood culture, French intellectual culture, Chinese immigrant neighbourhoods).
(1995: 10)

It surprised me how many diverse 'cultures' and interpretive frameworks criss-crossed through these women's ideas and experiences of
ultrasound. I had expected both ethnic and religious identity to be
clearly reflected in the voices of the women I interviewed; I found
instead that their accounts of pregnancy, ultrasound, and the fetus
drew from a rich interpretive palette that included ethnic 'tradition,'
popular guides to pregnancy, Hollywood movies, relationships with
family, friends and physicians, reproductive history, and local identity
politics. Their accounts were shaped further by institutional agendas,
by obstetrical traditions, and by sonographers' beliefs and perceptions. Diverse though their accounts were, they were also remarkably
similar in many ways, particularly so when I compared them to the
voices of women having ultrasound in other countries.

The notion of criss-crossing cultures, or intersecting frameworks of
meaning, offers an alternative to static analytic categories and a means
of moving recursively through multiple levels of identity and experience. But much more than the discovery of multiple meanings is at
issue here. Being 'an ordinary Canadian woman' masks the location of
women, collectively and individually, in particular relationships of
power and control.

The women in this study live in a nation ranked by the United
Nations (1999) and by several other international agencies as the world's
best place to live. Life expectancy for Canadian women is eighty-one
years, which places us slightly ahead of the United States, and roughly
even with France and Sweden, although behind Japan (United Nations 1999: 138). Both fertility (1.6 live births per woman) and infant
mortality (5.5 per thousand births) are among the lowest in the world
(Statistics Canada 1998). Per capita income, even after several reces-
sionary years, is about C$25,000 (Statistics Canada 1999), and the Ca-
nadian health care and social services systems are widely regarded

as models that other industrialized countries, including the United States, should follow.

Despite its favourable overall international ranking, there is significant gender stratification and discrimination in Canadian society. Canada's international ranking by the United Nations drops considerably when gender issues are included. Recent analyses by Statistics Canada showed that women working full-time in 1998 earned about 72 per cent of what men earned (Statistics Canada 1999); that percentage fell to about 62 per cent for women who did not finish high school (Gadd 1995: A5). Women continue to be underrepresented in economic and political positions of power: only 23 per cent of the parliamentary seats in Canada's House of Commons are occupied by women, and only 42 per cent of managerial positions are held by women (United Nations 1999: 142). Although more than half of all Canadian women work outside the home, women are responsible for most of the domestic labour. Canadian women prepare 76 per cent of the meals, do 71 per cent of the child care, and undertake 59 per cent of the shopping and housework (Philp 1995).

Most of the women in this study defined themselves as 'ordinary.' This reflected and condensed an idealized picture: a 'happy' marriage, a 'middle class' family, supportive friends and family, and a 'fulfilling' or at least financially rewarding job. Nearly all the women interviewed defined themselves as 'middle class' – an identity confirmed by the fact that most were neither poor nor wealthy by Canadian standards. Yet 'being middle class' encompasses a range of lifestyles, homes, educations, occupations, and incomes. Their work worlds were diverse, spanning the range from service and labour jobs (cashiers, garment workers, file clerks) to professional careers (accountants, social workers, entrepreneurs).

Each of the women was married or was living in a common law relationship with a male partner. Each envisioned her relationship as a 'partnership' based on romantic love, in which the man and the woman had relatively equal economic roles and responsibilities, were emotionally supportive of each other, and were able to pursue individual interests and career goals. Although the women stressed the equality and cooperative nature of 'partnership,' their everyday lives revealed a somewhat different picture. By and large, they were living a division of labour much like that of the previous generation: they did most of the cooking, laundry, and housecleaning, while the men *helped* with these tasks and looked after the car and yard (Wilson 1991). Each of the women expected they would be doing most of the child care, as well. Most of the women had long-term career goals and believed they were making an important and necessary economic contribution to the partnership: 37 of the 49, or 76 per cent, were employed outside the home. Importantly, within this framework of Canadian middle-class life, the women pictured themselves as agents, able to influence the course of their lives, make their own decisions, and reach their own goals.

The conflicts, contradictions, and vulnerabilities in these women's tales of 'ordinariness' were reinforced during pregnancy, as I will show in more detail in chapter 5. Pregnancy signalled that the woman's economic contribution to the household could become secondary (i.e., the couple could make do without it for a time) while her reproductive role and contribution to domestic labour took on more importance. At the same time, leaving the workforce for a short-term maternity leave or 'until the kids are grown' increased the anxiety of these women about finances and career goals. They felt empowered by pregnancy, although nearly 40 per cent (18 out of 49) said they had not intended to become pregnant at that time. The physical experience of pregnancy underscored their social and emotional connection to a particular man, and their distinctiveness from men in general. Also, pregnancy signalled to them that they were normal, that their bodies 'worked.' They described themselves as 'healthy' and 'strong,' yet they worried a great deal about what might go wrong during pregnancy and childbirth. Most of them believed they could choose the interventions used during pregnancy and labour, and even influence the course and outcome of the pregnancy. Yet at the same time, they expressed a tremendous sense of vulnerability and anxiety, and exhibited dependence on the advice and authority of others, especially medical experts.

I first met each of the forty-nine women interviewed in this study either in the waiting room of their obstetrician's office or at the hospital when they came for blood and urine tests early in pregnancy.[1] As are, presumably, most Canadian women who undergo ultrasound, the women I interviewed were considered by obstetricians to be at 'low risk' for fetal anomalies or complications. Each woman was awaiting the birth of her first child, and each woman had two 'routine' fetal ultrasounds. In fact, about one-third of the women had at least one additional scan, and 20 per cent of these 'low risk' women had four or more ultrasounds during pregnancy. I interviewed each woman several times: before and after her first routine scan, before her second routine scan, and post-partum. I observed their ultrasounds, including the first routine ultrasound, which takes place sixteen to twenty weeks into the pregnancy, the second scan, which occurs around week thirty, and any additional scans. I also interviewed the male partners of seventeen of the women.

Generally, the women welcomed me into their homes and into their pregnancies. They showed me – often with pride and enthusiasm – their growing bellies and the items they had purchased in anticipation of the baby. At other times they were subdued and exhausted by the changes in their bodies and in their lives. But they were always eager to talk. In addition to our scheduled interviews, we chatted on the phone – me calling to make sure they remembered I was coming, them calling to update me on the progress of the pregnancy, or to ask about something the doctor had said, or, post-partum, to ask for advice about wakeful or unhappy babies. With two of the women I acted as an impromptu *doula*, providing support and encouragement during childbirth.

Conversations about 'what was going on inside their bodies' were sometimes awkward, but I will not try to mask the ambiguity, inconsistency, or uncertainty either in my own voice or in the voices of the people I interviewed. One of my concerns was how to go about eliciting people's ideas about the fetus without shaping those ideas. I was strongly aware that my presence and questions were part of the process of creating the fetus as a social entity. Moreover, I was asking women to reflect on and articulate an aspect of their experience that was not only unfamiliar to them (being pregnant), but also politically charged (fetal subjectivity). In the hope of eliciting women's own ideas in narrative form, I used a semi-structured interview protocol of open-ended questions, each with a series of more direct supplementary queries. I tried as much as possible to encourage the women to talk freely and at length, and to avoid leading questions and predictable answers.

Although I worried that my questions, note taking, and tape recorder would increase their inhibitions, the women were remarkably frank during our conversations. They told me about abortions, their decisions to stop using contraception against a husband's wishes, the shock of unplanned pregnancy, the resentment of having to put careers on hold and of 'feeling fat,' and the frustration with husbands who lost sexual desire for them as their bodies grew. They talked of their experiences and often said, 'Well, you know what I mean,' establishing that we shared common kinds of bodies and common challenges to our sense of selves as women, wives, and workers. Many women complained that everyone they knew had advice, telling them what to do, and what not to do, and what to feel or not feel. I hope that the interviews offered them an opportunity to talk without being instructed, with someone who was interested more in how they felt than in what they should be feeling.

The Clinic

The Metropolitan Hospital (a pseudonym) is a medium-sized acute care and teaching hospital. Although the Met is still regarded as an 'English' hospital,[2] its staff and patients are culturally and linguistically diverse. Shortly after I arrived in Montreal, I began to hear the stereotypes about the styles of obstetrical care at the Met and other hospitals in the area. Some have a reputation for encouraging 'natural childbirth' – the use of birthing rooms, and so on – and for applying less technological intervention. At least some of the women delivering at the Met, including some of the women I interviewed, were attracted by that hospital's reputation for having the 'big guns.' As these women explained it to me, the Met had 'the best doctors for pregnancy' and 'all the machines, painkillers, and stuff to help you in labour.' This reputation is borne out in the hospital's obstetrical practices and statistics, which indicate that childbirth at the Met routinely involves an IV drip, chemical or manual acceleration of labour, epidural analgesics, and an episiotomy. Moreover, a recent survey of Canadian maternity practices by the Canadian Institute of Child Health indicates that the management of pregnancy and births in Quebec in general continues to be conservative, interventionist, and technology-driven (Levitt et al. 1995).[3]

During the period of my fieldwork at the hospital clinic, December 1989 through February 1991, I watched roughly 1,000 scans, most of them routine, some of them emergency, high-risk, or amniocentesis ultrasounds. I talked with a variety of people involved in ultrasound, including obstetricians, technicians, radiology and obstetrics residents, visiting physicians, and the clinic receptionist. Part of this book is based on observations of and conversations with six of the sonographers: two ultrasound technicians and four obstetricians.

I gathered some of the data from the sonographers through formal interviews; more often, I simply spoke to them informally in the interstices of the day, while we readied the clinic for the first patient, between patient sessions, and over coffee or lunch. I spent most of my time with the technicians, since they did the bulk of the routine scans. We talked the everyday talk of the workplace – home lives, sick kids, television shows, and the stresses of their work. The technicians would complain to me about the pressures of working with a heavy caseload and with anxious, uncomfortable, and sometimes impatient women. They confided their fears of 'missing' an anomaly during a scan and their feelings of helplessness when they detected fetal anomalies and miscarriages. I never came to know the professional or personal worlds of the physicians as well as I did those of the technicians. In part this was because each physician was at the clinic but once a week, while the technicians were there every day. The technicians tended to remain in one place and to have one task (at least for the duration of each scan), so it was easy for me to stand and talk with them. In contrast, the clinic physicians often changed locations and tasks: they went back and forth between the cubicles to assist technicians and residents with the scanning, they sat briefly at the doctors' desk to write ultrasound reports, they consulted with other physicians by phone, and they made trips to the delivery room.[4] Although I did try to minimize the effects of my presence on the process and interpretation of the scans, the sonographers would often relieve the monotony and pressure of their work by chatting with me while they scanned, and the patients would sometimes join in our conversation.

Throughout the research, the clinic staff knew I was comparing maternal and clinical perceptions of ultrasound fetal imaging, and were aware that I was studying them as much as I was studying the women. For the purpose of ensuring that the women in the study and those outside it did not receive differential care, the hospital ethics committee stipulated that the staff must not know which of their patients I was interviewing, unless the woman herself disclosed that fact; only one did so. I don't believe this requirement had a significant impact on the findings. The sonographers never asked me if particular women were in the study, and aside from some initial questions about my research, they were probably too busy dealing with their heavy caseloads to give it much thought.

I had volunteered in a hospital as a teenager and had done fieldwork among geneticists and genetic counsellors for my master's degree, so I was not entirely unfamiliar with the sounds, smells, and routines of a hospital and with the languages of medicine. But prior to my arrival at the Met clinic, I had never attended a hospital delivery, or watched an electronic fetal heart monitor, a 'non-stress test,' or an amniocentesis, and I certainly did not know how to interpret an ultrasound image. During my first few weeks of fieldwork, the sonographers patiently explained the ultrasound images to me. They pointed out interesting bits of fetal and maternal anatomy, and artefacts of the machine. They explained how they conducted an examination, and talked about the factors that increased or decreased the clarity of the image. Before long, I was able to recognize the fetal head, femur, and spine on my own. Yet I was also aware that I was learning to see from a particular standpoint: to read the grey echoes as landmarks for measurements, and as signs of abnormality, and to do this in relation to normalized growth charts. Thus, I found myself learning to read ultrasound images while trying NOT to become habituated to the conventions of a sonographic gaze. My field notes record my impressions of other possibilities of seeing:

> I got the giggles – the ultrasound suddenly struck me as odd and silly. A group of otherwise rational adults gathered round to coo and praise a grey blur. (26 February 1990)

> I'm getting bored and my feet hurt! They are all starting to look alike. (17 July 1990)

> An awful day ... I felt like a voyeur lurking at the end of the [examining] bed, recording women's pain and pleasure. (20 November 1990)

> Sometimes the images look really weird. The dark orbits [eye sockets] are creepy, the movements are jerky – like a puppet on a string – and the fetus has this organs-and-bones look. (5 January 1990)

> It bothers me that the techs use the term 'cutting' or *'couper'* to describe the 2D view of the ultrasound. Each time they say, 'It's like cutting,' I wince. (23 July 1990)

Although the sonographers encouraged me to try scanning, I never did. I knew that women were often uncomfortable with a full bladder

and anxious during the ultrasound, and I didn't like the idea of pro-
longing their discomfort while I fumbled around with the transducer.
I was also vaguely ill at ease with the physicality of rolling a piece of
hard plastic through the jelly on women's exposed bellies. Just watching often felt like an invasion of privacy.

Ultrasound in Quebec

As I spent more and more time at the clinic, the health care culture of
Montreal and the local tradition of ultrasound imaging gradually came
into focus. That context is characterized by pro-natalist government
policies, a distinctive health care system oriented toward disease pre-
vention and health promotion, and the conservative, technological management of pregnancy and childbirth (Renaud 1981).

   In Quebec, the rendering of bodies into reflected sound began around
1970 when several hospitals in Montreal acquired B-mode ultrasound
machines. The first applications of those ultrasound machines were
outside of obstetrics, for studying the brain, abdomen, and heart. According to several radiologists and obstetricians, obstetrical ultrasound
did not appear in Quebec until a few years later, when it was used to
detect twins, localize the placenta, and measure biparietal diameter. In
the mid-1970s, interest grew in using ultrasound routinely for all
women. There were probably a number of reasons for this. Ultrasound was becoming more widely used in prenatal care in Great Britain, France, and the United States at this time; also, the 1970s and
early 1980s were a period of significant health care reform, demographic change, and social change in Quebec.

   Since the 1970s, Quebec's health care system has focused on social
and preventive medicine. This has involved greater public participation in health care, greater equality among health care professionals,
and an emphasis on community-level care that bundles together medical services, social services, and public health programs (Rodwin 1984:
122; White and Beal 1994). As part of this agenda, early and frequent
publicly funded prenatal visits were institutionalized. Also, prenatal
care was redefined so that it no longer focused on detecting potential
complications of labour and delivery, and placed more emphasis on
screening and monitoring maternal health and fetal development
throughout pregnancy (Hanratty 1996; Savard 1987). In 1970, after
publically funded health insurance was introduced in Quebec, 'the
percentage of women [in Montreal] receiving prenatal care in their

first trimester increased from 27 to 56 per cent, and the percentage receiving care in their first five months increased from 73 to 94 percent' (Hanratty 1996: 277).

A common contention in sociological, anthropological, feminist, and historical writings about reproductive technology is that the routinization of ultrasound and other forms of prenatal diagnosis was, first and foremost, a means for obstetricians to maintain and extend their professional territory and control. Arney (1982: 51), for example, has argued that obstetricians in Britain and America, self-defined as specialists of abnormal childbirth, 'had to develop ways to "foresee" pathology and act prophylactically because they could not always depend on pathology being obviously present.' The extent to which challenges to physicians' authority and a desire to further medicalize births drove the routinization of ultrasound in Montreal is not clear. By the early 1970s, when obstetrical ultrasound was first used in Quebec, midwifery had been effectively suppressed in urban Quebec for several decades, and virtually all births were taking place in hospitals (Laurendeau 1987: 129). The 1970s, the period in which prenatal ultrasound became routine, coincides with a 17 per cent rise in the number of obstetrician-gynecologists in the province and a 20 per cent increase (from 41 to 49 per cent) in pregnancies supervised by specialist physicians rather than general practitioners (Laforce 1990; Laurendeau 1987: 129). That same period also saw increased use of medical interventions such as electronic fetal monitoring, artificial rupturing of the amniotic membranes, epidural anesthetics, and episiotomies (Laurendeau 1987). The routinization of ultrasound during this decade would certainly have extended the dominance of obstetrics in the management of normal pregnancies in Quebec.

We must also consider the changing context and meaning of reproduction and childbearing in Quebec. The francophone birthrate in Quebec, once the highest in Canada, has fallen by over 50 per cent since the 1950s (Rose 1990). The declining influence of the Catholic Church, economic growth in the province, the entry of women into the paid labour force, and legislative changes that have made contraception and abortion legal and available, have contributed to this demographic shift. Yet this decline in fertility rates was not restricted to francophones; by the mid-1980s, fertility rates for Quebec's anglophones were just as low (1.5 children per woman) (Lachapelle 1990: 158). Arguably, this demographic shift has strengthened the cultural constructions of family, motherhood, and childhood that now are dominant in Quebec,

Canada, and the United States. The present day's ideological model of the family, which began to take shape in the early decades of the 1900s, and solidified after the Second World War, is based on what Sharon Hays (1996: 8) describes as 'intensive motherhood' and 'child-centered expert-guided, emotionally absorbing, labour intensive and financially expensive' child-rearing. With a reduction in family size, the 'value' of each child intensifies, as does each child's capacity to offer the parent a pathway to moral worth, self-fulfilment, and emotional riches. From this perspective, the routinization of ultrasound, with its promises of closely monitoring the age and development of the fetus, has supported the notion of child-centred reproduction and extended the demands on women as mothers back through the prenatal period.

The new focus in Quebec on the early detection of problems in pregnancy coincided with the arrival of ultrasound in Montreal. By the mid-1970s, grey-scaled real-time machines had been acquired by several hospitals; once they appeared, interest grew quickly in using ultrasound routinely for all women, or repeatedly throughout each pregnancy. With its distinctive capacity to 'visualize' the fetus, ultrasound was well suited to state-supported moves toward early and regular prenatal care. Between 1978 and 1982 the number of prenatal ultrasounds in Quebec more than tripled (Braun et Valentini 1984: 7). The birthrate in Quebec continued to decline during the 1980s; at the same time, the average number of scans per pregnancy in that province almost doubled, from 0.86 to 1.52 by 1988 (Renaud et al. 1991: 40). A few years later, the figure was 1.9 scans per pregnancy (Renaud et al. 1993: 246).

Local Traditions

Prenatal ultrasound has been routinized in Canada; however, the practice is not uniform throughout Canada, or even within Quebec. Although this is not well documented, there are a wide variety of local traditions of ultrasound practice in Canada. Two prenatal ultrasounds are routine in Canada's most populous provinces (Quebec and in Ontario); in the other eight provinces, most women have only one scan during pregnancy (Anderson 1992; Renaud et al. 1993: 430). In Ontario, Canada's most populous province, most prenatal ultrasounds (61 per cent) are now conducted in physicians' offices or private clinics (Anderson 1992; RCNRT 1993: 817). Considerable variation exists between hospitals regarding whether husbands/partners or observers are permitted to watch, whether fetal sex will be disclosed to interested parents, whether a fetal image will be made available to parents, what the cost will be to parents for this photograph, and whether parents may videotape the ultrasound.

In the absence of national regulations, as ultrasound has spread across Canada, it has not been used in the same way. This issue does more than highlight that there are obvious differences in how decision makers perceive the 'best way' to use ultrasound. While medical technology may come with a manual, its actual implementation is shaped by local priorities, agendas, and meanings. Clearly, any discussions about 'Canadian ultrasound practices' or impacts must show some caution. How a technology is used is not simply a matter of whether it is available. The uses and impacts of ultrasound must be contextualized within a careful analysis of local health care cultures.

In Quebec, there is evidence that physicians take a distinctive approach to prenatal diagnosis, including ultrasound. Quebec physicians are generally more supportive of the routine use of ultrasound during pregnancy, and are more likely to conduct serial or multiple ultrasounds. Quebec leads Canada in providing ultrasound to pregnant women (97 per cent receive it; Manitoba trails all other provinces, at 62 per cent) (RCNRT 1993: 816). Furthermore, while '40 per cent of physicians [surveyed] in Manitoba and Alberta did not think it essential to order an ultrasound scan during pregnancy ... in Quebec, only 4 percent of physicians shared this opinion' (RCNRT 1993: 816).

The heavy use of ultrasound in Quebec, and the strong support in that province for serial ultrasound, may reflect the fact that Quebec's medical association has consistently endorsed the routine use of ultrasound, while guidelines in other jurisdictions have at various times not done so. For example, in 1987 the Quebec medical association's guidelines stated that it had 'no objection to ultrasonographic screening between the 16th and 20th weeks of pregnancy, even in a woman whose pregnancy appears to be evolving normally' (Corporation Professionnelle des Médecins du Québec 1987: 24).

Additional factors are suggested by the findings of a survey, conducted by Renaud and colleagues (1993) under the auspices of the RCNRT, of Canadian physicians' attitudes regarding the use of prenatal diagnostic procedures, the seriousness of various conditions, and the acceptability of abortion. Two key factors emerged from that study. *First,* 'it is only in Quebec that the great majority of physicians

(89 per cent, compared to 60 per cent elsewhere in Canada) find it acceptable to use ultrasound to screen for anomalies' (816). This finding is in line with others from the same survey, which indicate that physicians in Quebec are more likely than physicians in other provinces to use prenatal diagnosis (ultrasound, amniocentesis, and CVS), to perceive anomalies as serious, and to say that abortion following the detection of an anomaly is acceptable (302, 387). Quebec has the greatest proportion of Catholic physicians, who potentially might be resistant to abortion; however, physicians in that province are also least likely to claim that they practice their religion (392).

In fact, the picture in Quebec is more complex, since francophone physicians tend to order only one prenatal ultrasound, whereas anglophone physicians tend to recommend two (Renaud et al. 1991: 41). The physicians I interviewed reported that doctors at Montreal hospitals associated with the English medical school generally referred women for two ultrasounds, while women at the French teaching hospitals often had only one scan. Greater utilization of ultrasound among anglophone physicians in Quebec is in line with the finding that, in comparison to both non-anglophone physicians in Quebec and to physicians elsewhere in Canada, they appear to be more supportive of prenatal diagnosis and 'more technology-oriented' (Renaud et al. 1993: 399).[5] In part, the distinctiveness of Quebec's anglophone physician culture may rest with 'their connection to U.S. culture and their Protestant or Jewish religious backgrounds [which] make them more sensitive to individual liberties and especially to free choice' (Bouchard et al. 1995: 79). While it may well be possible to identify differences between anglophone and francophone medical culture, readers should be careful not to weight the role of language too strongly, since there are francophone doctors at 'English' hospitals and anglophone doctors at 'French' hospitals.

A *second* factor that the Renaud study found was strongly linked to greater willingness to use ultrasound was the specialty of the physician. In Canada, while '23% of GPs and 18% of paediatricians said they believed no ultrasound scanning is necessary during pregnancy, only 12% of obstetricians and 8% of radiologists shared that opinion' (Renaud et al. 1993: 312). Also, obstetricians and radiologists were more inclined than GPs and paediatricians to trust ultrasound (312). In Quebec, although the number of specialists overall is comparable to that in other provinces, the provision of ultrasound and other forms of prenatal diagnosis is dominated by specialists. This is particularly true in Montreal. As one respondent in the RCNRT survey explained, 'You won't understand your finding unless you know that Toronto is a city of general practitioners, while Montreal, like Boston, is a city of specialists. As for the rest of Canada, [prenatal diagnosis] is clearly dominated by GPs, with a few specialists in the large cities' (272).

The 'local tradition' of obstetrical ultrasounds at the Met can also be explained as a function of demographics, professional agendas, and health care economics. Although Quebec's birthrate of 1.6 babies per woman was still below replacement level at the time I began my research (Maser 1991: B2; Wadhera 1990), it was beginning to edge up. Obstetrical services, which had been pared down during the late 1970s and 1980s, were straining to accommodate what one physician called 'a mini baby-boom.' The obstetrical unit at the Met was delivering almost twice the number of babies it was designed to handle. This mini-boom enabled obstetricians at the Met to expand their administrative control over prenatal ultrasound services by having their own staff, rather than medical imaging staff, do more of those scans. Obstetricians now have more control over how prenatal ultrasounds are carried out, and retain a portion of the receipts from this outpatient service, which goes to research and development.[6]

Part of the history and contemporary practice of fetal imaging involves the competition between radiologists and obstetricians – and, more recently, family practitioners – for resources (patients, equipment, funding, scientific data, medical prestige, selection and training of residents), and also for the authority to produce and interpret ultrasound images.[7] At the Met, obstetricians' claims to authority over radiologists in producing and interpreting those images were grounded in what they called 'the obstetrical perspective.' In part, that perspective refers to using ultrasound to the fullest extent possible to diagnose, treat, and prevent problems during pregnancy. It also means 'knowing how to talk to patients.' These obstetricians acknowledged that radiologists were better at obtaining technically proficient images and accurate, precise measurements, but then commented that they lacked this 'obstetrical perspective.' In this turf war, obstetricians marshalled a longstanding stereotype: radiologists are better with machines than with patients.

'Knowing how to talk to patients' condenses a number of assumptions about pregnant women. The sonographers I talked to at the Met believed that pregnant women and their partners were anxious about 'something going wrong' and wanted the reassurance that ultrasound seems to offer. At the same time, pregnant women were perceived as willing to sue obstetricians in cases of missed anomalies and neonatal death. Furthermore, the sonographers believed that pregnant women wanted more than just reassurance; they also wanted pregnancy and childbirth to be a rich and fulfilling experience, and so were very interested in some of the non-clinical aspects of ultrasound, such as finding out the fetus's sex. In carrying out obstetrical ultrasounds in their own department, these sonographers believed they were providing fetal imaging that was both clinically superior to that provided by radiologists and more in tune with patient needs. Some of the sonographers believed that their attempts to make the ultrasound personal and friendly, their willingness to converse with expectant couples about the baby, and their efforts to ease women's anxieties set them apart from other practitioners in Montreal. Although their approach was in fact very common, when they knew I had been observing ultrasounds at other hospitals, the staff at the Met clinic would ask if I had noticed 'how we do things here.' They were careful to point out that their ultrasound practice was not 'zip-zap, you're done.' As I will discuss in more detail in chapter 5, the sonographers at the Met prided themselves on taking time to 'show women the baby.'

'Knowing how to talk to patients' and 'showing the baby' links sonographers at the Met to a set of ideas articulated within biomedicine about ultrasound's impact. Specifically, it has been argued for several years that seeing the fetus through ultrasound has certain 'psychological' or 'psycho-social' benefits for women – namely, reduced anxiety about fetal health, and maternal 'bonding' with the fetus.

The notion of women 'bonding' with their offspring is a cultural artefact of the last thirty years. The notion of mother–infant bonding arose in the 1970s, and was based on the idea that there is a brief 'sensitive period' (Klaus and Kennell, cited in Eyers 1992: 30) immediately after delivery during which close physical contact fosters a mother's deep emotional attachment to her child. As Eyers (2) suggests, bonding is the creation of a conservative ideology that constructs women as the primary caretakers of children and holds them responsible for their offspring's well-being. Women have responded enthusiastically to 'bonding' as a means to address their own growing conflict, of being "liberated" to work outside the home and feeling entirely responsible for the psychological health of their children. Full-time motherhood was out of the question, yet bonding provided the possibility of having it both ways in case the old ideology were true' (127–8).

The idea of bonding *before* birth, through ultrasound, first appeared in clinical journals during the early 1980s. In a letter to the *British Medical Journal*, one physician suggested that ultrasound should help women view the fetus 'as a companion aboard rather than a parasite responsible for the symptoms of pregnancy' (Dewsbury 1980: 481). A more widely cited promoter of ultrasound bonding had a somewhat different goal in mind: to resolve 'any ambivalence toward the pregnancy itself in favor of the fetus' (Fletcher and Evans 1983: 392). Bonding with the fetus during ultrasound rapidly became a new area of research.[9] A maternal–fetal attachment standardized scale was developed to 'measure' the extent to which 'the woman engages in behaviours that represent affiliation and interaction with her unborn fetus' (Kemp and Page 1987: 179). There have also been efforts to determine which types of ultrasound practices enhance this bond. Detailed explanations of the fetal image, for example, are said to stimulate a woman's 'positive feelings' toward the fetus (Reading et al. 1982).

'Bonding' with the fetus, like its antecedent, mother–infant bonding, reinforces conservative values related to the impact of a woman's behaviour and body on her offspring's development and welfare. 'Bonding' through ultrasound, however, is not about unmediated skin-to-skin contact, but rather about visibility mediated by technology. The visibility of the fetus is not the only issue; so is a woman's response/reaction to that fetus. A woman's reaction to the image might then be used to gauge her emotional commitment to the fetus (Bralow 1983: 114), as was mine during my first obstetrical ultrasound. The power of the ultrasound fetus to stimulate a woman's 'natural' mothering response is also assumed to reduce her anxiety and improve her compliance with such things as medical advice, regular dental care, and avoiding cigarettes and alcohol (Reading et al. 1982).

As discussed in the next chapter, 'bonding' is now seen as essential not only to the immediate post-birth period and to the ultrasound examination, but also to the duration of the pregnancy.

Chapter Four

Being Pregnant and Coming to Know the Fetus

In pregnancy I literally do not have a firm sense of where my body ends and the world begins ... the continuity between my customary body and my body at this moment is broken.

Young (1984: 49)

Fetal subjects are only partially the product of the technologies, legal discourses, and professional agendas described in the previous chapters. They also emerge through the diverse lives, actions, words, sensations, and imaginings of pregnant women. In this chapter, I begin to discuss women's experiences with and perspectives on fetality and ultrasound, with a focus on how women talk about being pregnant prior to the first ultrasound. Chapter 5 examines sonographer's narratives about the fetus during ultrasound, and chapter 6 examines how women apprehend the fetal subject through ultrasound imaging.

Each of the following three chapters includes narratives from four of the interviewed women – Rosa, Julie, Marie-Claude, and Tamara.[1] These narratives, and the other statements from women, are intended to convey something of the commonalities and varieties of women's experiences of pregnancy and fetal imaging. Moreover, by drawing from women's accounts from before the first routine ultrasound to post-partum, I hope to indicate both persistent assumptions and themes, as well as ambiguities, inconsistencies, and changes, in their thinking about the fetus. Pregnant women are not objects on which ultrasound is carried out, so I hope these narratives highlight that women do not simply have or undergo ultrasound. Rather, women actively feel, interpret, think about, and use this technology from within particular subject positions.

Julie

Julie, twenty-nine, and her husband, Tom, are anglophones, born in Montreal to parents from Quebec's neighbouring province, Ontario. Julie has had the same job for several years: 'long hours, for low pay' as a secretary. Until recently Tom had 'gone from job to UI [unemployment insurance] to job to UI.' Although he now has a part-time factory job, they find it difficult to make ends meet and afford their two-bedroom apartment. 'Money is tight and that couch you are sitting on is still unpaid for,' Tom laughs tightly. This is Julie's second pregnancy. As a teenager, she had an abortion, knowing that she would be 'thrown out of the house' if her parents discovered the pregnancy. The early weeks of her current pregnancy were also stressful. At eight weeks, bleeding vaginally and experiencing considerable abdominal pain, Julie was sent for an ultrasound to look for a 'tubular' [ectopic] pregnancy. Although that was ruled out and her pregnancy has continued without further bleeding, Julie says she is still 'nervous' and 'anxious.' Although she is bothered by respiratory problems, Julie does not want to take her asthma medication in case it hurts the fetus. She is also anxious and frustrated that she is still smoking cigarettes:

> I still smoke. I used to smoke more than a pack a day, sometimes two packs a day. This is an ongoing argument between me and him [Tom], and he's right. I know he's right. I went down in [early pregnancy] to ten cigarettes and then it progressively went up and up. Now I'm trying slowly to go down, down. Do you know the commercial on TV? ... There's this pregnant woman and every time she tries to light her cigarette it goes out and it says, 'Don't you think someone is trying to tell you something.' But it's easier said than done. It's an awful habit and it's hard to get rid of. But hopefully ...

Tell me about this pregnancy. How are you feeling?
Now? For the past four hours – great! [laughs] I don't think I've had a really easy time for the past four months. I've been sick a lot. Headaches. Sick in the afternoon and the worst times are at night. The more overtired I am, the worse it is.

Are you more tired than usual?
   Yup.

Have you noticed any emotional changes?
   Oh boy ... Fear, ecstasy, happy, sad, scared, thrilled. Everything! It's
   hard to pinpoint because there's so many ... If you give me a dirty
   look, that's it, you don't like me anymore and I cry and I find that
   really frustrating ... At the beginning of the day I feel really good.
   But I'm having a hard time getting through work, which is odd
   because I used to work until 7 or 8 at night. By 3 or 4 in the afternoon I'm tired and the more tired I get, the more irritable I am.

   [*Tom.*] It's like when a little child gets really tired. First it's all smiles
   and everything else, then a little cranky and then passes out.

Do you think about what is going on inside of you?
   A lot!

Tell me about that.
   Oh every day. What's developing now? What's it doing? Is it moving and I can't feel it? Is everything that has developed, developed
   properly and working properly? Stuff like that. We have the *Nine
   Months for Life*. I got it from the doctor's office. That's our bible.
   [laughs] We read that a lot.

Do you have an image of the baby?
   At this point? E.T. Small body, big head, big eyes. Cute, but not
   exactly what I want my baby to look like ... I figure it's in there,
   having a good time, listening to us, growing. Actually, I know you're
   gonna laugh, but I have this image of it hanging off the inside of my
   belly button. That's what it feels like! ... I don't know how much it
   can sense at this point. But I apologize to it for smoking and for
   getting upset when I feel so sick and we play a tape of our voices,
   just in case it can hear ...

Have you felt fetal movement yet?
   Yeah. Yeah ... The first time I felt it, I was at work. I dropped my
   pen, stood up and said, 'Baby alert!' [laughs] And I call him [Tom]
   when I get it. It's exciting ... Like there's aliens. Like there's chipmunks on a wheel. Or someone's tickling you from the inside. For

the past couple of days I've felt, oh this is really weird. You're going to laugh at me. I feel like someone is, well obviously someone is, like someone is hanging on my navel from the inside. It's really weird.

Are you worrying?
I'm worried about everything that you could possibly be worried about. I'm not neurotic!! It's not always the same thing. Sometimes it's, 'Tom, what do you think? Think everything will be okay?' He's so relaxed all the time. 'Yeah. Yeah. Don't worry about it!'

What can you tell me about the ultrasound?
I know that I've read and heard that it can tell you about the physical development. If there's deformities or whatever. Brain development, I'm not sure. I don't know if it can do that or not. I don't know if it can show mental retardation ... I also know it's gonna look like the negative of a snapshot. There's a girl at work who went about a month ago and she sort of described it to me. I'm anxious to see if you can see it moving. I don't know if it's going to be a still picture or if you're gonna see the baby actually moving. That would be so neat!

Do you want to know the sex?
I didn't. I was really against this. Come on, it's part of the excitement when it comes out. 'Julie – it's a girl.' Now I'm confused. I don't know. If it's the second one I'd probably want to know if it was a girl or ... but I don't know. I'm still not sure. He's [pointing to Tom] wanted to know since day one.

Why?
[*Tom.*] So I can stop saying 'it.'

[*Julie.*] Yeah, that's probably for me the main reason why, if I decide to find out. Because of that. I don't like, it bugs me, I don't why. It shouldn't. I don't like referring to my baby as 'it.' ... I'll wait until they're doing it [the ultrasound]. That's probably when I'll decide, at that split second. [pause] Would they be able to tell him and not me?

If you give your permission.
But then I'll know anyways, because he'll say 'he' or 'she.' I'll decide right then and there when they ask me.

Rosa

Rosa, twenty-two, and her husband, Mario, are the children of Italian immigrants. They have been married for about three years and live in a new home in the same neighbourhood as Rosa's family. Both have physically demanding jobs: Rosa works as a cutter in a garment factory, and Mario works in construction. She is happy about being pregnant, but at sixteen weeks is alarmed that her physician says she is 'carrying low.'

> When I first heard that, I was worried I was gonna lose the baby. And for Italians a big family means a lot. Even though it's still early and it's not born yet, I'm very attached to the baby. Like I don't know the sex or anything, but ... But now is it normal? I worry sometimes about that. I'm probably worried for nothing, but you are never sure that you won't lose your baby. I know one woman who lost hers at seven months and that's almost born ...
>
> I'm always talking and singing to it. The baby can feel it. It makes it feel more relaxed. Especially on a hectic day. When I'm in bed or sitting in front of the TV, I get to spend time with my baby. And I can say, 'Now I'm all yours' ... I pay attention to the baby. For women it hits them faster. I'm excited, but for the husband, it doesn't hit them. He's embarrassed to talk to my stomach, and I don't feel embarrassed.
>
> I got a book from the doctor, but to tell you the truth, I don't look at it that much. I did at first, you know, the pictures are kinda interesting, but its not like I'm studying it or anything. Besides, if I got a question, I can always ask my mom or my sisters. And two of his [Mario's] brothers are married and have kids.

Tamara

Tamara, twenty-six, is seventeen weeks along in her first of what she hopes will be 'three pregnancies for three babies.' She and her husband, John, are first-generation Montrealers born to Polish-Jewish parents. Tamara and her husband are dentists. We talk in the living room of their spacious apartment on the night before her first ultrasound.

How are things going?
> I'm feeling great! My breasts have changed a lot, they are sore and swollen. My abdomen is just starting to swell a bit, otherwise I look the same ... The nausea has been a trial, but I've been keeping a

record of what makes me really ill – like fried foods, fish, and spicy foods, definitely. Then I'll know to avoid them ... Other than that, well, I'm really getting worried if it's healthy. I think maybe I am worrying about this because I know too much ... I've done tons of reading and so, it's like when you are in medical school and each time you learn about a new disease you figure that you have it! ... And on New Year's Eve before I knew I was pregnant I had two Bloody Marys and I feel terrible about that! ... The first few months, the cardinal twelve weeks, I was very aware of all my movements and anything I did. I was thinking if I move this way, I might have a miscarriage or if I go too fast or if I go too slow. So I was just making an effort and being careful and not running for the bus. Things like that. Stupid, I know. Completely irrational ... Every time I go to the bathroom, I'm checking my underwear – 'Am I bleeding?' Typical, I guess, eh?

Do you think about what's inside of you?
Yup. I talk to it, I talk to my stomach. I blow kisses, my husband blows kisses at it. I'm sure it can hear. Not necessarily hear and understand but vibrations and movements. I'm sure that if I'm stressed, my blood pressure and heart rate will definitely be felt in the uterus.

What do you do when you are stressed?
I try to calm down. I just don't think it's a good environment. I don't know if it's true or not. If I get pumped up or get angry at my assistant or at myself, I'll say, 'relax.' It's not good for either myself or ... it's taught me how to relax a little more, also. I try not to get angry or yell. Not that I ever was that type of person. It's just that would bother the fetus.

What do you know about ultrasound?
Very little. Just that it's an image portrayed on a screen of what is inside of me by soundwaves. They put a cream on your stomach and they use sort of a microphone wand and rub it. And the vibrations – the sound waves – are portrayed on the screen ... You can't really discern who it is, but you know it's a person. And then photocopied fifty times! [*laughs*] I'm not expecting it to be like a portrait or anything.

Why do women have ultrasound?
Because their doctors tell them to! ... I guess it can tell you about any congenital abnormalities that are present. Any problems with the placenta or uterus. It can tell you if you are not pregnant, it can rule out pregnancy. Detect if you are carrying twins or multiple pregnancies. If the fetus is developing at the time that you think you are at, if you are on schedule? ... I don't think it can tell you if the child is retarded, if the child has some genetic problems that aren't visualized, emotional problems, that would affect their development outside the uterus. Can't always tell you the sex.

Has your doctor talked to you about having the ultrasound?
Not at all. The nurse in her office told me to make an appointment.

Do you want to know what sex it is?
No. I don't want to say that I have a son or a daughter. I like the fact that although I'm very attached to it, I don't want to attach a name yet. Because I know that something could still go wrong. I think it's easier if you have to let go.

Marie-Claude

Marie-Claude is twenty-seven and a third-generation Québécoise. Her husband, Andrew, is an anglophone of American- and British-born parents. Marie-Claude and Andrew finished high school; she works periodically as a sales clerk, and he is a postal worker. They live in a large, sparingly furnished apartment: 'We're still saving up for a dining room table and chairs.' This is Marie-Claude's second pregnancy; last year she miscarried at about ten weeks. This second pregnancy has caused her considerable anxiety; she started bleeding during her second month and was 'afraid that everything would just fall out.' After two weeks of bed rest, the bleeding stopped. At the time of our first interview, Marie-Claude was eighteen weeks pregnant.

How have you been feeling?
It hasn't been too bad. I've been moody, that's for sure. Short-tempered. But not too much nausea. I broke out in pimples, I had really sore breasts. Now it's pretty much at a standstill. I haven't really gotten big yet. Right now it's like before I was pregnant with the

added bonus that I don't have my period ! [we laugh] ... I was very very tired. I could have slept twenty-four hours a day.

Any worries?

I'm still worried about the general health of the baby. We're going for the ultrasound this week and it's gonna make a big big difference in terms of that ... I worry about the usual things, what women worry about, that everything will be all right. The little things that they do at the hospital. You know, you read so much material and you wonder will the hospital let me do this, will the hospital let me do that. I'm worried mostly about how open the hospital is ... We've [M-C and her husband] sat together with the books and I had him read a lot. We sat down and wrote down a lot of things so that he would know. Not only so he would know but so he would know how I felt about it and whether I wanted it or not. He's memorizing that right now! [*laughs*] ... I guess, too, I'm anxious 'cause everybody is assuming everything will be okay with this one, and I'm just waiting for the ultrasound ... Another thing – I'm tired of people patting me on the stomach! I keep telling them, you can pat the baby when it's born! That's the one thing that's really a strong point for me ... I want to get a T-shirt that said, 'Do not touch! Mother bites.'

What can you tell me about ultrasound?

To tell you the honest truth I don't know why they are done. I can see why, like at first they were done with me because I had some problems. The only thing I can think of, although it must be fun to see, but it must be extremely expensive for the hospital to give every single women two ultrasounds for no apparent reason.

What will they will be looking for?

They haven't specifically told me what they will be looking for. But I assume they will be looking for the size of the baby. Maybe the movement of it, the size of the heart, the size of the different ... the arms, the legs ... I hope I can see the whole baby because it's small enough to see the whole picture. I think we'll be able to see pretty much everything. I don't know about the sex of the baby, I think they'll be able to see that. I think you'll be able to see the fingers, the legs, the toes, the nose, the mouth, the eyes.

Being Pregnant

During the first interviews, I invited Julie, Rosa, Tamara, Marie-Claude, and each of the other women to talk about 'being pregnant' – how they were feeling, what were their thoughts, how others were interacting with them. The significance of their answers eluded me when I wrote this research into my dissertation. Although I had detailed and analysed the 'beliefs' and 'practices' common to their narratives, one of my dissertation examiners pointedly asked why I had not attended to 'women's embodied experiences of pregnancy.' This chapter, I hope, begins to redress that omission.

In the present chapter, I am writing about how these Montreal women lived the early weeks and months of being pregnant. In addition to, or in place of, Julie's sensation of 'aliens,' 'chipmunks' and 'someone hanging on my navel from the inside,' how do women *feel* their pregnancy? In a society obsessed with the appearance of the exterior of the body, what does it mean to think 'a lot,' as does Julie, about the events within the body? Are they thinking about what Carol Bigwood (1991: 68) describes as 'being inhabited by a growing sentience that is not truly "other"?' What does the loss of the familiar body mean for a woman's sense of her own self? What are the personal and the political ramifications of experiencing pregnancy in terms of 'symptoms' and anxiety about fetal normality? What are the implications for our relationships with others when we are perceived as the 'cranky little child' Julie's husband describes? What messages of wisdom and morality are conveyed by the secular 'Bibles' or advice books read by women?

Pregnancy as rite of passage

Pregnancy and childbirth are regarded by cultures around the world as 'life changing events' (Davis-Floyd 1992: 1). They involve potential physical dangers (e.g., discomfort, pain, death) and significant changes in social status and role (e.g., from woman to mother, from man to father, from couple to family). Also, significant ontological challenges are posed by the creation and emergence of a new being from a woman's body. The conceptual boundaries and categories that may be challenged vary through time and across cultures, but often include the distinctions between self and others, fetus and infant, non-human

and human, nature and culture, woman and mother, normal and abnormal (Davis-Floyd 1992; Jordan 1993).

In the context of this notion of pregnancy and childbirth as a year-
long rite of passage, Robbie Davis-Floyd has studied contemporary
middle-class women's experiences of hospital birth in the United States.
In her systematic analysis, she draws attention to the ritual aspects of
hospital gowns, fetal monitoring, cervical checks, and other standard
obstetrical procedures of normal births. In the following passage, she
discusses the ritual purposes of having women give birth lying on
their back with their legs in stirrups:

> This lithotomy position completes the process of symbolic inversion that
> has been in motion since the woman was put into that 'backwards' hos-
> pital gown. Now we have her normal bodily patterns of relating to the
> world quite literally turned upside down: her buttocks at the table's
> edge, her legs widespread in the air, her vagina totally exposed. As the
> ultimate symbolic inversion, it is ritually appropriate that this position be
> reserved for the peak transformational moments of the initiation experi-
> ence: the birth itself. The [physician, the] official representative of soci-
> ety, its institutions, and its core values of science, technology, and patri-
> archy stands not at the mother's head nor at her side, but at her bottom,
> where the baby's head is beginning to emerge ... The cultural value here
> is clearly on the baby, who is emerging at the 'top.' As Lakoff and Johnson
> (1980) point out, in this culture, 'up is good down is bad,' so that babies
> born of science and technology must be born 'up' toward the positively
> valued cultural world of men, in opposition to the natural force of grav-
> ity, instead of 'down' toward the negatively valued natural world of
> women. (1992: 123–4)

Davis-Floyd (1992: 2) rejects the argument that these procedures are
required by the physiological realities of birth, and argues instead that
they are repetitive and symbolic practices that 'effectively convey the
core values of American society to birth women':

> [These rituals] are profoundly symbolic, communicating messages through
> the body and the emotions concerning our culture's deepest beliefs about
> the necessity for cultural control of natural processes, the untrustworthi-
> ness of nature and the associated weakness and inferiority of the female
> body, the validity of patriarchy, the superiority of science and technol-
> ogy, and the importance of institutions and machines ... At the same time

that they attempt to contain and control the inherently transformative process of birth, they also transform the birthing woman into a mother in the full social sense of the word – that is, into a woman who has internalized the core values of American society: one who believes in science, relies on technology, recognizes her inferiority (either consciously or unconsciously), and so at some level accepts the principle of patriarchy. Such a woman will tend to conform to society's dictates and meet the demands of its institutions. (152–3)

In thinking about Davis-Floyd's analysis in the context of my own research in a similarly technocratic and gender-biased society, I wondered whether women experience ontological challenges to body, self, and society during *early* pregnancy, *before* they begin to 'show,' and to feel fetal movement, and *before* they make their pregnancy public. How are women socialized into 'core values' and practices during the early weeks and months of pregnancy, long before they undergo the dramatic rituals of hospital birthing? Davis-Floyd does describe the early separation of pregnant women from their former social identity, and their gradual transformation to a new identity guided by physicians, advice books, childbirth education classes, and other pregnant women (23–38); however, her analysis says little about fetality in this transformation. How are ideas about the fetus embodied and experienced during early pregnancy? How are the ontological dangers of simultaneously *being* one and *becoming* two felt and negotiated by pregnant women? With these questions in mind, I focus in this chapter on women's experiences of their bodies and of fetality during early pregnancy.

On Being Pregnant

Much like Julie in the opening narrative, most of the Montreal women I interviewed experienced pregnancy – especially in the early months – as a time of bodily discomfort, heightened emotions, marked anxiety, increased restrictions, and explicit social scrutiny. Reflecting findings for Canadian women in general, about 40 per cent of the women I interviewed had not intended to become pregnant when they did (CARAL 1998: 6). The fact that a pregnancy wasn't planned often heightens women's anxiety and ambivalence. These feelings are not necessarily erased by a decision to continue the unplanned pregnancy, nor are they qualitatively different from those surrounding a planned pregnancy. At the first interview, few of the women were 'showing,' or had felt fetal movement, or had told more than close family and friends that they were pregnant. Expressing a sentiment shared by other women, Sara (27, office manager) remarked, 'I know I'm pregnant, but hardly anyone else does. I feel different, but I don't really look pregnant yet. It's totally weird.' As the women talked to me about this 'weird,' liminal state, I was particularly struck by the recurrence in their narratives of talk about the 'symptoms' of pregnancy, especially 'losing shape,' and by their concerns about making the pregnancy public, and by their mixed feelings about motherhood. As I elaborate below, these themes do more than reflect common feelings about the bodily realities and social changes of pregnancy; they also highlight how women's experiences of being pregnant are shaped by historical forces, social relationships, and dominant meanings.

Bodily changes

Each woman regarded pregnancy as a 'normal' and 'natural' process, a part of being a woman; for some, it was also a sign that their bodies worked properly. Yet during pregnancy they found their bodies acting in unpredictable, unfamiliar, and sometimes unpleasant ways. When I asked, 'How are you feeling?' or 'How is the pregnancy going?' they responded with what soon became a familiar litany of complaints: fatigue, headaches, nausea, irritability, feelings of being bloated, breast tenderness, weight gain, food cravings. All of the women expressed mixed feelings about the changes in their bodies during the first few months of pregnancy:

> I know it's all worth it, even though when I get up in the morning I feel like vomiting. And the smell of coffee makes me sick. I know it's okay, because of the baby.

You're still feeling sick?
> Sometimes, yeah. Toothpaste makes me sick – weird, eh? Every time I brush my teeth, I throw up after that. Then I have to brush my teeth again! (Lena, 28, accountant)

> I feel exhausted and nauseous. Yesterday I spent the whole day in bed. I got up at one point and had a glass of water; ten minutes later I was throwing it up. I tried crackers and it still didn't [stay] down. During the week I am very tired as well ... I go to bed very early.

Nine-thirty and I'm in bed ... Other than being tired and nauseous, well, even with all that, I'm very happy about being pregnant. I smile more. (Michelle, 27, data systems analyst)

I like it, but I don't like it. There have been lots of changes in my life. Usually, I work a lot; now I can't even do housework because I'm so tired. I'm not the same person any more. (Marie Louise, 31, sales clerk)

The women's descriptions of how they felt during the first four months of pregnancy were couched in the language of discomforts, anxieties, symptoms, and complaint, and varied little with bodily, reproductive, and social circumstances. Likewise, the sensations of being pregnant varied little among them. Nausea and exhaustion, in particular, are often welcomed as the earliest signs of pregnancy, yet they may also be constraining, restricting a woman's activities and even isolating her. These sensations and others signalled the continuing pregnancy, but often made the women feel anxious about whether they were 'normal.' Bodily changes also provided evidence of a woman's growing difference from others, including her male partner. Yet at the same time that a uniquely female bodily experience of reproduction was highlighted, nearly 40 per cent of the women said their husbands were also experiencing physical changes, such as weight gain, nausea, and fatigue.

Of particular concern to the women in Montreal were the changes in the size and shape of their bodies. Attuned as they were to the social preoccupation with slimness and fitness, they worried that they were 'just getting fat' and were not really pregnant, that they might gain too much weight during pregnancy, and that they might not be able to lose it after the baby was born. They used terms such as 'blimping' or 'blowing' up, 'losing shape,' and 'losing my waist' in expressing their concerns about the impact of weight gain on their sense of self and self-control. They talked about the need to monitor the rate of gain, as well as the total amount:

I've put on so much weight.

How much?
Twelve pounds already and I'm only fourteen weeks. I heard you're supposed to put on, like, no more than twenty-five in total and my doctor says too much isn't good for the baby. But it's, like, I can't

stop eating. It's the only thing that stops the nausea, and when I'm not eating I'm asleep. (Olivia, 28, shipping manager)

I didn't put on anything at first, but then last month, I ballooned four pounds. I'm starting to worry 'cause I don't think you're supposed to put on that much, so fast. I can't remember what the book said, but I think it's only a bit each month until the end. (Claudette, 27, secretary)

For some women, pregnancy offered a release from maintaining constant vigil over their weight. As one woman put it, 'Being pregnant is great! I can eat whatever I want, and nobody says "Don't eat that, you'll get fat!' Yet even in late pregnancy, none spoke of the 'power' or the pleasurable sense of fullness or 'volume' that some authors have noted (e.g., Bigwood 1991, Millner 1999, Young 1984). In a culture that values slender and athletic bodies as a sign of youth, health, self-discipline, eroticism, and moral worth, women's experiences of gaining weight, 'getting fat,' or 'losing their shape' suggest more than a concern with bodily aesthetics. Weight gain, even in the context of pregnancy and expectations that they should gain weight, may threaten a woman's sense of control, identity, and self-esteem. Enlargement of the body's boundaries may be particularly threatening in early pregnancy when it occurs 'illegitimately,' that is, before a woman has announced the pregnancy, donned maternity clothes, 'passed' the ultrasound, and thus become socially as well as physiologically pregnant.

Telling others

Although the women told their husbands and close family and friends within hours or days of a positive pregnancy test, they often delayed by several weeks or a month disclosing the pregnancy to others. Publicly announcing oneself as pregnant carries tremendous social and symbolic weight and thus needs to be managed. For example, couples may delay the announcement if they are unsure how their parents and in-laws will react. Some of the couples who had not planned to become pregnant kept the news to themselves until they had decided not to have an abortion. Fearful of being laid off, some of the women in low-paid service and clerical jobs were reluctant to tell their co-workers. For many women, however, the delay arose from their concerns about miscarriage or fetal anomaly:

I guess we want to wait a bit [before we tell our friends]. The first couple of months are a big risk, right, so we'll wait a bit longer. Like, I don't think other people need to know yet, like if, knock on wood, there's a miscarriage or something. That's ... that's really private. (Rita, 23, university student)

My sister lost a baby and that was so hard, you know, after telling everyone and my parents were all excited. My mom had even bought stuff and then it was really hard for my sister to put it away. It's better to wait ... Like, I think once we've passed the ultrasound, then we'll be more like, 'we're having a baby.' I mean, I guess that's kinda what we're thinking it [the ultrasound] is for. (Sandy, 27, secretary)

For the mothers and grandmothers of these women, the symbolic meanings of pregnancy may well have revolved around a woman's marital status and sexuality (good girls versus bad) and her commitment (natural duty) to her husband and a family (Petchesky 1990). Among the women I interviewed, concerns about when and whom to tell were interlaced mainly with concerns about having to terminate a pregnancy, 'in case something showed up on the ultrasound' or 'in case something went wrong.' Women who found it difficult to conceive, and women who had miscarried in an earlier pregnancy, expressed a similar hesitancy. While the current pregnancy was joyous news – proof that they could indeed get pregnant – these women were cautious, saying they didn't want to 'jinx' the pregnancy by being too confident. These statements reveal both the social stigma of disability and abortion, and the fact that fetal identities are contingent on diagnoses of normality.

Becoming mothers

Women also expressed conflicting feelings about becoming mothers. All of the women expected motherhood – especially during the first year – to be 'hard work,' and exhausting, and to change their lives markedly. They were certain that having a baby would mean at least temporary changes in their employment and financial circumstances, their leisure time, and their relationship with the husband or partner. Worry about the stresses of parenting, a reduced income, and the loss of freedom and mobility conflicted with their view that these changes were natural and inevitable, 'just part of being a mother.' The transition to motherhood can also be fraught with anxiety about how motherhood can be balanced with the demands of work:

> I'm dying to have a baby and I know Costa [her husband] and his family are really excited. This is the first grandchild and his parents are really excited. I mean, they're buying baby presents already. It's like, you know, I feel sort of, like it's too much already. I start thinking can I do this? What if something goes wrong? What if I'm dying to get back to work, like, in three months? (Dorothea, 28, office administrator)

> I'm really looking forward to being a mother, but I know the changes will be huge. Like, the demands on my time, no sleep, all that. And I'm going to miss my job – I know that. (Alison, 28, data systems analyst).

The tensions and uncertainties expressed by these women draw attention to the ambiguous and contradictory meanings attached to motherhood in contemporary Canada.[2] Despite the steadily rising number of women in positions of political and economic influence in Canada, women are still expected to subordinate their needs to those of their children. Even before they had given birth, several women expressed their anxiety about 'balancing' employment and motherhood. How would they find affordable and trustworthy daycare? Who would look after an ill child during working hours? Could they afford to spend the first year at home with the baby? At issue here is a woman's status as a 'good mother' in a society that perceives motherhood as central to a woman's self-definition, while at the same time devaluing motherhood as politically insignificant, and blaming mothers for how children turn out, and making the combination of career and motherhood an exhausting and not entirely laudable ideal.

To some extent, women's attention to bodily discomforts during early pregnancy, and their anxiety about motherhood and things 'going wrong' may be a socially acceptable way of drawing attention to the somatic and social inequities which mean that women bear the brunt of the responsibility for childrearing, as well as for less than normal children. From this perspective, the complaints and anxieties of pregnant women can be seen as examples of somatization, or the expression of social distress through the body.[3]

Managing Pregnancy: Husbands, Family, Friends, Physicians, and Advice Books

As with other rites of passage involving physical, social, and ontological disruptions, pregnancy and childbirth are often the site of intense ritual activity, social attention, and guidance by cultural authorities. Before the baby showers, childbirth education classes, and ultrasound examinations of the second and third trimesters, women's anxieties and ambivalence about pregnancy are typically dealt with through advice from husbands, other family members, and friends, through questions to the physician, and through close reading of guides to pregnancy.

Husbands, family, and friends

At the first interview, when I asked women what they liked about being pregnant, two-thirds replied, and most without hesitation, 'the attention.' Twenty-five-year old Vicki, a dental assistant, elaborated her response in this way:

> Everyone pays attention to me now. They all want to take care of me. Like, I always get the most comfortable chair now! The best food. Everyone asks me how I'm doing, if I'm okay, if I feel okay. It's nice, you know. It makes me feel good, you know. Like everyone is looking out for me.

This attention, or what Davis-Floyd calls 'specialness,' validates the pregnancy and locates the woman in a social network; at the same time, it confirms that she is no longer the same person. Her transformation from one social category to the other is underway. The attention also generally brings advice. Husband, family, friends, and (occasionally) strangers on the street offer instructions and advice to pregnant women about diet, exercise, rest, doctors, childbirth, and so on. Not all of these prescriptions and prohibitions echo the language and logic of biomedicine. Women reported being cautioned not to scratch their own bodies lest they mark the baby, not to use scissors lest they sever the cord, and not to sneeze or cough too forcefully lest they expel the baby. They often questioned the validity of this advice but few were willing to ignore it and risk the consequences. Twenty-two-year-old Rosa recounted the advice of her Italian-born mother:

My mother told me not to mop.

Mop?
  Yeah, you know – mop. Don't stretch your arm out, cause you'll
  pull the cord around the baby's neck. I don't know if it's true or not.
  But I figure I'm not gonna mop until after the baby is born. You
  know. Why take chances? And Mario [her husband], he don't want
  me to mop either. So what? I don't have to mop for a few months.
  That's good, right?

Welcomed, reassuring, and helpful though some of it might be, the
increased attention and advice could also be restrictive. Like many of
the women, Olivia chafed under the watchful gaze of husbands, family, and friends:

  My husband, he's got nieces and nephews and he's close to his
  sisters. So he's like the one who knows what to do, what I should
  eat, what I gotta do, how I should place my back. Yah, you know,
  it's great 'cause we don't need to ask no questions. But it's hard, too.

Hard?
  Yah. Like he's always telling me how to sit and watching me. Well,
  not watching me, but, like, worrying over me. It's like I need to go
  to work to get away!

Regular Medical Care

Women's experience of pregnancy and of the transition to motherhood is also shaped by their contact with biomedicine. All the women
in this study believed that despite the normality of pregnancy, and
their own status as 'low risk,' having a healthy baby was going to
depend on 'regular medical care.' Nearly all the women I interviewed
conducted a pregnancy test at home or at a local pharmacy within a
few days of missing a menstrual period. Shortly after, they went to
their physicians for confirmation, via another hormonal test and an
internal cervical exam, that they were 'really pregnant.' 'Regular medical care' is initiated once the physician confirms the pregnancy, and
continues through the series of monthly and then weekly doctor's
visits that mark the passage of pregnancy for middle-class Canadian
women. Although the women complained about the hours they spent

waiting for each 'three-minute' doctor's visit and for laboratory tests, ultrasounds, and fetal heart monitoring (non-stress tests), and although some found their physician's manner abrupt, 'brisk,' or *pas gentil,* they considered this medical supervision essential to, in their words, 'reduce risks' and 'ensure a healthy baby.'

As Davis-Floyd (1992) suggests, in societies like Canada and the United States, which privilege biomedical and technological knowledge of the body, physicians play a significant role as both ritual authorities and key symbols in shaping women's experiences of pregnancy. The attention the women in this study paid to their bodies illustrates this point very clearly. When they narrated pregnancy through lists of bodily changes and bodily discomforts, it did not mean that they disliked being pregnant or even that they disliked the bodily changes. Nor was it an inevitable effect of the location of pregnancy in their bodies. Rather, their self-descriptions in terms of bodily symptoms and hormonally induced emotions, and their careful attention to diet and weight, and the importance they assigned to medical supervision, clearly indicated that they were well-disciplined to the norms and conventions of medicalized pregnancy. The acceptance of medicalized pregnancy in Canada should not be surprising, given both the dominance of biomedicine in the health care system and the existence of universal health insurance. Other physiological changes - menstruation and menopause – for instance, are similarly pathologized and medicalized for North American women (Davis 1991; Lock 1993). As Canadian women, we know and experience our bodies largely through the 'vocabulary of signs and symptoms' (Low 1994: 140) and as the objects of medical management. In Montreal, the influence of obstetrical knowledge and practice may be especially powerful. At least for some women, the first visit to an obstetrician-gynecologist during their teens marks their social transition to womanhood. Moreover, in Quebec, and especially in Montreal, the primary practitioner during pregnancy is often an obstetrician rather than a general practitioner or family physician. This is in contrast to other provinces such as British Columbia, where women generally see an obstetrician only if they are deemed to be 'high risk.' None of the women interviewed had considered either home birth or the assistance of a midwife in the hospital, declaring it 'too risky' or 'dangerous.' Furthermore, some women had specifically sought out obstetricians with delivery privileges at the Met, a hospital with a reputation for having the 'big guns.' Within this context, we can understand the women's narratives of bodily discomfort and change not only as descriptions of physiological processes, but also, and perhaps mainly, as reflections of the culturally inflected and socially located power and significance of biomedical knowledge and practice.

From talking with these women, I came to understood that much of the cultural work of socializing women into the norms of technologically managed and biomedically organized reproduction is not carried out by doctors directly but rather by another, more readily accessible source of ritual wisdom and authority – advice books on pregnancy.

Pregnancy by the Book

Written materials on pregnancy that are aimed at women have proliferated since the early 1980s. Information pamphlets, magazine articles, and books on the topic are almost unavoidable if you are a pregnant woman in Canada today. Nearly all of the women I interviewed had a booklet titled *Nine Months for Life*, published by the Quebec physician's association and distributed free of charge by physicians and childbirth educators. The most common guide that the women purchased was an American book, *What to Expect When You're Expecting*, by Arlene Eisenberg, Heidi Murkoff, and Sandy Hathaway (1991). A handful of women had other books, including *Pregnancy and Childbirth* (Hotchner 1984) and *The Complete Book of Pregnancy and Childbirth* by British author Sheila Kitzinger (1989).[4]

The guides appeal to women on multiple levels. The advice is authoritative, at the same time it is offered in an upbeat and conversational tone. The women, who typically described their prenatal visits as 'lasting three minutes' and as consisting mainly of weighing in, testing urine, and measuring fundal height, welcomed the friendly tone and wealth of detail in these guides. Although women often had questions for their obstetrician, they didn't always ask them: 'I forget my questions as soon as I get there.' 'I don't want to waste his time.' 'It's over so fast, I'm just getting ready to ask her something and she's already out the door.' Guides to pregnancy are not overworked and preoccupied; they require no appointment, and no waiting; and they promise 'comforting answers to hundreds of questions' (Eisenberg et al. 1991: back cover).

The guides are aimed at heterosexual, married, middle-class, ideal-weight, able-bodied women, and the authors presume that their readers have both the time and money to eat right, reduce stress, and learn how to be pregnant 'properly.' The 'Every Woman' of these books is actively and effectively engaged in lessening the demands of work, marshalling the support of husband and family, receiving medically supervised prenatal care, and otherwise arranging her life to ensure the right conditions for her pregnancy. Women who do not fit this model – either the bodily different ('obese,' diabetic, disabled, epileptic) or the socially different ('drinkers,' 'smokers,' 'users of illicit drugs') – require special treatment: a separate chapter, or a special group (e.g., AA), or more medical care. Single mothers are also marked as different from what one guide calls 'the majority of ... readers [, who] are in traditional families' (Eisenberg et al. 1991: 28). Presumably to keep up at least the appearance of that 'traditional' family, single women are enjoined to find someone to 'play the role of the father' (Eisenberg et al. 1991: 28).

Strategically deploying the rhetoric of individual choice,[5] the advice books reinforce biomedically managed childbearing while simultaneously making pregnancy a uniquely personal experience. Constructed in these terms, a successful pregnancy seems to depend on women 'being informed' and making the 'right choices.' Marketed as 'bestsellers' and 'required reading,' and endorsed by physicians and medical organizations, these guides were avidly and eagerly read by the women I interviewed as 'essential information.'[6] Several women, like Julie in the opening pages of this chapter, referred to one guidebook or another as their 'bible.' In explaining why they read these books, these Montreal women referred not only to their desire to understand what was happening to their bodies, but also to the importance of that knowledge for improving their chances of having a healthy baby (see Browner and Press 1997 for similar ideas among American women). Especially in the early months, these women described reading the guides as a way 'to get involved' with the pregnancy happening in their bodies. 'Getting involved' meant tracking the progress of their pregnancy and evaluating its normality, following the books' advice about how to be pregnant, and learning about the fetus. In short, the physiological presence of pregnancy was not in itself enough for having a child and becoming a mother; rather, the women needed instructions on how to be pregnant.

In the guides, women's experiences of pregnancy are reduced to checklists of physical and emotional symptoms. These checklists focus mainly on excretion, digestion, the appearance and sensation of the breasts, weight gain, fatigue, and sleep patterns; and, especially, on the pregnant woman's anxieties, worries, and fears. Echoed through women's voices, these symptoms are organized in the guidebooks into a version of a widely accepted North American medical-scientific narrative on human conception, fetal development, and the effects of pregnancy on women. Canadians learn this account in school, read about it in books and magazines, see it on television, and hear it from others, including physicians and other pregnant women. In this narrative, pregnancy is rationally ordered into segments, usually three 'trimesters' (each about thirteen weeks in length). Yet women soon learn to think of the pregnancy in terms of weeks and days, describing themselves as 'fourteen-and-a-half weeks pregnant' or 'sixteen weeks yesterday.' The rational ordering of pregnancy into segments, particularly into weeks and days, strategically 'synchronizes' a woman's individual pregnancy with physicians' normative models (Georges 1997: 103; Jacoby 1995). That synchronization often caused some confusion among the women in this study, who generally counted from the date of conception or intercourse, whereas physicians count from the first day of a woman's last menstrual period. In locating themselves along the time line of medically managed pregnancy, the women were deploying a linear grid against which they could evaluate their own pregnancy on a daily basis and assess their normality; they saw this activity as making choices. This construction of pregnancy as a day-to-day experience of knowledge and choice is prefaced on notions of fetal risk, maternal insufficiency, and the need for self-monitoring.

Within both medical science and popular wisdom in Canada, pregnancy is conceptualized as a time of risk and potential danger. Beliefs about the risks of pregnancy are, in part, a reflection of problems that sometimes do occur during pregnancy, labour, and delivery. In Canada, however, these ideas are organized, institutionalized, perpetuated, and given authority through a medico-scientific discourse that focuses on risks to the fetus and that tends to locate the source of those risks in the bodies and behaviours of women. In her discussion of pregnancy and amniocentesis among Quebec women, Quéniart (1992: 164) writes: 'It is not just the mother's genetic background, but other variables such as age, weight, blood pressure, overall health, etc., as well as data related to personal habits and lifestyle, that are used to create multiple categories among pregnant women: namely those at risk, (read 'those whose *fetus* is at risk') – be it high or low – and those who aren't.'

In fact, the logic of risk as it is voiced and practised in Canadian biomedical practice precludes this latter category; all pregnancies include some risk of anomaly or complication, so there are no women classified as 'no risk.'

Each of the advice books read by the women I interviewed portrays pregnancy as a time of risk, uncertainty, and potential harm to the fetus. Women reading these guides learn about the randomness of genetics, the ubiquity of environmental hazards, and the unpredictability of fetal development. Gambling and risk-taking metaphors are especially apparent in *What to Expect*, wherein pregnant women read about 'the best odds diet,' 'tempting fate' with a second pregnancy, and playing 'baby roulette' (Eisenberg et al. 1991: 80, 26, 76). Women read that risks are everywhere and that there are no guarantees of a healthy baby, and then, reading on, learn that many of the dangers in pregnancy are located in the bodies, histories, and activities of pregnant women (see also Daniels 1997). Choices made long before pregnancy, activities engaged in before pregnancy was suspected, and behaviours during pregnancy may all pose a risk to the fetus. Yet, promise the books, women can reduce these risks.

More than just 'going to the doctor' is required to safeguard against fetal harm, minimize the discomforts of pregnancy, and prepare for childbirth. The guidebooks urge women to pay careful attention to excretion, digestion, bodily appearance and sensation, and mood swings, as well as to diet, sleep habits, exercise, employment, leisure time, clothing, shoes, sexual activities, skin and hair care, medications, interactions with others, and even the air they breathe – all require careful attention and surveillance. Weight and diet come in for particularly extensive discussion. While this is familiar terrain for women accustomed to 'counting calories' and 'watching their weight,' the stakes are raised during pregnancy: 'There's a tiny new being developing inside you. The odds are already fairly good that he or she will be born healthy. But you have the chance to improve those odds significantly – to come as close as possible to guaranteeing your baby not just good health, but excellent health – with every bite of food you put in your mouth' (Eisenberg et al. 1991: 80).

Women are repeatedly told, 'You've got only nine months of meals,' and are urged to make 'every bite count' (Eisenberg et al. 1991: 81). They are made aware not only that they bear the responsibility for producing a healthy baby, but also that they have only a limited time in which to do so (see also Michie 1998). One guide reassures women that they don't need to count calories (Eisenberg et al. 1991: 84); and another cautions that weight control 'should not become an obsession'

(Kitzinger 1989: 86); both guides then instruct women to choose 'good' calories over 'empty' ones, and to 'never, never skip a meal' (Eisenberg et al. 1991: 81), and to weigh themselves or measure their upper thighs every week (Kitzinger 1989: 87). As Susan Bordo (1993: 166) has pointed out regarding how women attend to hair, makeup, clothing, and other normalizing disciplines in their everyday lives, the calculus of calories, pounds, and inches inscribes on our bodies 'the feel and conviction of lack, of insufficiency, of never being good enough.' During pregnancy, the stakes are raised for women as they worry about the effects of their bodies and actions on the health of their baby.

Choice and *being informed* are tropes that resonate throughout other aspects of women's lives. Many Canadian women are confident that gender discrimination is a thing of the past, a problem of their mother's generation, and have been socialized to believe that given the right information, a woman can make the right choices. Appropriately informed and making the right choices, she can lose weight, be fit, look beautiful, make her marriage work and her sex life sizzle, have a lovely home and garden, be fulfilled by her job, *and* be a good mother.

Ironically, the language of choice, being informed, personal preference, and women's control over the experience of pregnancy permeates Canadian discourses on pregnancy care; yet at the same time, the self-monitoring and medical surveillance thereby engendered serve to increase women's anxiety, self-doubt, and compliance with medical regimes of prenatal care. Furthermore, because risk and responsibility are now individualized, women's attention has been deflected away from the *social* causes of discomfort, suffering, and risk during pregnancy – causes that include poverty, poor working conditions, double-shift of workplace and home, and, for many low-income women, lack of quality health care (Bordo 1993). Current psychosocial and medical narratives often parcel out the responsibility for miscarriage and fetal impairments, marking these down to the randomness of genetics or the vagaries of bilateral descent. Yet in practice, women still shoulder much of the blame when something goes wrong in pregnancy. When I asked women in Montreal about risks during pregnancy, the list of potential harms emanating from a woman's body was long. When I asked about risks posed by the father, most women shrugged off the question, saying, 'only if there is some inherited disease in his family.' Many regarded the question as puzzling or nonsensical.[7]

For all the attention that women are supposed to devote to their bodies, there are surprisingly few images of intact women in these guides.[8] The Quebec Medical Association booklet read by about three-quarters of the women I interviewed has multiple, lush, colour photographs of the fetus, but no images of women (Corporation professionnelle des médecins du Québec 1990). In *What to Expect*, the other guide popular among this group, descriptions of each month of pregnancy begin with a profile drawing of a headless, armless naked woman. Her breast is bared, and her transparent torso contains only vagina, rectum, bladder, and uterus, and the fetus. The caption reads, 'What You May Look Like.'

As Helena Michie (1998: 268) has cogently argued, the woman is often represented as if she is transparent, and the pregnancy is over, and 'the baby [is] in some sense already born.' Thus, the authors of *What to Expect* remind us that 'even if you're not hungry, the baby is' (Eisenberg et al. 1991: 81). If offered a celebratory drink, women are urged to say: 'Thanks, but I'll toast your birthday with orange juice – my baby's underage.' (Eisenberg et al. 1991: 63).

Looking at pictures: reading subjectivity

A powerful contributor to this representation of women as fetal containers, and of pregnancy as a matter of risk management, is the work of Lennart Nilsson. Nilsson is a Swedish photographer whose photographs of conception and embryonic and fetal development have been reproduced widely in electronic and print media around the world. While I was doing my research, a new edition (1990) of Nilsson's own book, *A Child is Born*, arrived in Montreal bookstores, and his photographs were featured on the cover of various news magazines including *Life* (August 1990), *Time* (30 September 1991), and the Quebec weekly *L'Actualité* (15 November 1990). Produced with a complex technology of endoscopes, fibreoptics, and scanning electron microscopes, Nilsson's photographs are strikingly clear and detailed, as if they were neutral, 'scientific' recordings of *in utero* events. His images, nonetheless, look more like 'baby photos' than scientific or clinical images. The 'natural' meanings of these images have in fact been carefully constructed (Condit 1990; Hartouni 1993; Petchesky 1987) through a variety of culturally inflected strategies. For example, each image is greatly magnified so that from the first month, the fetus seems to be the size of a five- or six-month fetus – presumably of uncontestable personhood. Even in the earliest stages, the fetus appears as a distinct and complex individual rather than a mass of tissue. Culturally salient elements of personhood and individuality figure prominently in Nilsson's photographs – fetal faces, hands, feet, and genitals. In some of the most widely reproduced images, the fetus seems to be sucking its thumb. We know from premature deliveries that fetal skin is a deep red colour until about the seventh month (Kantrowitz et al. 1988); yet, in Nilsson's photographs, and especially in those reproduced in the Quebec guide, the early fetus appears golden or pink skinned, fragile, soft, and translucent. In Nilsson's photographs, women are absent and the fetus seems to be suspended inside the soft 'veil' of the amniotic sac against an opaque, dark background. In some of the photographs the golden fetus appears in its amniotic bubble superimposed on a star-filled background. The obvious parallel in these photographs with an astronaut floating in space has been discussed by several writers (e.g., Condit 1990; Duden 1993; Hartouni 1991, 1993; Petchesky 1987). Reminiscent of the transparent female torso in *What to Expect*, the cover of Nilsson's (1990) book depicts an impossibly large pink fetus glowing within an orb that is identifiable as a woman's pregnant belly only because it is beneath a bared breast.

As Condit (1990: 85) shows in her analysis of fetal images, visual elements and written commentary work together to convince the viewer that the fetus is human, visually appealing, and a person. In each guide, the fetus is described in terms of the appearance or near appearance of certain physical parts, especially the heart, brain, spine, and arms and legs. Continuity from embryo through fetus to baby is established visually with a series of images, and textually by drawing attention to fetal features that are 'buds,' or 'forming' or 'will soon develop.' Small features are given special mention – for example, the genitals, tooth buds, ankles, wrists, hair, eyelashes, and nails. Smallness of size, complexity and completeness of anatomy, and rapid development are combined not to draw attention to the fetus but rather to dramatize the baby inside the womb:

[week three–conception] Your baby is a cluster of cells which multiply rapidly as they continue the journey along the fallopian tube. (Kitzinger 1991: 372)

By the end of the first month, your baby is a tiny, tadpole-like embryo, smaller than a grain of rice. In the next two weeks, the neural tube (which becomes the brain and spinal cord), heart, digestive tract, sensory organs and arm and leg buds will begin to form. (Eisenberg et al. 1991: 101)

[At 7 weeks the] primitive embryo becomes a primitive, well-propor-
tioned small-scale baby, less than one inch long; face is flattening; eyes
perceptible through closed lids; shell-like external ears; mouth opens –
has a human face with eyes, ears, nose, lips, tongue; chest and abdomen
completely formed; heart is internal, lung buds appear; arms, legs, hands,
feet are partially formed: the arms are as long as a printed exclamation
point and have fingers and thumbs; the toes are all stubby but the big
toes have appeared (Hotchner 1984: 68).

These guides reinforce this carefully constructed physical appearance by conferring a specific and unambiguous identity to the fetus: it
is 'the baby.' The terms 'embryo' and 'fetus' do appear in these guides,
but almost always in definitions, captions, and topic headings. In most
summaries of fetal development, and whenever a relationship or interaction between the fetus and someone else (the woman, her partner, or the physician) is implied, the term 'baby' is used. Significantly,
the guides refer to 'your baby,' and only rarely to 'your fetus' or 'your
embryo.' This language and imagery appeals to women in a society in
which words like 'fetus' and 'embryo' are regarded as 'cold,' 'clinical,'
or too closely linked to the abortion debate.

Guidebooks portray the fetus, even during the early weeks of pregnancy, as sentient, active, and socialized. In the imagery and language
of these guides, the fetus is articulated as a distinct self, an active and
aware individual. The fetus has emotions and experiences distinct from
those of the woman. It is described as active and intentional, able to
swallow, yawn, suck its thumb, frown, blink, and 'look around' (Hotchner
1984: 70), and even 'leap around energetically' (Kitzinger 1991: 32).

Fetuses are only human. Just like us they have 'up' days, when they feel
like kicking up their heels (and elbows and knees), and 'down' days,
when they'd rather lie back and take it easy. (Eisenberg et al. 1991: 201)

The baby [at 20 weeks] measures 25 to 30 cm (10 to 12 in) and weighs
about 500 g (1 lb). A few hairs have appeared on its head. Although its
eyelids are still closed, the baby is starting to become aware of sounds
coming from outside: your voice, and your partner's. (Corporation
professionnelle des médecins du Québec, 1990: 12)

[At 12 weeks, the] the baby is moving vigorously. You cannot yet feel
these movements, but it is kicking, curling its toes up and down, pressing its lips together, frowning, and making other facial expressions. The

baby is also swallowing the amniotic fluid, gurgling it from its mouth or passing it out through its bladder. There is still plenty of room in the uterus, so the fetus can swoop and undulate in its own enclosed sea. (Kitzinger 1991: 67)

Alongside these extended descriptions of the embryo and fetus as a miniature, volitional person, the authors describe maternal–fetal bonding as a sentimental private communication mediated by medical expertise. This bonding is positioned as central to women's proper experience of pregnancy. Women are given a particular identity, that of the 'selfless' mother who is nurturing and sensitive to the nuances of her body (her baby). Women's emotional and physical symptoms of pregnancy are equated with a fetal voice expressing its own needs. That voice represents a vulnerable, dependent fetus. The depiction of that interaction carries a clear message of normative maternal behaviour:

After the first few days of euphoria, once your pregnancy has been confirmed ... [there] are moments of inner questioning ... Will you make a good mother? ... As soon as you think you're pregnant, even before your doctor confirms it, get comfortable with the idea that you are going to have a baby. (Corporation professionnelle des médecins du Québec 1990: 4)

[At two months] the tiny human being attached to you is beginning to make demands on your body. These are harmless, but can cause you some discomfort. It will take time for your body to adjust to these new conditions, to the new being living inside of you. But you'll see. In just a short time your body will adapt and you'll be pleasantly surprised to find out how easily the two of you can live in harmony. (Corporation professionnelle des médecins du Québec 1990: 6)

Your thoughts are starting to turn inward, and you may find yourself day-dreaming. Your priorities have changed, your attention increasingly focussed on the being developing inside you. (Corporation professionnelle des médecins du Québec 1990: 14)

Enticing women with their claims to authority, these advice books powerfully map out a normative experience of pregnancy for women. They represent pregnancy as complex and inherently risky, but also as controllable with proper guidance and with the proper behaviour and attitude on the part of the woman. They define pregnancy mainly in terms of fetality, a fetality in which the fetus is visually and textually scripted as the fascinating, adorable, and vulnerable 'baby.' Women are instructed on how to be altruistic, fetocentric, self-disciplining mothers – living fetal monitors.

The Fetus on the Big Screen

The cultural narrative of fetal agency, risk, and maternal–fetal bonding encountered in guidebooks appears in a variety of forms and at a variety of sites. There is even a movie version. Amy Heckerling's 1990 film *Look Who's Talking* is one example of what Lauren Berlant (1997: 129) calls 'fetus driven comedies.' In the early scenes of this movie, a talking sperm encourages other sperm in a race along a pinkish, obstacle-ridden path (a woman's vagina) toward an enormous, luminous-white, mute egg that has just been released and awaits their arrival. At the moment of fertilization – depicted as a crescendo of music, fireworks, and electricity radiating from the egg – the winning sperm breathes an audible sigh of contentment. Later in the film, the fetus makes its first appearance, in the form of a large-headed doll with widely spaced eyes and short arms and legs, blinking its eyes as it floats gently within a warm-looking pink uterus. As it catches sight of its hands, the fetal voice-over remarks: 'I've got two of these things.' Fetal gender is soon established. Not only is the fetal voice male, but in an early scene the fetus looks at his hands and then at his body, remarking that he has a 'another little arm coming in down there.'[9] Throughout the film, the fetus experiences and comments on events in the woman's life, including her diet, her actions, and her choice of boyfriend. Considerable agency is attributed to the fetus. For example, when the doctor palpates the woman's uterus during a routine examination, the moving fetus blinks rapidly and shouts in surprise. In another scene, the pregnant woman gulps down a glassful of juice after the thirsty fetus tugs on the umbilical cord and calls out, 'Yo! Let's get a little apple juice down here.'

Many of the women I interviewed rented this movie on video while they were pregnant, although not all did so during the first few months of pregnancy. While a few of them found this cinematic portrayal of the fetus 'silly,' nearly one-third of the forty-nine women incorporated images and dialogue from the film into their own accounts of being pregnant. In particular, this movie offered them evidence in support of their ideas about the relationship between a pregnant woman and her fetus, and suggested what the fetus could hear, sense, see, and do. As twenty-five-year-old Annabella remarked, 'I found that a terrific movie to get an idea of what the baby is feeling.' The compelling nature of these images is unsettling. So is the blurred boundary between entertainment and education. So is the apparent ease with which the message of attentive women and demanding fetal subjects is read as authentic and natural. (Kaplan 1994: 129)

The Fetus Within

Although the women in this study were clearly fascinated by the descriptions and photographs of the fetus in their guides, before their first ultrasound they generally did not refer to the physical fetus, or to the fetal anatomy, shape, size, or appearance, except in response to my questions about 'what is developing or happening inside you.' Although they were willing to answer my questions, they explained that they rarely thought about their pregnancy in terms of the stages of fetal development. For some women, the descriptions and images of fetal morphological development provoked anxiety: 'You realize how much can go wrong.' Some of the women felt detached from the *in utero* photographs, referring to them as 'amazing,' 'ET,' or 'aliens,' or 'too weird for words,' and asking me, 'Are these [fetuses] real?' During the first interview, I asked each woman to draw the fetus and talk about what she had drawn. Of the forty-three women[10] who agreed to do so, only one-quarter visualized a developing or partially formed fetus, or what some called an 'embryo,' 'tadpole,' 'shrimp,' or 'alien.' Two-thirds of them said they imagined a 'newborn' or 'a baby, any baby.' Similarly, although the terms 'fetus' and 'embryo' were found in their guides to pregnancy, only three women – significantly, each with a university science degrees – used them to refer to what was inside them. Rejecting the term fetus as 'clinical' or 'too closely linked to the abortion debate,' and resisting the term 'baby' for the peculiar-looking stages of fetal development, many women took refuge in the impersonal and unemotional pronoun 'it.' However, when they talked about the individual they envisioned would eventually be born and with whom they were forming an emotional attachment, women were at ease using the term 'baby':

I don't think of this [pointing to her abdomen] as a fetus. This is my baby. (Sylvie, 25, chef)

I'm not having a fetus. I'm having a baby. (Jennifer, 31, counsellor)

At the time of the first interview, around eighteen weeks, most of the women (40, or 82 per cent), had not 'quickened' or felt fetal movement. Among the nine women who had felt fetal movement, the sensations were often not just unfamiliar but fleeting, leading some to wonder if they had 'really felt anything' or if it was 'just gas.' Most of the women said they knew they were pregnant because they had had a chemical pregnancy test. Some weeks later, nearly all had heard the fast 'thwump, thwump, thwump' sound of the fetal heartbeat through Doppler ultrasound. Eight of the women (16 per cent) had an 'early' ultrasound before twelve weeks of pregnancy, usually after an episode of vaginal bleeding. Significantly, before the first routine ultrasound, women did not regard either hearing the heartbeat or the early scan as an introduction to the baby or as 'meeting' the baby.[11] Rather, they perceived these as diagnostic events confirming the existence of the pregnancy and a live fetus. Nonetheless, most women were actively engaged in thinking about, learning about, and developing a 'relationship' with what was inside their bodies.

Heeding the advice they had found in their books, the women made various changes in their lives. Mainly, this meant eating nutritious foods, getting plenty of rest, avoiding stress, abstaining from alcohol and cigarettes, and staying away from various 'chemicals' (including medications, recreational drugs, and household cleaners). Besides all this, three-quarters of them had begun to 'communicate' with what lay inside their bodies. As they understood it, by rubbing or prodding their abdomens, 'sending good thoughts,' having their partners 'listen' at their bellies, and talking aloud, they were communicating with the fetus:

When I talk to the baby I say, 'Baby, please don't make me sick today. I want to go out tonight and I don't want to be sick.' (Annabella, 25, office clerk)

I know it can recognize voices now. My boyfriend talks to it, he says, 'Hi. I'm Daddy.' And sometimes at work I say, 'We're gonna get those customers.' Just stupid things like that. You know, 'We're going home now' and, 'I hope you aren't tired like me.' (Norma, 24, cashier)

I saw the movie *Look Who's Talking* ... And he [the fetus in the movie] says, 'Hey I need some juice down here' and she drinks juice. And that's the conception I have. Like the baby is coughing every time I have a cigarette. And she has a glass of wine one time and he says, 'Like this is really neat' ... So that's why every time I have a cigarette I pat my tummy and say, 'Sorry.' [*laughs*] ... That's why when I get upset, I get pains and I keep saying, 'I'm sorry.' Like if I yell at my husband or something ... I speak to the baby all the time. I'll even put earphones on my stomach and play my favourite music. (Sophia, 31, graphic artist)

Bonding both presumes and mobilizes particular notions of fetality. Not surprisingly, the thirty-seven women who were communicating with the fetus said that the sixteen to eighteen week old fetus had 'some' sensory ability, that it could hear, see, and sense movement and touch, and that it had 'some' cognitive ability. Most of this group (84 per cent) believed that the fetal eyes could open and close and distinguish light and dark at sixteen to eighteen weeks, although many remarked that there was 'nothing to see' inside the uterus. Similarly, most (89 per cent) said the sixteen to eighteen week old fetus could hear the sounds of the woman's own body and voice, as well as loud external noises such as music, cars honking, and people shouting.

Describing their ideas about the fetus in this way – as the percentage of women who believed such-and-such – masks the fact that this was not knowledge that could easily be articulated or elaborated. Resistant to words, this knowledge surfaced in their actions and gestures and in inexplicable bodily knowledge: it was something they just 'knew' or 'felt.'

Talking to the fetus, thinking about it, and touching it were perceived by women as ways to make the fetus aware of their presence and their feelings toward it. As one woman said, 'I want this baby to know I'm here and that I care.' Many women believed that the fetus could not understand words but absorbed their meaning or the emotion conveyed by sensing 'vibrations' or the 'tone of voice.' That being said, the above examples indicate that their talk and thoughts to the fetus included salutations, words of encouragement, and commentaries on their activities, moods, and surroundings (the weather, noises, people nearby). Women apologized aloud to the baby if they swore, or forgot or delayed a meal, or coughed, or had a cigarette, or if they became emotionally upset or physically stressed. They also talked about doing things together with the fetus ('we're going home now'). Some described their communication with the fetus to me as, 'We talk to each other all the time.'

Men were also involved in this 'communication.' Occasionally as the initiator, but more often acting on a suggestion from their partner (i.e., as a way to 'get involved' and 'feel connected to the baby'), a man might massage the woman's abdomen to make the fetus aware of his presence, or listen at her belly for the fetal heart beat, or talk quietly against her belly so the fetus would 'recognize dad's voice.' Several women had read that it might be possible to influence the scholastic or artistic potential of the child by reading to it, playing music, or repeating simple calculations or spellings *in utero*. A few women thought this was possible, but early in pregnancy none were inclined to try these types of prenatal learning. However, a few women repeatedly sang or played a particular song to the fetus, hoping that once the child was born, the song would have a calming influence on it:

> My Mum, when she was pregnant with me she used to listen to a lot of Johnny Mathis, and to this day I love Johnny Mathis. It drives him [her husband] crazy! ... It's gotta have something to do with it. There is one song I'd like to find and to play over and over, so that when the child isn't feeling well, it will know that this is its song and it'll feel better. (Michelle, 27, data systems analyst)

Five of the couples had prepared audiotapes, which they played regularly against the woman's abdomen. Hoping the baby would 'recognize' their voices, these couples recorded introductions of themselves and other family members, descriptions of their houses (especially of the room that would belong to the baby), favourite songs, lullabies, and stories. Julie played her tape while watching television: 'I still feel kinda stupid sitting there talking to my stomach, so we made the tape. He [the fetus] gets to hear us, and I don't feel stupid.'

Most of the women I interviewed believed that the fetus was sentient, and capable of experiencing things through its senses; not only that, but many envisioned an empathetic fetus that was able to share the emotions of others. Most of the women (86 per cent) were confident that by sixteen to eighteen weeks the fetus could sense their emotional state. However, some women believed that the fetus could sense their moods only near the end of pregnancy. Invoking an association that goes back several hundred years in Europe (Huet 1993), women moderated their own emotions to avoid harming or upsetting the fetus or making 'a nervous baby':

> I don't want to argue with my husband, because I don't want the baby to feel anything bad and aggressive. I don't want to scare the baby. (Naomi, 31, accountant)

> If I'm tense, it's tense. So I say, 'I'm sorry' to the baby. Then I talk to myself and tell myself to control myself. It can hear me. (Suzanne, 27, secretary)

> My little baby there needs me very much and he needs me to feel good. I think about that. I'm trying my best ... My husband and I we don't want to scream too much to each other or fight because we know that this little kid can hear it and we don't want a nervous baby and a baby that is disturbed. We are trying our best to be calmer ... I lost my mother a year and a half ago and my father five years ago. My father – I got used to it, but my mother – it is harder. So sometimes, two or three times, I really cried hard, but I explained everything to the baby. I tell the baby what is happening to me. That I'm sad, that something is bugging me. I have a good relationship with my baby. (Natalie, 27, office clerk)

Women also envision the fetus as an agent, capable both of influencing the woman and of doing things because it wants to:

> I know that this little baby is really strong-minded. It's making itself felt so early and so strongly.

Have you felt it move?
> No, not yet. But just the way it has taken over my body and makes me do what it needs. Like, 'sleep now,' 'eat now.' Like, I'm just along for the ride and the baby is calling all the shots. (Sandy, 27, secretary)

While they often attributed the physical and emotional sensations of pregnancy to 'hormonal changes,' almost three-quarters of the women also described their nausea, fatigue, appetite, and changes in their appearance as if they were caused directly by the fetus. In some cases, bodily changes were seen as a kind of corporeal communication from the fetus, telling the woman what it needed:

> So far this baby is not giving me a hard time. I'm not sick, I don't have morning sickness. I'm not gaining weight. I'm a little tired, but that's it. (Jennifer, 31, counsellor)

> I look at my tummy and say, 'Okay, so you want more room.' I throw up and I say, 'Okay, so you didn't like dinner last night?' I feel like my body belongs to the baby. It's not mine. It's not my husband's! [laughs] He doesn't like that! It's all the baby's. (Cheryl, 33, office manager)

> When I overexert myself, I get cramps and I think it's the baby telling me to slow down. (Kate, 24, bookkeeper)

> I can tell how the baby is by the way I'm feeling with my stomach. Like when I get nervous I tend not to be very hungry. I eat just to keep the baby going, but it's as if the baby doesn't even want it. (Annabella, 25, office clerk)

In summary, well before the first ultrasound, as the women imagined the appearance, gender, and character of their baby and made conscious attempts to 'eat better,' 'rest more,' and 'take care,' they began to create an individual, a baby, from their pregnancy and to think about themselves differently. Yet, they were also attentive to the possibility that 'something' might go wrong that would end the pregnancy. The underlying contradiction or as Janelle Taylor (1998: 24) phrases it so well, '"the prenatal paradox" is that, ironically, pregnancy is constructed more and more as a "tentative" relationship, and the fetus as a "commodity," at the same time and through the same means that pregnancy is also constructed more and more as an absolute and unconditional relationship, and the fetus as a "person" from its earliest stages.'

Women simultaneously enable and constrain the extent to which they see the fetus as a person. Prior to the first ultrasound, relatively few women had told anyone other than close family and friends and their physician about the pregnancy. Most women had not begun to display the material items that symbolized a social identity for themselves as mothers, or for the early fetus as baby – wearing maternity clothes, preparing a room, purchasing toys, clothes, cribs, and other 'baby things.' And they still talked much more about 'being pregnant' than about 'having a baby' or about what was inside their bodies. In this context, the women interviewed held high expectations for ultrasound.

'Expecting': Hopes and Worries about the First Routine Ultrasound

Among the Montreal women I interviewed, the presence of ultrasound in their pregnancy was expected, reassuring, and eagerly anticipated. Through their conversations with friends and by reading their advice books, they learned about the procedure, what it would feel like, why it was done, and what the image would look like. They expected to have at least two ultrasounds during pregnancy; that they did so was interpreted by some as a reassuring sign that they had chosen a 'good' doctor. Most women had seen a copy of an ultrasound fetal image belonging to a sister, friend, or co-worker, or in a book, so they knew that the image would be black-and-white and blurry, like a photographic 'negative,' a 'snowy black-and-white television' or an 'X-ray.' A small group of women, including several recent immigrants to Canada, had never seen an ultrasound image; they wondered if the image would be like the *in utero* colour photographs in their guidebooks.

The topic of how ultrasound images were produced held interest for only a few of the women – the ones with a science or health profession background. More compelling to them was the issue of whether ultrasound was safe. Half of the group were concerned that the ultrasound might be harmful, and worried that it might cause cancer, ear infections, hearing loss, or nervousness in their infants. Despite their concerns, only four women asked their physician about the safety of the procedure. Most of the women reassured themselves by reasoning that 'everyone has them now' and that doctors 'wouldn't be doing ultrasounds if they were dangerous.' Whatever the risk of harm from the ultrasound, it was perceived as small, and as less significant than the benefit gained from finding out that the fetus was normal. None of the women refused an ultrasound; and as far as I am aware, none seriously considered doing so.

Since I was by then well-versed in the controversies about ultrasound's safety and efficacy, I found it unsettling to hear women say that their physicians had told them little or nothing about ultrasound, only reminding them to book an appointment. When I asked each woman whether her doctor had asked if she wanted the ultrasound, or had requested consent for the procedure, the response was nearly always the same: 'No.' Most women seemed taken aback by my questions, and a few admitted that they thought the test was 'compulsory' or 'mandatory.' My questions were perplexing to them because they *wanted* and looked forward to the ultrasound. Implicit in their puzzled expressions was the response, 'What mother wouldn't want ultrasound?'

When I began the interviews, I was intrigued to discover that women were excited and eager to have ultrasound. Their enthusiasm struck me as odd: why would women look forward with such eagerness to a procedure that might detect a problem with their pregnancy? Ultrasound fetal imaging straddles two worlds: it is both a medical procedure and a social ritual. These women viewed ultrasound as a 'routine procedure,' as 'another one of those tests they do when you're pregnant'; at the same time, their enthusiasm signalled its social significance. What made this test distinctive and desired was what they called 'seeing the baby.'

I want to see the heart beating, to see that life is there. (Clara, 30, university student)

I just want to see the baby and know that everything is all right. That everything is there and what it's doing, if it's sleeping or swimming or whatever. I just want to see how it's doing in there. (Claudette, 27, secretary)

I want to be assured that it is totally routine with respect to the results and that there is nothing wrong with respect to the development ... I really hope there will be time to bond with it. I mean, this is my first chance to see my baby and I don't want it to be too clinical. I want there to be some time just to watch it and get to know it. (Tamara, 26, dentist)

Women's expectation to 'see the baby' has two primary meanings, which parallel two broad claims about ultrasound made by sonographers and advice books. *First,* women assert that 'only ultrasound can tell me if my baby will be normal.' Nearly all the women in this study (92 per cent) said that physicians send women for ultrasound merely to determine fetal normality. The sonographers claimed that the principal reason for the procedure was to determine fetal age, yet relatively few women were unsure of their dates, or listed fetal age as a reason to do ultrasound. Women's belief that ultrasound would 'determine' normality was not unqualified: stories from a sister, a friend, or someone at work about missed anomalies, wrongly assigned gender, rushed examinations, and various false alarms raised their anxiety. Yet the moral of these stories was not that sonographers were prone to making errors. Ironically, the women generally felt that these stories indicated *too much* reliance on the technology: 'ultrasounds can't tell you everything and you shouldn't expect it to' (Rita, 23, university student). Other women offered stories about anomalies and stillbirths among babies born to women who refused ultrasound, as testimony that women should have ultrasound, since 'it's better to be safe than sorry.'

Second, 'seeing the baby' also refers to women's expectation that they will see 'what the baby looks like.' The women assumed that with the help of the sonographers, they would at least be able to see the shape or form of the fetus and rule out the possibility of twins. Ultrasound also held out the possibility of seeing something that would personalize the fetus. Thus, women wanted to find out 'what the baby looks like' and 'what kind of baby it is' – to learn if it was a boy or girl, to observe thumb sucking, and to see fetal movement and position and the 'build' of the baby, as well as facial features and hair:

> I already know I'm pregnant. So it's not like it's gonna be a big surprise or anything. But I'm gonna see what it really looks like. My brother and me were bald babies so I really wanna see if it's got hair. (Natalie, 27, office clerk)

> I'm dying to know the sex ... I have to know. I hate surprises. I want to know if I should be calling it a 'she' or a 'he.' (Elaine, 28, social worker)

'Seeing the baby' was often articulated by women in the lexicon of meeting a new person. Some described the ultrasound as a 'sneak preview' or 'a chance to say hello.' One woman expressed her excitement about the ultrasound by saying, 'I feel like I'm going to meet my baby.' In a disquieting echo of their reasons for reading books on pregnancy, some women said it offered a chance for them to 'get to know' or 'bond with' the baby. The pictorial apprehension of the fetus held the possibility of 'putting it all together,' making the abstract and intangible, concrete and experienced.

> You hear the heartbeat and you are really excited because you know there is a baby there, but at other times, it just seems your pants are getting a little tight. So while you realize that there is a baby there, it's hard to realize that it's true. It's hard to make the connection. I think about it cognitively, but not really psychologically that it's inside of me. Maybe when I see the ultrasound it will help me put it all together. (Karen, 26, university student)

In short, among these women ultrasound held the promise of enabling them to see something – activity, character, family resemblance, gender – that would personalize *their* baby and thereby clarify its identity. What they were shown during the ultrasound is the topic of the next chapter.

Chapter Five

'Showing the Baby': Sonographers' Accounts of Fetal Images

> Producing a 'good' ultrasound image is not as simple as snapping a picture; neither is reading one.
>
> Barad (1998: 101)

All ultrasound examinations are, borrowing Haraway's terms (1991: 164), acts of 'translation' or 'coding' in which technologically produced signs (reflected echoes) are translated into meaningful statements about the world. Some of the work of translating ultrasound echoes into a picture of the fetus is accomplished through historical and social processes such as technological change and the institutionalization, routinization, and dissemination of fetal images (see chapters 2 and 3). In the present chapter, I focus on how that translation continues as sonographers produce and talk about routine prenatal ultrasound images. During these scans, sonographers must translate the physics of echoes – that is, distinguish maternal and fetal anatomy from 'artefacts' (echoes be caused by the machine rather than by any maternal or fetal structure); but at the same time, they must also translate the clinical and social meanings of these different shades of grey. Specifically, sonographers translate ultrasound echoes and maternal history into clinical information expressed as percentages, numbers, rates of growth, and statements of normality or abnormality, and also into social evidence of fetal and maternal selves. Embedded in the domains of meaning that are enabled and engaged by this translation process engender are contradictions and tensions that sonographers must negotiate in order to present a coherent image. In this chapter I argue that translating the greyish echoes into compelling and meaningful images involves more than expert sonographers offering explanations to passive, non-expert viewers. The meaning of the images emerges through the dialogue and interactions that arise between the sonographer, the pregnant woman and her companion, and other viewers.

My analysis is woven around an ethnographic narrative of the ultrasound clinic at the Metropolitan Hospital. The narrative is a composite constructed from different days during my eighteen months of fieldwork at the clinic, and includes lengthy observations of ultrasounds of the four women – Rosa, Tamara, Marie-Claude, and Julie – introduced in the previous chapter, as well as shorter segments from the scans of other women. In the following pages I use the term 'sonographer' except where the distinction between technician and obstetrician is important to the discussion. At the Metropolitan, the vast majority of routine scans and a portion of each non-routine scan were done by technicians rather than by obstetricians. This division of labour meant that technicians spent more time with parents and talked to them about a wider range of subjects; obstetricians' conversations with parents often focused on diagnostic matters. In general, however, during routine scans, the descriptions of the fetal image for parents given by obstetricians were similar to those given by technicians.

The Metropolitan Hospital Ultrasound Clinic

Outside the hospital, the winter air is clear and cold. As I walk down the corridor, the air of the hospital seems stale by comparison, and heavy with the smells of institutional cooking, floors still damp from mopping, and an unsavoury blend of medication, disinfectant, and sickness. The narrow halls in this part of the hospital are always crowded with men and women in uniform pushing carts laden with food trays and bins heaped with sheets and towels. I pass an orderly pushing a wheelchair and catch a glimpse, farther down the corridor, of the usual group of men standing around the door to the ultrasound clinic. The men watch the steady flow of people along the hallway while they wait to be summoned inside for a brief look at the ultrasound. I step through the doorway into the clinic and understand why the men have chosen to stand in the hall. It is barely nine a.m. but the clinic's waiting area is already full; women in various stages of pregnancy sit on the chairs, their hands clasped around extended bellies, talking with other women, some holding squirming toddlers. A few men lean against the walls, reading magazines or newspapers. I nod 'hello' to Rosa's husband, Mario, as he sips coffee from a styrofoam cup.

'Lavoie. Carole Lavoie,' the receptionist calls, and a woman crosses the room to sit next to the reception's desk.[1] I follow until I can wave 'good morning' to the receptionist. A corner of her desk is covered with toys for diverting impatient children in the waiting room. The wall beside her has a growing collection of photographs of newborn babies sent by women who have had their ultrasounds at this clinic. I turn back toward the examination rooms and hear the receptionist asking a woman for her health insurance card.

Outside the ultrasound rooms three women sit below a manufacturer's poster illustrating what can be visualized by ultrasound during each month of pregnancy. These women have another fifteen to twenty minutes to wait before they will be scanned. Their bladders are full with the required four glasses of water, and they squirm uncomfortably. For many of the women in the outer reception area, it will be another hour before they are called into this inner waiting area.

Past the ultrasound rooms is an office used mainly by the supervising obstetricians, to write up ultrasound reports, which are sent on to each woman's referring physician. Farther along the corridor, fetal heart monitoring is conducted. Sometimes the amplified sound of fetal heartbeats – a rapid *woosh woosh* sound – is audible in the ultrasound clinic.

At the physicians' desk, I take off my coat and pull a notebook and pen from my briefcase. I take lots of notes during the scans; the sonographers shake their heads in amazement that I can write so much about what seems so ordinary and routine to them. I turn to a new page, record the date, and enter one of the ultrasound rooms. Another day of observations has begun.

Rosa

The narrow room is dark, the overhead lights are off, the window blinds are closed. Light from the ultrasound monitor illuminates the technician's face as she looks over her shoulder to greet me. I stand at my usual place, at her back near the foot of the bed, facing the ultrasound machine and the monitor above it. On my left is a desk and supply shelves. I say 'hello' to Rosa, who is just lying down, settling herself on the bed to my right, and she smiles in reply.

The technician swivels her chair to look at Rosa's ultrasound requisition form. Written at the bottom of the form is 'G1P0,' which indicates that Rosa is pregnant for the first time (Gestation 1) and has not yet had a live-born child (Parity 0). 'Maternal history' is an important element in how ultrasound echoes are made meaningful. This history is begun during a woman's first visit to her physician, when a file is created to record the events of her pregnancy. At the ultrasound clinic a similar file is compiled that includes the woman's age, the date of her last menstrual period, number of previous pregnancies, number of live-born infants, and any specific reasons for having the ultrasound (e.g., vaginal bleeding, suspected breech presentation, previous infant with impairment). During an ultrasound the woman's maternal history is used as a context for interpreting the echoes; initially, it serves to distinguish 'routine' scans – 'normals' as they are sometimes called at the Met – from 'high-risk' or 'detailed' scans.[1] Routine scans are those which sonographers believe (at least initially) involve only one fetus and no amniocentesis, and for which there is no reason to suspect either fetal demise or fetal impairment. Routine scans generally last about fifteen minutes; detailed scans can last much longer.

Facing the screen, the technician squirts blue transducing gel on Rosa's abdomen, picks up the 'probe,' or transducer and begins the scan.[2]

TECHNICIAN. [*Looking at the sheet that indicates this is Rosa's first pregnancy*] This is your first one, eh? How's it going?

ROSA. So far so good. I've had some morning sickness, but not too bad. And I'm finally getting over that tiredness. My God! I could'a slept all day for weeks.

While Rosa is talking, the technician quickly and silently checks to see that there is a fetus and that the fetal heart is beating. Then she continues:

TECHNICIAN. So I'll give you a quick look at the baby and then I'm gonna do my measurements. Then I'll ask your husband to come in. Here's the heart. You see the heart beating? It's clear, eh? [*Rosa nods and watches the screen intently.*] The head. The baby's head.

ROSA. [*Shakes her head. The technician traces the outline of the fetal head with her finger on the screen.*] Oh my God! That's the head? How come you're all the way up here? [*Points to near her navel.*]

TECHNICIAN. The baby's head is up here. [*As Rosa watches the transducer on her belly, the technician watches the screen and traces the position of the fetus with the transducer.*] Head. Spine. Legs over here. He's sleeping, all in a ball.

ROSA. It's not low? [*The technician shakes her head.*] My doctor said I was carrying low, so I figured it was like all the way down.

TECHNICIAN. Okay, now I'm gonna do my exam. This is the bladder.

ROSA. Baby's bladder?

TECHNICIAN. No, your bladder. I have a look at your cervix. You're really full! Just a minute and you can go empty a bit. [*Rosa looks at her blankly*] You're too full, so you can go empty halfway.

As the exam begins, the technician examines and records an image of the maternal cervix and vagina and the placenta. After this the fetus is examined from the head down, first the cranium, cerebellum, and face, then the spine (particularly the lumbar and sacral regions), and finally the arms, hands, legs, and feet. Internally, the stomach, bladder, and kidneys and the four chambers of the heart are identified. The volume of amniotic fluid is estimated (high, low, average), and the blood vessels of the umbilical cord and the site where the cord attaches to the fetal abdominal wall are visualized. Toward the end of the examination, the technician may try to determine the fetus's sex.

When Rosa returns after a few minutes, the scan resumes. She rests her head on one arm crooked behind her head, and with her other hand holds her hospital gown away from the gel. With her right hand the technician holds the ultrasound probe against Rosa's abdomen; her left hand rests on the scanner keyboard. The probe is cylindrical with a rounded end, and is attached by a heavy cord to the ultrasound machine. Another probe, narrower and operating at a higher frequency, rests on a holder at the edge of the keyboard. The technicians use this second probe to examine fetal structures that are closer to the surface of the woman's abdomen. On a lower shelf is a case that holds an endovaginal probe, which is used for scans earlier than twelve weeks' gestation. The technician moves the probe over Rosa's belly, pressing deeply at times to get the right angle.

We all watch the television-like monitor in front of the technician. For the technician and I this is not difficult, since we are facing the monitor. Rosa, however, must crane and twist her neck to look at the monitor above and to the right of her head. Midway through the research period, an additional monitor was placed at the foot of the examining bed, making it easier for women to watch. The image is shaped like a wedge of pie; the upper, narrow part of the wedge corresponds to the woman's abdominal surface, and the lower, wide part to her back. Indistinct grey, black, and white patches swirl around in this wedge, occasionally coalescing into shapes, some of which I can now label – fetal head, leg, spine.

No two ultrasound examinations are exactly alike. They vary with the stage of the pregnancy and the fetus's position. Also, twins may be present, or a possible fetal impairment may have to be investigated. And, of course, different women ask different questions. What goes on during ultrasound is also affected by the sonographer's scanning style, whether he or she feels talkative that day, fluctuations in caseload, the presence of a novice sonographer, changes in clinic protocol, and equipment quirks. Even so, as I show in the following pages, there are many recurring elements in how sonographers conduct and narrate routine fetal images.

The technician continues the ultrasound examination, locating, examining, and recording standard anatomical landmarks and structures. Some parts of fetal anatomy are assessed qualitatively by location, size, shape, and appearance (dark or light, uniform or mottled, etc.). Landmarks are connected on-screen by means of dotted lines or '+' marks, which are converted into measurements of fetal biparietal diameter (ear to ear through the head), length of the femur (and sometimes humerus and radius), abdominal circumference, and so on. 'Sonographic' measurements are compared automatically with standardized charts of fetal growth.[3] Thus fetal landmarks, having been transformed into measurements, are transformed yet again into numeric estimates of fetal age and size and into assessments of cranial growth and of the symmetry of fetal long bones.

Every so often the technician freezes the image on the screen, then touches a button on the nearby printer. The small printer hums quietly and adds another black and white 'photo' to the dangling strip of ultrasound images. I glance at the strip and see images of Rosa's bladder, her closed cervix, the placenta, and the fetal cranium. The technician turns the probe, brings the white circle of the fetal cranium into view on the screen, and taps at the keyboard. The image freezes, and a small cross appears on the screen. She places the cross on one side of the fetal cranium and then rotates a small tracer ball on the keyboard to draw a line across to the other side of the cranium. She taps another button; numbers appear on the lower left of the screen indicating that the fetal biparietal (ear-to-ear) diameter is 37 millimetres. These measurements are compared with standardized tables of fetal size and growth to estimate fetal age and assess fetal growth.

TECHNICIAN. Now, we see the cerebellum, the lower part of the brain. [*Long pause. The image swirls each time the technician moves the transducer. As the sonographer works, Rosa's gaze moves back and forth between her and the screen.*] The two white lines is the spine of the baby. [*The technician is quiet again for several minutes as she moves on to the internal organs of the fetus.*] Now we look inside the baby. The heart beating again. The stomach. Baby's bladder – he's full, too. That's good, baby's kidneys are working.

ROSA. So can you see what it is? You said '*he's* full.'

TECHNICIAN. No, no. I'm not there now. I'm gonna do my measurements and then I'll see. Do you want to know?

ROSA. No. We want the surprise.

TECHNICIAN. Yeh. It's different when it's your first. You can always try again. [*Several minutes pass in silence as the technician completes her examination of the fetal internal organs and then measures the femur.*] Now I'm looking at the femur. That white line.

ROSA. What's that?

TECHNICIAN. [*Pats her own thigh.*] La cuisse.

ROSA. Thigh?

TECHNICIAN. Yes. We measure that to see how the baby is growing.

Measurements of the image are not automatically assumed to be 'good' and thus worth saving in the computer as clinical data. Each measurement must be evaluated in the context of standardized charts, normal variation in fetal growth, measurement error, and gestational age based on the woman's last menstrual period. Ordinarily, the sonographer tries to resolve discrepancies by redoing measurements and getting them to 'fit.' For example, each measurement is repeated until the technician has two that do not differ by more than one or two millimetres. She may also question the woman about her last menstrual period in order to determine whether it can be used as an indicator of gestational age. Estimates of fetal age based on the starting date of the woman's last period may be discarded if ultrasound measurements indicate a different fetal age. Alternatively, if her dates are 'good,' the ultrasound measurements may indicate that the fetus is not growing normally. If there is something in the image that the technician cannot account for as 'normal,' she may return to that portion of the anatomy to 'try again.' If she is still unable to make the image 'normal,' she will ask the clinic obstetrician for assistance.

Once the fetus has been examined and measured, the woman's companion is called in to see.

TECHNICIAN. Okay. I'm gonna ask your husband to come in now.

In earlier days, the clinic permitted male partners, friends, and others to watch the ultrasound only after the diagnostic examination was finished. After a few months, to save time, the staff allowed a woman's companions to watch the entire scan. There is still considerable variation between hospitals on this point. Once he is admitted into the room and the scan resumes, Mario leans forward across the bed to watch the technician's screen, and Rosa twists and cranes her neck to see.

TECHNICIAN. I'm gonna start with the baby's head. Oh, he's awake now. 'Good morning baby.' [*She speaks in a high voice.*] '*Allô Maman. Allô Papa.*'
ROSA. [*Looking back and forth between the transducer on her belly and the movement screen.*] Is that you? Or the baby?
TECHNICIAN. The baby's moving. See. I'm not moving. There's his arm and his hand. [*Touches the screen.*] Right by his head. See, his mouth is open. [*Laughs.*] He's yawning. [*The technician mimics the yawning stretch of someone who has just awakened. Rosa and Mario laugh.*]
MARIO. He's stretching, eh?
TECHNICIAN. Hold still so we can see you.

This part of the scan, when sonographers have completed their examination and are 'showing the baby' to parents, is generally similar from scan to scan. The heart, head, legs, arms, and spine, often in that order, are indicated to most parents. Internal organs such as the bladder, stomach, kidneys, and brain may be noted, as well as facial features, hands and feet, and fetal genitalia. Near the close of 'showing the baby,' or when a particularly clear or 'cute' image appears, the sonographer will freeze the screen and print out a copy for the parents.

TECHNICIAN. Now I'm gonna take a picture for you. Can you see the head here? He was in a better position before to see, but I'm gonna take my picture here. [*She concentrates for several minutes, trying to get a good picture. Then she puts down the transducer and hands Rosa the print-out.*] The head is here and spine here, like a train track. [*She wipes the gel from Rosa's belly.*] Okay. That's it. Your dates are good. Everything looks fine. Your doctor is gonna get the report in a few days. [*As Rosa and Mario leave, the technician places the ultrasound photos and report on the physicians' desk.*]

Exams that sonographers consider 'negative' are indicated on the ultrasound report as 'no anomalies seen' (in French, 'Rien à signaler'). Obstetricians at the Met prefer to telephone the referring physician if fetal anomalies are detected; 'questionable' or 'anomalous' findings are also described and included on the written report, as are recommendations for additional ultrasounds or separate tests. A copy of the report is then sent to the woman's own physician; another copy and the photographs remain on file at the ultrasound clinic for use in interpreting subsequent ultrasounds in this or later pregnancies.

Showing the Baby

'Seeing' is not a natural activity; rather, it is focused in culturally and historically specific ways (Crary 1990; Romanyshyn 1989). What one sees depends on how one looks. As sonographers look at the ultrasound screen, they translate the echoes (i.e., 'look') in specific ways – to search for anomalies, to improve the ultrasound resolution, and to find 'a cute picture' for expectant parents. Janelle Taylor (1998: 25) has described routine prenatal ultrasounds as 'hybrid' practices; that is, what is seen and said about the images straddles and engages multiple domains of meaning – clinical diagnosis, psychological reassurance, and entertainment. The hybrid character of ultrasound is evident in a variety of ways. For example, the current indications for routine ultrasound emphasize searching for anomalies, as well as reducing parental anxiety and fostering parental–fetal 'bonding.' Ultrasound's hybrid character also emerges in the actions, gestures, and words of sonographers and expectant parents.

Tamara

I stay in the examining room, unrolling a clean sheet of paper over the bed while the technician calls in the next patient. Tamara comes in and settles on the bed. When we talked last night, she said she was 'really nervous' about the scan and relieved that her husband, John, would be there: 'I'll definitely need hand-holding.' The technician looks over the requisition form and types Tamara's name and patient number into the computer. Then she asks Tamara to pull up her gown, covers her pubic region and thighs with a towel, and squirts transducing gel onto her belly. We all look expectantly at the screen.

TAMARA. [*Looking at the screen size.*] I was hoping for a twenty-six inch!
TECHNICIAN. No, just a monitor and no colour. [*She quickly looks over the fetal heart, head, and limbs.*] Okay. I'll give you a quick look at the baby and then I'll do my measurements. [*She moves the transducer over Tamara's belly.*] Here is the baby's heart beating.
TAMARA. Great!
TECHNICIAN. This is the head. Okay. The baby is lying head down. [*She scans the fetal head very quickly and then moves on to look at Tamara's bladder.*] Okay. Now I will do my measurements. Can you lie back please? [*Tamara has raised her head off the pillow to see the screen.*] How is the pregnancy going?
TAMARA. Great! Can you see the hands? Will you be able to see the hands?
TECHNICIAN. Yes. Later.

During the first few minutes of a scan, sonographers quickly and silently search the image in order to 'document fetal life.' Although they may not tell parents that is what they are looking for, sonographers make a point of showing the heartbeat to parents, often describing it as 'a beautiful sight.' Having established that the fetus is alive and 'viable' at this level, sonographers treat the scan as 'routine,' and begin to do what they call 'showing her the baby.' One of the sonographers described the first few seconds of scan this way:

Usually everything is okay. But I always feel good when I see that heart. You know ... [*lets out a big breath and visibly relaxes her shoulders*] like okay, I can relax a bit.

Tamara's remark at the beginning of her ultrasound – 'I was hoping for a twenty-six inch' – underscores the contradictions and tensions that inform contemporary routine fetal imaging. Ultrasound has been routinized as a means of screening for clinical problems; and that very routinization has made it a means of reassuring women that there are no problems, and of transforming the fetus into a form of entertainment that women are supposed to desire and enjoy. While the first few moments are particularly stressful in terms of documenting fetal life, the possibility of finding some further fetal impairment remains, so fetal viability and normality are contingent. Paradoxically, as sonographers search for the very anomalies that may suspend or constrain fetal personhood, they are constructing that personhood by talking about the image and encouraging the parents to see and to bond with a sentient and acting 'baby.'

The tension that arises from this contradiction was managed by sonographers at the Met in specific ways, not unlike those observed by Taylor (1998: 29) in her research at an American clinic. Sonographers in both locations separate the clinical from the entertainment portions of the exam, semantically and structurally, by telling patients, 'First I'll give you a quick tour and then I'll do my measurements' or, 'After I do my measurements, I'll show you the baby.' In other words, once fetal life is documented, women are to be reassured that the fetus is alive with the 'quick tour.' But, they must then wait until the full examination is finished to 'see their baby.' At the Met, while they are doing the measurements, technicians tend to have the monitor directed toward themselves; when they are 'showing the baby,' they swivel the monitor to make it easier for the woman to see and enjoy the image. While this boundary between medical procedure and entertaining spectacle is actively managed, it is not rigid or impermeable. Over the course of the research, as the technicians gained more experience and the clinic caseload grew heavier, the boundaries between these two domains of meaning became increasingly blurred. Sonographers continued to say, 'First I'll do my measurements and then show you'; but in practice, they narrated fetal personhood throughout the scan. In addition, providing an additional 'patient' monitor, admitting husbands and other people for the entire scan, allowing women to wear their street clothes, and charging a small fee for the print-out of the fetal image all worked to blur 'diagnostics,' and 'entertainment,' the 'medical' and 'non-medical' portions.

Tamara's ultrasound proceeds, with the technician examining the bladder and cervix and then moving on to examine maternal fetal anatomy. The sonographer tells her which parts of the fetus she is examining and which measurements she is conducting. Sonographers can articulate the basic 'principles' of ultrasound scanning (how sound waves are transformed into an image, when to switch to a different probe or transducer, when to adjust the grey-scale contrast, etc.), but that knowledge is largely hidden in their everyday work of translating echoes into fetal facts. Occasionally, when the equipment fails to work properly, when obtaining the correct orientation of the fetal image is difficult, or when an 'artefact' appears in the image, sonographers draw consciously on their knowledge of how ultrasound works. With ultrasound equipment becoming ever more sophisticated, less and less of the work of producing and interpreting images involves the sort of calculations, figuring, and knowledge about physics that were part of doing a scan during the 1960s. While sonographers can and some-times do discuss measurements, anatomy, and clinical indications with women, little of that knowledge is made explicit during a routine scan. Ultrasound equipment software even automates some of the work of labelling fetal and maternal anatomy and (with built-in compara-tive charts) evaluating ultrasound measurements. Routine obstetrical ultrasound is more about screening – locate, identify, measure, and record – than about diagnosing clinical pathologies. Like other assem-bly line or 'prescriptive technologies' (Franklin 1999), its use is repeti-tive, stressful, and exhausting. The impact of the routinization of fetal imaging is felt mainly by the bodies of sonographers – technicians in particular – who often suffer repetitive stress injuries. Finally, more and more emphasis is being placed on sonographers' communication skills. As the obstetricians at the Met explained to me, their techni-cians had been selected not just for their technical skills, but also be-cause they were 'friendly and knew how to talk to patients.'

Sometimes ultrasounds are carried out in relative silence; the clinic is busy, and there is a long line of patients, so sonographers work quickly and quietly. But sonographers like to talk to patients – to describe the image, ask questions about this and other pregnancies, answer questions, and engage parents in conversation. Some of this talk is intended to help non-expert viewers 'read' the image; and some of it helps the sonographer clarify maternal history (especially gesta-tional age, vaginal bleeding, fetal movement); but much of it touches on topics that are not diagnostically relevant. For example, the sonographer may ask the woman whether she (or her husband) would prefer a boy or girl, and whether a name has been selected and a room readied for the new baby. Indeed, sonographers regard the 'talking' of ultrasound as a signature part of the 'distinctive care of obstetrics' and of 'how things are done at the Met.' When sonographers discuss the importance of 'talking to patients,' they say it reassures parents and minimizes anxiety. The casual and light-hearted dialogue masks the hierarchical relationship between sonographer as skilled professional and woman as inexpert viewer; it also blurs the boundaries between ultrasound's various facets: diagnostic, psychological, and entertainment. 'Talking to patients' is something that technicians in particular enjoy and take pride in doing. Clearly, it also helps sonographers. To some extent, conversing with patients alleviates both the fatigue of translating ultrasound's echoes into the fetus over and over all day long, and the stress caused by the fear of seeing – or worse – missing anomalies.

TECHNICIAN. So this is your first? [*Tamara nods.*] You want a boy or a girl?

TAMARA. It doesn't matter to me. My husband's family is really hoping for a boy. They don't have any grandsons yet.

TECHNICIAN. My husband's family was like that. But after the baby is born, they don't care! They spoil them all. [*Tamara and technician laugh. There are several minutes of silence while the technician proceeds with her examination.*]

TAMARA. What is that? [*She reaches out and touches the screen.*]

TECHNICIAN. The leg.

TAMARA. They're so cute. Like flippers! [*Laughs.*] What's that?

TECHNICIAN. The thigh bone.

TAMARA. Oh! You measure the femur, right? [*The technician nods. The examination continues.*]

TAMARA. Where are you now?

TECHNICIAN. Now I'm looking inside the baby. It's like cutting, you know, we see in slices.

To most untrained viewers, ultrasound images are confusing. Women and their partners depend heavily on sonographers' accounts of the image in order to see their baby amidst the swirling grey mass of echoes. At her second routine ultrasound, one woman commented to the sonographer: 'Let us know if we see anything!' Sonographers endeavour to help parents to 'see,' and thus to bolster the reassurance and bonding effects of ultrasound, by offering advice on how to read the image. To help women discern the fetus within the swirling grey, sonographers may say, 'The white is bone ... the black is liquid.' They may also draw the parents' attention to the least ambiguous elements: the beating heart, the white line of the cranium, the white blocks of the spine, the dark fetal bladder and stomach. Paradoxically, their advice generally draws attention to the diagnostic aspects of ultrasound. Women and their companions often haven't realized that ultrasound 'sees' inside the fetus as well as inside the woman's body. Some people, perhaps recalling photographs of translucent fetal skin in advice books and media images, ask, 'Is the baby transparent?' At the Met, sonographers responded by explaining: 'With ultrasound we don't see the whole baby. We see in slices. It's like cutting the baby in slices.' I have heard ultrasound described this way elsewhere among anglophone sonographers; however, it is worth noting that the term 'cutting' is a translation of the French verb *couper*. Although one of the obstetricians preferred that the technicians use the English term 'looking at' rather than 'cutting,' the dissection metaphor may well pose no problem for physicians and ultrasound technicians accustomed to cross-sections in anatomy texts, and to other ways of seeing into bodies. Some of the women I observed, many of whom were unsure about how ultrasound works and were worried about whether this technology would harm their infants, were clearly startled by this terminology.

While these hints about the technology of ultrasound help some parents see the ultrasound fetus, and provide reassurance, they also constrain that vision in particular ways. The fetus emerges as the product of expert intervention, confirming popular beliefs that pregnancy is risky and not something a couple can or should do on their own (Taylor 1998). Specifically, the sonographer's directions for seeing emphasize the fetus as a collection of diagnosable and thus potentially abnormal parts.

TAMARA. Is that the heart?
TECHNICIAN. No, the stomach.
TAMARA. Can you see the kidneys?
TECHNICIAN. The bladder, both kidneys. [*The series of measurements is completed, and the technician is scanning the kidneys again. Several*

more minutes pass as the technician looks intently at the image of the brain on the screen, twisting her body and the transducer to get the 'right angle.']

Obstetricians and technicians emphasize ultrasound's ability to detect anomalies and to indicate the health of the fetus; yet sonographers' accounts of the image contain little information for the parents about the results of examinations. During a routine first scan most women are told the fetal age (in weeks); at the second routine scan they learn the fetal weight and position, and (sometimes) the estimated weight at delivery. Usually, the clinical information given to women is non-specific.[4] Sonographers may mention that a particular observation – fetal breathing or a full fetal bladder, for example – is 'un signe de bonne santé' (a sign of good health), or that a full bladder 'shows that the kidneys are working,' or that 'we look at the spine to see if it is okay.' During my fieldwork at the Met, the sonographers I observed generally did not refer to the specific pathologies screened for during ultrasound, nor did they often use the term 'normal.' Instead, if no anomalies were found, women were simply told, 'Everything looks fine,' or 'Tout va bien.'

None of the questions surrounding the usefulness of routine ultrasound for fetal well-being are mentioned in routine scans (see chapter 2). While women may be told that fetal age and size are estimates, they are rarely told that determining the age of the fetus through ultrasound may not be useful. The diagnostic limits of ultrasound – what can and cannot be seen, and with what degree of accuracy or error – are rarely spelled out for parents. Several publications now recommend that women be told that a pronouncement of 'normal' after ultrasound refers only to those kinds of anomalies which can be seen or for which the sonographer is searching (Royal Commission on New Reproductive Technologies 1993; Toi 1990). This recommendation was not routinely followed at the Met while I was doing fieldwork there. Women who asked about ultrasound's limitations might be told, 'We cannot see if the baby will be deaf or blind,' or 'We cannot tell the colour of the eyes.'

TECHNICIAN. I'm gonna get your husband. What's his name?
TAMARA. John. [*The technician goes out, and Tamara turns to me.*] You wonder how they see. It's not very clear, is it? [*John enters and stands next to Tamara. The technician resumes the scan.*]

TECHNICIAN. Here is the baby's heart – beating there. Baby's head. The spine, it looks like train tracks.

TAMARA. What do you look for? The vertebrae?

TECHNICIAN. To see that the lines are parallel. You can see the outline of the baby here. The arm up here.

TAMARA. Is it sucking its thumb?

TECHNICIAN. No. no. We rarely see that. The hand is near the head, near the face. [*She points to the screen.*] The face is up towards you. [*Tamara smiles and waves at her stomach.*]

TECHNICIAN. [*Smiling at the screen*] Hello!

TAMARA. When you measure the head, that gives you the age, right?

TECHNICIAN. Yes.

TAMARA. Because my periods are thirty-two days apart, so I figure I ovulated at seventeen days. So I figure it's about four days later than what my LMP gives.

TECHNICIAN. Well I get sixteen weeks and your dates are seventeen weeks. That corresponds. [*After a few more minutes of scanning, the fetal image comes sharply into focus – head, face, spine, and torso*]. Can you see? It is very clear. He's looking right at you! His head is turned here and back and little bum.

JOHN. That's the first thing I've seen yet!

TECHNICIAN. I take my picture quick. He's gonna go play again. You're gonna be busy, he moves a lot. [*The scan concludes. After Tamara and John have left, the technician tells me that one kidney 'looked different, not much, just a bit.'*]

As I have been arguing, the translation of ultrasound echoes (e.g., what was pointed out and said to Rosa and Tamara and to the other pregnant women and their partners about the fetal image) does not simply reflect the technical and diagnostic strengths and limitations of this technology. That translation process both enables and is constrained by its use as a screening and diagnostic tool, an instrument of psychological reassurance, and a source of pleasure, fun, and entertainment. The tension that results from these potentially contradictory domains shapes how sonographers conduct the ultrasound and talk about the image. To this point in the chapter, I have discussed how this tension underlies the guidelines that sonographers give to women about how to understand the image and the diagnostic information provided. Sonographers' accounts are intended to help women 'see' their baby amidst the echoes, and to reassure them. Identifying the anatomical parts being examined and measured underscores for women that this is a clinical procedure that may detect something wrong in what is seen. Yet the clinical and diagnostic information provided to women and their companions is characteristically non-specific, so as not to alarm them.

At the same time that the fetus is constructed as the object of clinical investigation, which may undermine its claims to personhood, the fetus is also constructed as an unconditional person. As I elaborate below, much of the sonographers' talk to expectant parents about the fetus includes statements about (1) its physical body, appearance, and activity, (2) its subjectivity, (3) its potentiality, and (4) its social connections to kin and to sonographers. These statements resonate with sonographers and with many pregnant women as signs of fetal personhood, and thus are integral to how the ultrasound image is made culturally meaningful as a 'baby.'

Marie-Claude

I move to another ultrasound room, arriving just after Andrew has been called in to join Marie-Claude for her second routine scan. A routine thirty-two-week scan is conducted in much the same manner as the eighteen-week one. However, this time the fetal measurements of the femur, head, and abdomen are used to assess the rate and symmetry of fetal growth rather than to estimate fetal age. Current fetal weight and (sometimes) expected weight at delivery are also calculated at this later scan. The fetal position, placental and umbilical functioning, and amniotic fluid levels are also noted during the thirty-two-week ultrasound.

MARIE-CLAUDE. We want a picture, too. If we can see it! [*She and Andrew laugh.*]

TECHNICIAN. Can you see the head? And the spine.

ANDREW. [*Looking at the screen.*] Too bad we can't do this in the evening when it's moving.

TECHNICIAN. Yeah, but I don't wanna do this in the evening! ... That's the top of the head.

MARIE-CLAUDE. It has no hair. So it's your head. Hey look! It's bilingual, English and French, two sides square and two round. [*Everyone laughs.*]

TECHNICIAN. Baby's sleeping with his hand by his head. Can you see that? [*She points to her monitor.*] See the elbow. [*She puts her own head on her hand*] Fait dodo bébé.

ANDREW. Boy! I was under the impression that you could see a lot. I guess if you've seen a lot of them, eh? ... What is that?

TECHNICIAN. Spine. All this is the spine. [*Andrew is leaning over the bed to watch the technician's monitor. Several times Marie-Claude motions him back because he is obscuring her view of the patient's monitor at the foot of the bed.*]

ANDREW. It's not moving around?

MARIE-CLAUDE. No.

ANDREW. I guess you would know.

TECHNICIAN. It's good your baby is tired today. I could do my measurements very fast. Here is the bladder.

ANDREW. The black spot?

TECHNICIAN. [*Nods.*] Turn on your side. [*Marie-Claude turns with difficulty and the technician scans for a few seconds.*] Okay now turn back. It's in breech, eh?

ANDREW. Breech? What's that?

TECHNICIAN. Bottom down.

ANDREW. Oh, instead of its head, right?

TECHNICIAN. I can't see 'cause it's in breech. It's so hard to see when they are like that.

MARIE-CLAUDE. I don't want to know, but even if it wasn't in breech I couldn't see what it is.

TECHNICIAN. It can move still.

ANDREW. It can move? Oh my God! There's no room.

TECHNICIAN. Do you want a picture?

MARIE-CLAUDE. I think we'll forget the picture. It looks like a deep sea animal.

TECHNICIAN. Can you see that? The foot. Little toes. [*Marie-Claude and Andrew peer intently at the screen*]. It's so cute. [*The technician leans forward and 'tickles' the toes on screen. Then she prints out that image and hands it to Marie-Claude.*] Okay. Everything look good.

The Corporeal Subject

Seeing the fetus as a subject, as more than a technological product or diagnostic entity, depends heavily on its corporeality – a set of assumptions about the human body and its functioning, normality, and capacity. This dimension of selfhood refers to locating the self in time (its onset and extinction) and in place (e.g., in the brain, in the heart). As I've already pointed out, the first objective of all obstetrical ultrasounds is to determine the 'viability' of the fetus. Most of what obstetricians and technicians say to parents during a routine ultrasound refers to the physical fetus (as Rosa's and Tamara's scans illustrate) and the basic descriptions of this anatomy are similar from scan to scan.

When sonographers describe fetal anatomy – especially those parts they consider appealing – they may simply say, 'Here is a foot,' or, 'Look at the arm.' Often, however, they identify fetal anatomy in language inflected with the sentimental imagery of babies and newborns: 'Here is the baby's foot.' 'What a cute little nose.' 'Look at those tiny little fingers.'

Descriptions of the physical parts of the fetus pass through a cultural sieve as sonographers select and describe those parts which they believe are most appealing and reassuring for women – the beating heart, the skull and brain, and the hands and feet, especially the fingers and toes. The beating heart signals viability and draws on the popular idea of the heart as the source of life, vitality, and whatever it is that animates people. Showing the fetal hands and feet takes direct aim at parents' anxiety about whether their baby has 'all its fingers and toes.' As metonyms for the whole body, fingers and toes send the reassuring message that even the tiniest parts are normal. The head and brain have long been perceived in Western cultures as a kind of synecdoche for the whole person. At various times in recent history, cranial form and dimensions have signalled race, class, sex, morality, degrees of intellect, and predisposition to criminality (Flavell 1994; Gould 1981). In the present age of organ transplants, life support systems, brain deaths, and 'breathing cadavers,' the head continues to be culturally overdetermined as the location of personhood (Ohnuki-Tierney 1994). During the routine ultrasound, the white oval of the skull and grey echoes of the brain signal normality, intellect, and even gender.[5] Since sonographers at the Met consider the early fetal face to be 'weird,' 'strange-looking,' and 'too much like a Ninja Turtle,' they prefer not to show it during the first scan. Several of the interviewed women referred to an ultrasound of the early fetal face as 'creepy' and 'like a skeleton.' The sonographers believe that the rounded fetal nose, forehead, and cheeks visible by the second routine scan are appealing enough to include in the parent's copy of the image.

The 'real time' of ultrasound is central to how the image is personi-fied. Fetal movement is presented as a sign of the physical aliveness and viability of the fetus and as evidence of its individuality. The beating of the fetal heart, the bending and extending of the fetal limbs, and the changes in position of the entire fetus as it twists and rolls form an integral part of the account for parents. This is especially true during the scan done at eighteen weeks – a time when many women have not yet felt fetal movement. Fetal movement seen during ultra-sound is often referred to as 'the baby moving,' and is often described in terms of particular activities. Thus, the fetus is said to be 'playing,' 'swimming,' 'dancing,' 'partying,' or 'waving.' Fetal body rolls are described as 'trying to get comfortable,' and the extending of the limbs and the arching back are referred to as 'stretching.' When the fetus is not moving, the sonographers may tell parents, it is 'sleeping' or 'rest-ing.' If the fetal hand is near the mouth, the parents may be told, 'The baby is sucking his thumb.' In conversations with me, the sonographers explained that it is rare to see the fetus sucking its thumb, but parents like to think that's what it is doing. Even internal organs are described in terms of fetal behaviour or activity. For example, if they see that the bladder is emptying or emptied, the technicians may say: 'Your baby just peed!' Although the lungs do not appear in the fetal image, the clinic staff refer to movement of the chest wall as 'breathing.' When the fetal stomach is hard to visualize, sonographers ask women to return for an additional scan, explaining, 'Maybe next time when you come back he will have just eaten.'

Fetal Boys and Fetal Girls

The contradictions and tensions surrounding the 'appropriate' use of ultrasound as a diagnostic tool, means of bonding, and source of en-tertainment are especially apparent when it comes to determining and disclosing the sex of the fetus. While there are times when knowing the sex of the fetus is diagnostically relevant, concerns have been ex-pressed about the distress caused when errors are made in fetal sex determination; also, some parents may decide to terminate a preg-nancy if the fetus is not what they want. In 1993 the Royal Commis-sion on New Reproductive Technologies recommended that fetal sex not be disclosed before the third trimester of pregnancy, 'except for medical reasons' (RCNRT 1993: 818). Some hospital ultrasound clinics I have visited since then have signs posted: PLEASE DO NOT ASK US TO TELL YOU THE BABY'S SEX. At the time of my research, before the RCNRT recommendations were published, the question of whether the fetus was male or female was part of nearly all routine ultrasounds at the Met, especially second and third trimester routine scans.

Julie

When I enter the adjacent room, Julie, who is now about thirty-four weeks pregnant, is just settling onto the bed. She is uncomfortable lying on her back, and sighs deeply several times, saying, 'It's hard to breathe.' Once the measurements are done, Julie's husband, Tom, is called in. He enters with Julie's young cousin.

TOM. So today's the day of the million-dollar question!
JULIE. Yeah, but I haven't got a million-dollar answer. [*Long pause.*] Can you tell what it is?
TECHNICIAN. Yes. Do you want to know?
JULIE. Oh! Don't ask me! Wait. Wait! Tom! Help!
TOM. It's up to you.
JULIE. Does it have all its parts?
TECHNICIAN. Yes. Everything looks fine. Here are the legs.
JULIE. Oh good. Last night I had a nightmare it didn't have any legs! Thank you! [*After a few moments.*] Oh! Okay. What is it?
TECHNICIAN. A girl.
JULIE. A girl? It's a girl. Oh my God! It's a girl. [*She looks at Tom. He smiles and holds her hand. Julie shakes her finger at her cousin.*] Don't tell anyone! [*Starting to cry.*] Oh, I'm such a suck!
TECHNICIAN. That's it. Everything looks good.
JULIE. Thank you.
TECHNICIAN. Do you want a photograph?
JULIE. Yes, please.
TECHNICIAN. I don't know what you're gonna see. [*She scans for several minutes, pressing deeply as she tries to get an image to photograph.*] Can you see the face here?
JULIE. [*Chuckling.*] Not really. But we'll take it anyway.

While they articulate their concerns about making errors, and the consequences of telling parents the sex of the fetus, the sonographers believe that knowing the fetal sex contributes to making ultrasound a pleasurable experience. Yet the message sent out to parents is a contradictory one. On the one hand, sonographers – especially the technicians – draw attention to this aspect of the examination by asking women if they want to know the fetal sex. In fact, they need only ask, 'Do you want to know what it is?' On the other hand, sonographers do not include sex determination among the reasons for conducting ultrasounds and they may tell women, 'That's not the most important thing,' or 'I check that after I make sure everything is all right.' As I discuss in more detail at the end of this chapter, this sort of statement underscores the tension between appropriate and inappropriate uses of the technology; it also reveals both the underlying hierarchical relationship between sonographer and woman, and ultrasound's use as a site for evaluating women's maternalism.

Disclosure of the fetal sex is not taken lightly by the sonographers. They carefully scrutinize the fetal genitalia before pronouncing the fetus to be a boy or girl, and if unsure, they prefer to say nothing rather than speculate. Similarly, sonographers at the Met generally believe that the first routine scan is 'too early' to be sure about fetal sex.

Disclosing fetal sex may bring into conflict popular and legal notions about the autonomy of women's bodies and 'ownership' of the fetus, as in the following excerpt from the thirty-three-week scan of another woman in the study.

CHRISTINA. A friend of mine, she had her scan and they said, we're ninety-nine per cent sure it's a girl, but don't buy pink. I guess that one per cent, they're not sure.

TECHNICIAN. You don't want to know and he does?

CHRISTINA. Right. So, we're both not gonna know.

LEO. No, you [the technician] can tell me and you [Christina] can not know.

TECHNICIAN. Can I tell him?

CHRISTINA. No.

TECHNICIAN. Okay, you're both not gonna know.

CHRISTINA. Hah!

LEO. Why can't I know? *C'est un loi provinciale ou fédérale?*

TECHNICIAN. If she don't want you to know, I don't say. It's her body.

LEO. [*Laughing in exasperation.*] Okay. Okay. This time I give you a break. But the next kid, I want to know.

TECHNICIAN. Besides, it's in a breech. So I cannot know.

LEO. [*Cynically, but smiling.*] Yeah, yeah. Sure.

If the woman and her partner are both present, the sonographer generally is careful to find out if both want to know. If only the woman wishes to know, the technician will tell her privately. However, if only the man wants to know, the sonographer will not reveal the fetal sex to him unless the woman gives permission. As above, when the spouses disagree about knowing, sonographers may simply say that the baby's position precludes determining the sex.

Fetal Subjectivity

'Showing the baby' to parents also brings a subjective dimension to fetal selfhood. It is often implied to parents that the fetus is aware of its surroundings and of being distinct from other selves, and has 'intentions,' moods, and emotions.

TECHNICIAN. [*As she searches for a 'take home' image.*] *C'est beau.* See how good he is. A perfect picture. [*Pointing to the screen.*] You see the head? *Et un bras avec le main* [*with an arm and hand*].
NICOLE. [*Nods.*]
RANDY. I see the hand.
TECHNICIAN. [*As the image is printing.*] Ahh, look. [*She puts her hand over her own face.*] His little hand is hiding his face. Maybe he's gonna be a shy baby.

Sonographers ascribe intention and emotion to fetal movement and body position. For example, a fetus with its hand near the head may be described as 'thinking' or, sometimes, as 'tired.' Fetal movement that impedes the process of conducting the ultrasound examination often is described as evidence that the fetus is 'shy,' or 'modest,' or 'doesn't like' something: 'He doesn't like it when I press,' or 'Look, he runs away when I do this.' As sonographers attempt to record the image, they may comment: 'He moves away when I try to take the picture,' or 'He's shy. He doesn't want his picture taken.' They may also refer to fetal shyness and modesty if visualizing the genitalia is difficult. Conversely, as in Nicole's scan above, a clear, easily attained fetal image may be offered as evidence that the fetus is 'being good' or 'very cooperative.' On particularly cold days, I would often hear the technicians explaining fetal position as a reaction to the weather: 'They're all in a corner today,' or 'All my babies are hiding today.'

Sonographers' interactions with the fetal image further suggest fetal subjectivity. They speak to the image, giving instructions and words of encouragement or reprimand: 'Move over, baby.' 'Smile for the camera.' Technicians may mimic fetal motion or position. They may wave to the image, greeting it, and sometimes encourage the parents to do the same. As during Marie-Claude's scan, sonographers may touch, stroke, and 'tickle' the image, especially the fetal feet. As during Rosa's ultrasound, technicians may create a voice for the fetal image by raising their own voice to a falsetto (I never heard obstetricians, male or female, do this). As in this exchange I observed at the Met, the fetal voice is part of a larger dialogue:

TECHNICIAN. [*Trying to get the fetus to change position, she speaks in a falsetto.*] I'm sleeping this morning. [*Then, in her usual voice.*] Move, move, baby. Move so Mummy and Daddy can see you. [*After a few moments, the fetal image changes and the technician resumes her falsetto.*] Allô Maman.
WOMAN. [*Hesitantly.*] Hello.
TECHNICIAN. [*In her usual voice.*] Okay, baby. Back to sleep.

The Potential Self

During ultrasound, the fetus is often perceived as demonstrating its potentiality; elements of individualism, membership in a family, cultural competence, language, moral sense, and a role as a 'productive' member of society are attributed to it. Just what kind of person the fetus will become may be revealed in the sonographer's explanation: 'With lungs like that he'll be a runner.' 'A big brain – he'll be smart.' Activity seen during the ultrasound may be described in terms of the future behaviour of the baby or young child. Like Tamara, many women hear, 'Your baby is moving a lot. You're gonna be busy!' Such statements are often gender-specific: 'What a big baby. It must be a boy!' 'With thighs like that it has to be a girl.' The fetal image is also described in terms of potential resemblance to certain family members.

OBSTETRICIAN. Look at that nose!
WOMAN. [*Chuckling.*] My husband has a big nose.
OBSTETRICIAN. [*To the fetal image.*] You're going to have a big nose like Papa, eh?
WOMAN. [*Smiling.*] Poor kid.

Explicit cultural stereotyping sometimes arises in joking banter between sonographers and parents. For example, when rapid movements of the fetal arms are observed, parents may be asked, 'Are you Italian?' In Montreal, where language is a powerful and highly politicized sign of identity, francophone sonographers may cautiously tease parents that they can detect an anglophone baby. A squarish fetal head is called 'un bloc de glace' (a block of ice, or an ice head), the French term for the stereotypical reserved and unemotional anglophone Montrealers. It is not just sonographers who express stereotypes and refer to potentiality. During her ultrasound, Marie-Claude evoked both kinship ties (from the fetus to her husband) and social status (bilingual fetus) when she saw the shape of the fetal head.

The Social Self

During the routine ultrasounds I observed, the fetus was spoken of as an idealized infant. Largely absent during these ultrasounds was the notion of *fetus* or *embryo* with its 'alien' appearance (as it was labelled by several of the women I interviewed), uncertain subjectivity, and contested personhood. Evoked instead was a social or moral dimension to selfhood; the sonographers and the women talked about the image in terms of culturally specific identities (e.g., 'mother,' 'doctor,' 'baby') associated with sets of rights and obligations.

At the Metropolitan, I rarely heard sonographers or parents use the term 'fetus'; both groups regarded it as 'too scientific sounding' and 'too cold.' Moreover, as the following example illustrates, some parents were even discouraged from using the term.

HUSBAND. [*Looking at the ultrasound photograph the technician has handed him.*] Great! Now I can put this on my desk and say, 'This is my fetus.'

TECHNICIAN. [*Surprised.*] Your *fetus*? Ugh! Don't say that! It's your *baby*.'

The term 'fetus' is generally restricted to diagnostic matters and to discussions among sonographers, although there is considerable variation among Canadian hospitals on this point. At the Met, 'fetus' was used when the clinic staff wanted to avoid referring to fetal gender. The term 'fetus' has been heavily politicized in Canada and is surrounded by cultural ambiguity, and at the Met was often inflected with uncertainty, or an air of amusement or even scorn.

TECHNICIAN. [*Pointing to the screen, after telling the parents she could not determine the fetal sex.*] *Il bouge beaucoup.*[6] ['He's moving a lot.'] Can you see that?

HUSBAND. Is that a Freudian slip ? [*Technician looks at him blankly.*] *Il bouge.* ['*He* moves.']

TECHNICIAN. [*Laughing.*] No. No. I don't know. The baby. No. No. *Le fetus.*

As the following examples suggest, while some women may be uncertain about what to call what lies within their womb, that uncertainty may be erased by sonographers' use of the term 'baby.'

WOMAN. Can you see the fetus yet?

TECHNICIAN. [*Points to the screen.*] The baby's back is here. The bum is here.

WOMAN. Can you see if the fetus, I mean, um ... Can you see the baby's head?

TECHNICIAN. Yes. See here. You see baby's spine and baby's head.

WOMAN. My God! I didn't think the baby would be so big by now.

This disciplining effect is not always initiated by the sonographer; sometimes it reflects a pervasive uncertainty and debate about the fetus in Canadian society.

WOMAN. [*Looking at the screen.*] Is that the baby? Oops! I shouldn't do that. It's the fetus, right?

TECHNICIAN. Right. [*Emphasizing the word.*] *Le fetus.*

WOMAN. Yup. The fetus. Because it's not anything yet, right? [*She and the technician laugh at this. The obstetrician comes in.*]

TECHNICIAN. [*Referring to the woman.*] She calls it the fetus. It's not the baby.

WOMAN. Right.

OBSTETRICIAN. [*Frowning.*] No. It's the baby.

Thus, sonographers describe the fetal image in terms of its social identity as 'the baby.' They also often refer to parents during the scan as 'Maman' and 'Papa.' The voice that sonographers create for the fetal image often speaks directly to the parents: 'Hello Papa,' or, 'I'm tired, Maman.' Family members who are present are encouraged, for example, to look at their 'niece' or 'grandchild' or 'baby brother.' This process of weaving the fetus into a network of kinship relations and conventionalized roles is not specific to ultrasound. For example, obstetrical nurses often refer to women who are pregnant for the first time as 'pregnant mums.'

The compelling nature of this on-screen 'baby' is especially evident when sonographers see an image they particularly like. Their postures, facial expressions, and voices change as they lean closer to the screen, often tilting their heads and smiling. Sonographers may even touch and stroke the on-screen image and create a voice so that the fetus can 'speak' and communicate its 'feelings.' Expectant couples watch, many of them delighted, as sonographers wave to the image, speak to it, and offer instructions and words of encouragement or reprimand: 'Hold still, baby.' 'Smile for the camera.' Often the instructions are for the fetus to do something for the parents: 'Say hello to Mama.' 'Don't move, so Papa can see you.' At these moments, sonographers and expectant couples closely resemble people admiring a baby in someone's arms. I want to emphasize that this communication and interaction with the fetal image is generally not viewed as 'silly,' or overdrawn, or a 'joke' by either the sonographers or the expectant parents; rather, these people see it as an enjoyable form of interaction or contact with the fetus that ultrasound makes possible.

In sum, when sonographers talk about the fetal image for parents, they often describe and interact directly with the fetal image, as if it *were* the fetus or, rather, 'the baby.' The fetal image is described, talked about, and sometimes talked *to* as if it were an individual – an intentional, conscious, appealing, and sentient person with meaningful ties to other people.

Shaping these accounts of the fetal image are normative and culturally specific expectations about the social relations of pregnancy, especially maternal behaviour toward the fetus. There is, for example, the idea that women who come for ultrasound – who avail themselves of the benefits of this technology – are doing what is best for their babies. Thus, ultrasound provides a site for monitoring *women* as well as fetuses. Among themselves, the sonographers refer to certain women as 'nice.' 'Nice parents,' for example, wait patiently for their appointments, follow the sonographer's instructions, and do not disrupt the examination with frequent questions. 'Nice patients' do not look 'funny' or 'strange,' do not have a 'bad smell,' and are not obese. Notably, 'nice' women are those whom sonographers believe 'care' about the fetus – that is who show interest in the image and concern about fetal health, and not too much interest in fetal gender. These women tend to receive detailed and personalized accounts of the fetal image, as described above. In other words, 'nice' parents receive accounts containing many of the elements I have been discussing (i.e., accounts that explicate the fetal image as a 'baby' possessing appealing physical qualities, intention, emotion, and consciousness, and that link the fetus to the parents both physically and socially). In contrast, abbreviated accounts of the image may be given to women believed to be disinterested in the image, women more concerned about fetal gender than fetal health, or women whose behaviour or appearance is considered inappropriate. For these women, accounts of the image tend to contain only brief descriptions of fetal anatomy and fetal agency.

Sonographers' accounts of the ultrasound image are infused with a powerful cultural script on 'natural' behaviour for pregnant women and mothers. According to this script, women from certain groups – 'races,' to use the sonographers' term – are assumed to be 'different' by nature: impassive, unemotional, or overly interested in the 'wrong thing.' For example, some sonographers described black women and First Nations women as unexcited or unmoved by the prospect of having a baby. 'They never show anything,' remarked these sonographers, who provided women from these groups with relatively brief accounts of the fetal image. Conversely, there are other women whose reactions – excessive joy, abundant tears, loud giggling – on seeing the fetal image or learning the fetal sex are considered 'too emotional.' They, too, often receive relatively brief descriptions of the ultrasound image.

Some women are perceived to be overly concerned with 'things that aren't important.' Sonographers told me that they don't like to do scans on these women, because 'the women don't care about the health of the baby.' In this category are women considered to be interested only in fetal sex, and thus, frivolously, in whether 'to buy pink or blue.' In particular, East Asian and South Asian women are assumed to prefer sons.[7] Women who appear too interested in learning the fetal sex are often admonished: 'Finding out the sex isn't important. The most important thing is that the baby is healthy.' Moreover, if sonographers are concerned that a woman may be sufficiently disappointed by the sex of the fetus to seek termination of the pregnancy, they may tell her simply that they are unable to see whether it is a boy or a girl.

This discourse on motherhood is played out not only along lines of cultural and 'racial' difference and gender preference, but also in terms of reproductive history, personal habits, and self-discipline. Women having their first child may be dissuaded from asking about the fetal sex by statements such as, 'This is your first? You don't want to know, do you? You can always try again.' Women in their teens or in their forties and women with more than four or five children may be asked about their decision to have a baby at this point in their lives. Women over thirty-six may be asked to give reasons if they mention refusing amniocentesis. Similarly, normative comments may be made to women whom the sonographers consider 'non-compliant' or 'not taking care of themselves.' For example, women who admit to smoking during pregnancy may be shown the image of the placenta and told, incorrectly, 'We can see the smoke in it.' Obese women may be told that 'it's hard to see,' the subtext being that their bodies are an obstacle to evaluating the health of the fetus.

In summary, in their accounts of the fetal image, sonographers encourage specific ways of seeing and mobilize particular kinds of physical, emotional, and social connections between parents – women in particular – and the fetus. Accounts for parents generally lack a detailed technical or diagnostic content. Instead these descriptions concentrate on explicating and transforming the fetal image in terms of human social characteristics. Most notably, dimensions of selfhood are included, and the fetal image is described in terms of its social identity, activity, intention, consciousness, and emotion, and a distinctive or potentially distinctive self. Sonographers' accounts of the fetal image also situate the fetus in a world of other selves. In particular, sonographers personalize their accounts of the image for parents, comparing parental and fetal behaviour and appearance, employing kinship terms to describe the image, creating a voice to enable the fetus to talk to parents, and encouraging them to reply. During routine ultrasounds, the fetus emerges as a social being, a social actor with a distinctive identity – 'the baby' – enmeshed in a social network of kin and sonographers. Women, too, are monitored during ultrasound, not only for physical conditions that may complicate delivery, but also for their own shortcomings, such as failure to monitor their bodies and behaviour, and failure to be compliant and selfless – in short, failure to be 'good mothers.'

In the next chapter, I examine how women's sensations, ideas, and images of pregnancy, of fetality, and of themselves are both shaped by and resistant to having 'seen the baby' through ultrasound.

Chapter Six

'Seeing the Baby': Women's Perspectives on Ultrasound

> Meaning is ... the product of particular cultural work, particular institutional arrangements, epistemological practices, reading conventions, and political contests (as well as subjective experience, desire and intention). No image speaks for itself in a clear, unmediated fashion; indeed no image merely contains or displays a transparent, self-evident, objectively fixed reality.
>
> Hartouni (1999: 300)

In this chapter, drawing from women's narratives on their experiences with ultrasounds, I continue to explore the links among technology, bodies, and thinking, feeling women. What do women 'see' during routine fetal imaging? Does this seeing shape the other sensations of being pregnant? What symbolic messages reverberate through the routine practice of having an ultrasound?

Julie

> They didn't do it until noon! I was too full and there I was waiting, in agony, from 10:45 ... They changed my due date! My God! First she said it was a little small. And I got all freaked out and said how much smaller. Then she said it's only seventeen weeks! I was so pissed off! [Laughs.] I made her check again! I was really upset! ... And I thought I was big, maybe it was twins or something, and I've gained seven pounds. I thought maybe I was two weeks further along. Then she tells me I'm only seventeen weeks.

What could you see?
The top of the head and something moving. Then I went, 'Oh my God! Tom! It's the baby moving!' She showed us the spine, stomach, head, two arms, and two legs and they were going all over. The hands and fingers. Not the face ... It was more developed than I expected. I mean, at four months everything is there. And I didn't expect to see movement ... They had trouble measuring the head, it was so active. I don't know. I have a feeling it's gonna be spunky ... At my first ultrasound [at eight weeks] it was a black dot and now it's a baby. It's a little person. Proof positive that there's a baby in there. It was weird.

Weird?
Well, like, seeing it was weird, because before it didn't seem like much. Nothing much was happening. Then seeing it is such a shock. I guess it will take me a while to get used to it.

Rosa

As soon as the picture came on, she told me right away, 'There's the baby.' And she pointed it out right away. "Cause you know you're upside down'[1] ... And then she told me to go to the bathroom because my bladder was too full. Whatever I drank I had to go let it out. And that, well, not that I didn't like it, but I suffered keeping it in and then I had to go let it all out. 'Cause she said the bladder was so full, the baby couldn't move. When I came back the baby had already, like, turned around ... I mean, even before I really focused on it she said go and pee.

You went to the bathroom and came back.
Yeah, I came back and then she started again. First she took the measurements and that was going very fast, and then after she just stayed with me five or ten minutes showing me the baby and pointing things out. Showing me where everything was.

What did the image look like?
It was all blurred. I couldn't really see clear. You had to really try to like, imagine it and whatever, like what was there. She was saying the white is the bone or whatever, so then we saw a bit more. Why different parts of the body were different colours [shades of gray]. The clearest thing was the heart beating. That I saw right away, the

heart beating. But after she pointed everything out, everything looked pretty clear. Like the baby opened his mouth and then he stretched and, like, going for a turn. That was nice to see ... Well, my husband, like when he looked at it, he said he got a feeling that it's like a boy. Maybe just by looking at it, something clicked. I dunno. But we'll see if that's right.

[*Mario.*] Right away I looked at it and I thought, it's a boy. It was built, so it had to be a boy! Its arms were big.

How did you feel after the ultrasound?
I felt more open. More like I really was pregnant, you know. Everything just kind of hit you. Even until now, like I still keep seeing the picture going over and over, like when he stretched and opened his mouth and closed it. And moving around. It's funny 'cause he's in like his own little world. Yeah. It's true. Sometimes you say, like, what's it doing in there, you know? Staying upside down for a couple of weeks. [Laughs.] You want to say, you know, get up, you might get a headache! Or the blood rush to the head ...

Do you have any worries?
No. I never really worried. I did everything I possibly could. Now, if something were to go wrong, well, it's destiny. I don't drink, I don't smoke, I don't take any medication. Like I had a cold and before I took anything I went to get checked. I try to eat well. I don't skip meals or eat corn flakes for lunch or something ... Well, the only thing I wanted to see – but I don't know if she coulda told that now – was the fingers, the hand, and the toes. 'Cause even when she zoomed in, you don't see the picture super clear. The only thing I forgot to ask her was if it had all its fingers and toes.

[*Mario.*]   She didn't say anything. So everything's OK.

[*Rosa.*]   Well, either that or she didn't see ...

Tamara

The first thing I saw when she put the wand or whatever you call it, the first thing I saw, right away, I saw the baby. Right away! I was shocked! All my fears disappeared! ... I recognized the head, the body, the trunk. I didn't see any limbs, nothing detailed. But I was too caught up in seeing the head and the eye and the profile and I also saw movement in the baby itself. So I knew it was alive and I knew it was a baby.

We went for lunch after and I started thinking, 'Did she see this? Did she see that?' I started worrying all over again! ... It was a little quick. Like, she basically said, 'Yes. It's normal, normal, normal,' pointed a few things out, like the important structures, the heart, the brain, and all that stuff. But I would have wanted to see everything that *she* saw. So I could know exactly what she is looking at. I more or less trusted her because I know that she's done this all the time, and I know that they don't have time to do that.

Was it as you expected?

Basically it was very technical. I would have liked to have had a chance to bond to it, just to see what type of a person it is, which I didn't get to do. I mean, it's so hard to see and it looks pretty weird, right? I know she [the sonographer] has her measurements to do, but I just felt like I wanted her to stop for a while and let me watch the baby.

Marie-Claude

How did you feel while you were waiting for the scan?

I was nervous and scared. I was afraid they would give me bad news, that the baby was dead. I guess because of what happened before ... Well, she [the technician] went very fast. She said she would explain it. I recognized some movement, but my husband was lost. When I saw the movement, then I knew it was the baby. I saw the head move and I knew he was alive and okay! ...

What did you see?

The top of the head, the forearm, the spine, the heartbeat. She showed me the eyes, nose, and ears but I couldn't see it. I saw the thigh, foot, and the stomach ... You know, I feel it is more in my court now. The baby is fine. Somebody's allowed me to have this baby and now it's up to me to stay healthy. I sleep easier at night. It's like I just got pregnant! Before I didn't dare be too happy. Now I can show that. My husband says, 'It's really a baby, now.' It's more real for him, too ... Before, my mother was worried about me. She kept asking me, 'Are you happy about the pregnancy?' I was happy to be pregnant, but I didn't want to show I was happy in case something happened. It was strange.

I think the baby will be very calm as opposed to seeing my sister's baby, which moved a lot during the ultrasound ... I know it's gonna have my attitude.

How do you know that?

It was calm and slow moving. If it was like my husband, the baby would move a lot more and pace around. I mean, my husband's a great guy, but I'm glad it's gonna have my personality ... And also when she first put the ball or whatever it is on my stomach, the baby moved, like, 'What the heck is this thing?'

'Now I've Seen the Baby'

During each interview after the first ultrasound, I asked, 'What was the ultrasound like?' Nearly all the women made positive and enthusiastic comments, describing the ultrasound as 'great,' 'exciting,' and 'wonderful.' What made the digitalized reflection of their bodily interior 'wonderful'? What, for them, was memorable, pleasurable, and meaningful about this procedure?

I cannot know precisely what each woman saw in the ultrasound image, but their comments during the scan and their descriptions in the follow-up interviews suggest that few saw as much as Tamara did. In fact, many women recognized little. As Rosa suggested, they 'had to really try to, like, imagine it and whatever, like what was there.' When I asked if they had seen the shape or form of the fetus, over three-quarters of the forty-eight women said they had not. Yet two-thirds described the ultrasound by saying that they had 'seen the baby.'

If 'seeing the baby' did not mean visually apprehending it, what did they mean when they said they had 'seen the baby'? 'Seeing' was often fleeting and unstable – a glimpse, amid the swirling grey echoes, of the outline of the head, the beating heart, the white line of the femur, or the white blocks of the spine. From the descriptions that follow, it is clear that 'seeing' was, for these women, inseparable from the sonographer's *explanation* of what was visible on screen.[2] And even with the sonographer's instructions about *how* to see ('white is bone, dark is liquid') and the descriptive labels of *what* to see ('the femur,' 'baby's bladder'), several women made distinctions along the lines of, 'I could see what she was pointing at, but I couldn't tell what it was.' Ironically, then, 'seeing with sound' may be more a matter of the sound of the sonographer's voice, as opposed to the ultra (high frequency) sound of the equipment. While the image itself may make little sense, the comments made by sonographers do.

> It was a bit confusing at first. I thought I would see the whole baby. But it was only parts. She explained it to me, but it was still hard to visualize. Without her explanation, I saw nothing. (Louisa, 28, counsellor)

> To tell you the truth, I couldn't see very much ... I saw the outline of baby's body, the head. The best part was the heartbeat, finding something that you could really see – you could see it moving. Other than that it was just kind of the outline, like, of the arm. The body you couldn't really make out, it was just a round clump. I guess the legs were up. I couldn't make out any legs ... I would never have known it was a baby. I would never have recognized anything if it hadn't been pointed out. If I were to look at it again, I doubt I would recognize it. (Esther, 27, office manager)

The fact that the women were unable to see the fetus through the technology alone, but instead relied heavily on the sonographer and the entire process of having ultrasound, shaped in specific ways their experiences of having an ultrasound. *First*, the women's descriptions of what they had seen often closely paralleled what they had heard the sonographer say. In our post-scan conversations, the women recounted – almost word for word in some cases – the sonographer's description of the image. The emphasis that sonographers placed on particular parts of the image – especially the beating heart, the femur and arm, and waving hands – re-emerged in women's descriptions. *Second*, the women often took the sonographer's language as their own and retrospectively said that they had 'seen' things that they had actually heard.[3]

> When I first looked at it, I couldn't see anything. Emptiness, whiteness. She showed me the head, spine, placenta, arms, and the heart. The heart was easy. But if she hadn't said, 'Here is the baby,' I wouldn't have seen. It was, like, okay, I'll take your word for it ... Now that I've seen it, I have a picture in my mind. To be honest, I

didn't have one before. I just couldn't imagine it. And I guess I have a different feeling about it. A better feeling. I feel more relaxed. I know they can't tell me everything about it, but I feel more reassured. (Adriana, 26, data systems manager)

Third, as I explore in more detail in the next section, the sonographer rather than the ultrasound machine was often the women's 'window onto the fetus.' This highlights the sonographer's powerful role as gatekeeper to the image, as well as women's dependence on the sonographer.

'Fingers and Toes': Fetal Normality

The women in this study often began their description of 'seeing the baby' by explaining that now they knew the baby was normal.

The baby is healthy. Everything is fine. She kept on saying the baby is wonderful, it's healthy. So I found that out and then, just that it was normally formed and stuff. (Dorothea, 28, Greek Canadian, accountant)

I'm disappointed I still don't feel anything. She tells me it's so active and yet I don't feel anything. But I'm happy. I'm sure everything's okay, because otherwise, well ... hopefully she would have told me ... It does relax your mind. You know that everything is okay and you know that there is something inside because people tell you that it moves and they've already felt this and they felt that. So it puts your mind at ease. So you know someone else is telling you that everything is okay. Someone with a white coat, so to speak, is telling you everything is okay. (Christina, 25, secretary)

Sonographers' indications such as 'everything is fine' and 'the fetus is normally formed' were accepted with relief by most women as evidence that they would give birth to a 'normal' or 'healthy' baby. While this news was especially welcomed by these women who had once miscarried or who were especially anxious about miscarrying, there is no question that 'passing' the ultrasound had a powerful reassuring effect on many others. Certain parts of the image – the heart beat, fetal movement, the 'fingers and toes' that Rosa wished she had asked about – held particular significance as metonymic signs of normality, and signalled to women that 'everything is all right.' Most of the women did not need to observe directly the normality of the fetus; it was enough to hear it from the sonographer or 'someone with a white coat.' Paradoxically, however, a procedure intended to alleviate anxieties often created them.

Writing about her fieldwork at a hospital-based ultrasound clinic in the United States, Janelle Taylor (1998: 27) suggests that 'the convention of "showing the baby" ... provides an opening for women to interrogate sonographers about the medical procedure, in a way that might be unusual in the context of other diagnostic tests or in the interaction with doctors.' Thus, as discussed in chapter 4, women may ask questions during the scan to clarify what is seen, to understand the reasons for and significance of the measurements taken, and to probe both the accuracy of the ultrasound and the sonographer's claims that 'everything is okay.' While some of the women I interviewed did ask such questions during the scan, the procedure and the prospect of 'seeing the baby' also generated anxiety and feelings of dependence and vulnerability:

I didn't get nervous until I was sitting there waiting for her to call my name. Then I started thinking, in a few minutes somebody is gonna be telling me if everything is there or not. If my baby is alive or not. I just sort of sat and panicked. (Louisa, 28, counsellor)

I didn't really have any worries until I got in there. I think she [the technician] brought them to the surface! I sort of assumed everything was normal and then she said, 'We'll measure this and look for this,' and I'm thinking 'Oh my God!' ... I mean, I have to be honest. I found the whole thing pretty nerve-wracking. There they are checking arms and legs. And is the spine there? My God! It was scary. (André, Michelle's husband)

Since the sonographer was doing the seeing *for* them, the women paid particular attention to her. Throughout the scan, the women were extremely sensitive to the sonographer's choice of words, tone of voice, topic of conversation, choice of language, body position, and facial expression, and to the presence of additional health care staff. Especially when the woman could not see or understand the image as the sonographer was describing it, she would turn her attention to the sonographer or other clinic staff. Anxiously reading the sonographer's behaviour and comments for clues to fetal normality, many of the women misinterpreted routine clinic practices as causes for concern. When the clinic physician entered the cubicle, or when the technician seemed to be 'quiet for too long' or 'looked at the screen and didn't say anything' the women were especially alarmed. Also nerve-wracking were sonographers' casual comments such as, 'I can't get the head,' 'It's taking a long time to find the leg,' and, 'Where's your leg, baby?' Even being sent to empty their bladder was enough to make a few women think something was wrong with the baby:

> When she [the technician] sent me to the washroom, I sat in there thinking that she was probably telling Martin [her husband] that something was wrong with the baby. (Sandy, 27, secretary)

Conversations about the fetus on the screen sometimes excluded the woman from knowledge about that fetus. This being Montreal, language sometimes intervened to increase both the woman's anxiety and her dependence on the sonographer:

> It really bugged me that they talked in French. They'd look at the screen and then talk to each other in French. They talked to me in English but I was sure something was wrong with the baby. (Rita, 23, university student)

> When the doctor came in I got a little freaked out. They were scanning for something and they couldn't find it. Then the doctor came in and she [the technician] said, '*Je peux pas le trouver.*' [I can't find it.] The doctor helped her zoom in, and then she said, '*Voilà.*' [There it is.] And I was kinda trying to eavesdrop. It was in French, but my French is very good and it was almost as if they were talking in code. (Cathy, 33, office manager)

'Now I've seen the person': Fetal Identity

'Seeing the baby' meant more than being provided with reassurance of its normality. Three-quarters of the women used what they heard and saw during the ultrasound to assign the fetus a social identity – as someone with gender, behaviour, character, and resemblance to others, and as someone to whom they felt closer. As the examples that follow make clear, the women generally perceived the fetal image as a reliable window through which to observe their baby, and the sonographer's comments as meaningful descriptions of that baby. The women also actively and imaginatively made their own interpretations of the images, even when those interpretations diverged from the sonographers' descriptions.

Women drew a variety of conclusions about the fetus. They based these in particular on what they saw of fetal movement, size, and proportions, and on sonographers' descriptions of these. Fascinated by the real-time images, which conveyed the sense that they were actually watching the fetus instead of looking at the screen, the women talked about how they had seen what the baby was doing. With phrases reminiscent of those used by sonographers, women described the movement, or lack of it, in a variety of ways: 'I saw the baby sleeping.' 'He was dancing.' 'I saw my child sitting so peacefully.' 'He was really going.' This combination of 'live' images, the sonographer's evocative narrative, and the woman's perception that the ultrasound images were photographs, created the impression that the fetus, too, was aware of the ultrasound and responding to its observers. In words that recalled sonographers talking to and waving to the fetus, some women described the movement of the fetal hand as a communicative gesture: 'It waved at us.' 'It was like the baby said "Hello" to me.' The image also provided an indication of their infant's personality or character, and an opportunity to 'connect' emotionally and genealogically:

It looked like a shy baby because we could never see the face. He was always turning away. He was shy or didn't want to be bothered. It was curious. Sometimes you see their hands or feet right on the screen, but this one was more shy. (Térèse, 29, accountant)

The baby's taken on a character that we didn't know before. The fact that she [the sonographer] mentioned the baby was sleeping with its hands over its head. That got to me, because that's exactly how I sleep. So that struck me as being very odd. And the character, the fact that it used its hands a lot. That gave us a kick because I use my hands a lot. (Cathy, 33, office manager)

I was amazed. It looks just like my husband. I mean, because of the bone structure, I guess. But right away I thought – that's like my husband ... It was moving and kicking, like a little spitfire, so I know it's gonna be just like my husband. (Angela, 27, secretary)

The first thing I saw, it's crazy I know, but this kid has my husband's legs. Everything about it was like my husband. Just the way it looked, the build, the bones, the proportions. It was incredible. (Sylvie, 25, chef)

Women's assertions that the fetus was 'like my husband,' 'a little spitfire,' or 'very calm' were often based on a passing comment by the sonographer or a fleeting observation by the woman. Yet in conjunction with the sonographer's statement that 'everything is all right,' these glimpses were tremendously meaningful for women:

It's like if you're talking to someone on the telephone and if you've never seen the person you can only say, you know, 'Yeah, yeah.' But if you've seen the person ... [Changes her expression and smiles broadly.] You can say, 'Hey! Hi! How are you?' It's the same thing [with ultrasound]. It [the fetus] is more like a human being now, because I've seen what it looks like. Now I've seen the person. (Michelle, 27, data systems analyst)

On Being 'Really Pregnant': The Fetal Image as Proof

'Seeing the baby' with all its intertwined meanings about fetal normality and fetal identity, produced a strong sense of reality for these Montreal couples. Over three-quarters of the women I interviewed talked about the fetal image as a form of proof: 'Now I know I'm really pregnant!' 'Now I know it's real!' 'Now I know there's a baby in there.' As the following quotes suggest, ultrasound's ability to legitimize changes in a woman's body shape and size is an important element of what makes this test both desirable and authentic for women. Moreover, the illusion offered by ultrasound of seeing the baby is far more powerful than the images a woman produces in her mind or senses through her body:

It's not my imagination. There really is a baby in there. I'm not just getting fat. (Jennifer, 31, counsellor)

Seeing the baby meant that it's really there. I'm not imagining things. It's been nearly four months and you can't really see any results. Yes, I'm nauseated and have sore breasts. I'm tired and my stomach is sticking out. But seeing an image of the child, it's reality. (Michelle, 27, data systems analyst)

It's a little more real. I can keep on with the preparations now. I guess it reassures me because it is something else the doctor can use, other than the heartbeat and the blood test and manual palpations ... So far I was just gaining weight and getting bigger. But seeing the image means it is not in my imagination. Because I haven't felt any movement yet. Other than that I feel I'm just getting fat. Now it is more real in my head. More like believing that it is actually happening. (Laura, 27, dentist)

The ultrasound image is so convincing in large part because it *is* pictorial: at least initially, the women regarded it as more compelling evidence of the existence of the fetus than either a hormonal test or hearing the fetal heartbeat. Certainly, the hormonal test could show the existence of a pregnancy (a physiological process), and a Doptone monitoring of the heartbeat could be taken as a sign of 'life' and a continuing pregnancy. The following dialogue between Julie and her husband, Tom, underscores the importance the women ascribed to the ultrasound, relative both to their own bodily changes and to other technologically produced signs of pregnancy:

JULIE. When I heard the heartbeat I knew something was there. Now [after the ultrasound] I know it's a baby.
TOM. [*Surprised.*] What did you think it was?
JULIE. I don't know! [*Laughing.*] I mean, you know you're pregnant; you've had your test. You don't have your periods, but nothing is different. You don't show, you don't feel different. Now, now it's different. I've seen it.

Before her ultrasound, Julie had simply said she 'felt' different since becoming pregnant. As it turned out, the reality of the ultrasound was more persuasive to her than her bodily sensations.

For the women in this study, the copy of the ultrasound image they received at the clinic was a tangible and portable sign that the fetus existed and was normal. They often displayed the ultrasound image at home – on the refrigerator, at their bedside, or in an album or frame – as 'Baby's First Picture.' Several women had the ultrasound print photocopied, and even enlarged, to pass around to friends and relatives. Several men put the image in their wallet or on their desk at work, as if it were a school photo. The symbolic value of the image was so great that even though many could not identify anything in the image, women and men showed it to friends, family members, and workmates as 'a picture of my baby.' When I asked the women what people said about these images, most admitted that the image was difficult for others to understand. One woman surmised, 'I guess only a mother can see her baby in that.'

For the viewer, the reality of the ultrasound fetus is unquestionable, compelling, and intensely pleasurable; ultrasound is perceived as a reliable and evocative window through which to observe the baby. Women's hopes that ultrasound will allow them 'to see what kind of baby' they have are not dashed by the unclear image, but rather are fulfilled by sonographers' descriptions of that image. Women do not see a 'fetus' in the ultrasound image, nor is the image presented to them as one of the fetus. Rather, most women see 'their baby.'

This technologically produced image of the fetus both shapes and is shaped by the experience of having a fetus in one's body. Compared to a woman's own bodily sensations and perceptions of being eighteen weeks pregnant, the ultrasound image seems concrete and absolute. Indeed, after the ultrasound, women say they 'feel' closer to the fetus, or 'feel' that the fetus is more real. The 'aliveness' and immediacy of the ultrasound image (Sandelowski 1994) masks the fact that women are viewing a digitalized reflection rather than their baby. As Nia Georges (1997: 99) has suggested, it is as if ultrasound imparts a 'tactile quality' to the fetus, which at this early stage of pregnancy is both unseen and unfelt. Given that this is a technology that 'sees' with sound, the fact that ultrasound also 'reconfigures women's senses' (Georges 1997: 99) is not surprising. Some women clearly find it empowering that ultrasound draws the disembodied fetus into the realm of their senses. The 'tactile quality' of which Georges speaks was powerfully evoked by Angela when she told me, 'When I saw the baby, it made me believe that I'm actually going to be a mother, like I held it in my arms.' That this ultrasound baby is a fiction is evident if one considers what holding an eighteen or twenty week fetus would be like. A fetus at that stage is only 16 to 20 centimetres long and cannot survive outside the womb; and its dark-red, spindly appearance is not particularly appealing, as several women commented as they perused their guide books.

Ultrasound's Possibilities

Convinced now that 'there really is a baby in there,' some women told me that they felt 'different' about themselves and about their responsibility to the baby. Several women said they wanted 'to take it easier' or 'slower' and to 'think more about the baby.' A few women remarked that when they saw how 'little' and 'helpless' the fetus was, they wanted to 'cuddle it' or 'help it.' After the ultrasound, half of the ten women who were smoking said they intended to try harder to stop or cut down. Empowered by ultrasound's proof, many of the women began to publicize the pregnancy by wearing maternity clothes, telling friends and family, showing the ultrasound photo, and making plans for the baby's arrival. In other words, for many women the pregnancy was no longer 'tentative' (Rothman 1986), and no longer private.

The confirmatory effects of the first ultrasound were not restricted to the women, who described – often quite graphically – how their husbands or partners reacted to the fetal image. Thus, the ultrasound was like 'cold water' or 'a slap in his face,' or 'really hit him when he saw it. It's real for him.' They attributed certain changes in the men's behaviour to the ultrasound: 'He wants to stay home more now.' 'He feels he has to work all the time so we have enough money.' The men I spoke with echoed these statements, saying they 'suddenly woke up' or 'realized a baby was on the way.'

During routine ultrasounds, the sonographer encouraged the male partner to 'move closer' to the screen and to take part in the conversation about the image. If the woman came alone to the exam, the sonographer might inquire, 'Your husband didn't come?' Typically, the woman would encourage her partner to attend the ultrasound, often in the hope of stimulating his 'bond' to both the fetus and herself. Calling upon the persistent idea that an understanding of technology is masculine, several women told me that their husbands 'could see better,' or 'understood more' than they did themselves. The presumption was that men possessed a 'natural' ability to see the technologized fetus, and would bond as a direct result of the ultrasound image. Margarete Sandelowski (1994a: 231) has argued that through ultrasound, 'expectant fathers' experience of the fetus is always enhanced, whereas pregnant women's experience may be enhanced or attenuated.' In other words, by privileging the technologically rendered *visible fetus* over the sensed, *embodied* fetus, ultrasound enables men to bypass their pregnant's partner's body, thereby enhancing their experience and knowledge of the fetus. The same technology can reassure and empower women; or it can undermine their embodied knowledge of the fetus by marginalizing such knowledge as 'anecdotal' and as a poor substitute for ultrasound-derived knowledge.

Some women use ultrasound to stimulate or engage their partner's interest in the baby, and to test his commitment to the relationship. During an ultrasound, women often watch closely their partner's reaction to the fetus. Here are two responses to my question, 'Why do you want your husband to come to the ultrasound?'

> I want him to know that this is a baby. It's not going to go away. He just can't get it yet. I guess it's a physical thing. Men don't have all the changes in their body ... The ultrasound changes that. It's like a slap in the face for him! ... Now he's got to get serious about us and this baby. (Vicki, 25, dental assistant)

> My husband hasn't said very much about this baby. He's older, he's got two other kids from his first marriage. So I guess I'd like him to show more interest. A friend told me her husband cried when he saw the ultrasound. I guess I'm kind of hoping that happens to Russ. (Gillian, 30, financial adviser)

Ultrasound offers some women a means of renegotiating their position in their network of family and friends. One woman gave an enlarged photocopy of the ultrasound image to her parents and in-laws:

> Our parents, especially his, they didn't really want us to get married. They said we were too young or not ready or something. I don't know. I mean, I think this baby shows them that, you know, we're really serious about each other. This isn't some boyfriend/girlfriend thing. We're a family now. (Erika, 24, small-business owner)

Another woman, who described herself as the 'last one on the block' to be having a baby, said:

> All my friends think they're Eve. The first ones to be pregnant, the first to have kids. They constantly tell me what I should be doing, how I should be feeling. If I say, 'I don't feel like that,' they look at each other and smile and say, 'Wait, wait. You will' ... Now I've seen my baby. I know everything is fine and I'm gonna ignore them. (Sophia, 31, graphic artist)

One-quarter of the women in this study had once miscarried or were especially anxious about miscarriage. For them, ultrasound echoes were especially and poignantly meaningful, as reassuring 'proof' that they were going to have a baby:

> It has meant a new calmness, I feel a lot more relief about it. I'm not as wary. Well ... before I would tell people I was pregnant, but now I feel a lot more confident telling people. Before it was like, 'I'm p-p-p-pregnant!' But now I'm more confident. (Tamara, 26, dentist)

A few women who miscarried in a previous pregnancy, like Marie-Claude, marshalled the physician-ordered ultrasound as evidence to convince those doctors of the normality and certainty of their pregnancy:

> I was so excited after the ultrasound. I took my picture in to my doctor the next week and said, 'See, see. I told you this time it would be all right.' She's very cautious, always saying, 'Let's take it one step at a time.'

Seeing Past the Sonographer

The dominant message sonographers convey through ultrasound is not 'this is a fetus,' or even 'this is *your* fetus.' Rather, what is communicated to many women is 'here is your baby' – a normal baby, vulnerable, active, sentient, and distinctive. Yet what is communicated through ultrasound is also contingent, uneven, and open to reworking by women. At the time of the first scan, not seeing a fetal subject, determining fetal sex, and worrying about the effects of the ultrasound on the fetus were three areas where women tended to 'see' differently than did sonographers.

Most of the women said they saw their baby during the first ultrasound and learned something of its identity; however, one-quarter of them left the clinic with a different impression:

> This test is for doctor to check baby. I thought ultrasound was like baby in book, not so dark and hard to see. But doctor knows what is there. (Nirmala, 30, homemaker)

Not all of the immigrant women I talked with viewed their ultrasound this way. That being said, Nirmala and three other women who were recent arrivals from South Asia or the Middle East generally regarded the ultrasound as a 'test' rather than a means of 'meeting' the baby. There were eight other women whose post-scan accounts were relatively unelaborated; while they had expected that the ultrasound would enable them to get to know their baby, the ultrasound left them disappointed.

It was very disappointing. She didn't say anything. I was very disappointed. I didn't see my baby ... I thought I would be able to see the baby's head, hands, and feet, but she didn't explain what was on the screen ... Maybe next time, I'll get to see. (Marie-Louise, 31, store manager)

We were pretty disappointed. I mean, after my sister's which I saw, and my friend whose ultrasound picture is, like, really clear. No question – it's a baby. This one was not like that at all.

Why do you think that was the case?
I don't know. Maybe it was like a better machine in Toronto. (Esther, 27, office manager)

Significantly, 'not seeing the baby' did not mean these women were less reassured with the sonographer's statement about fetal normality, or more critical of ultrasound's role in prenatal care.

Just as some women did not see as much as they had hoped, some women *and* men saw more in the image than what the sonographer said was visible. For example, although sonographers at the Met maintained that the first ultrasound was too early to determine fetal sex, some women drew their own conclusions, based on their perceptions of the ultrasound's echoes, about whether they were having a boy or a girl. Before the first routine scan, two-thirds of the women said they 'knew' or 'had a feeling' about their baby's sex. Then, during the ultrasound, a few women claimed that they *saw* (rather than felt) evidence of fetal sex. Others explained that they knew it was a boy because the ultrasound fetus was 'big,' 'sturdy,' or fast moving. In contrast, 'delicate', 'skinny,' and 'quiet' ultrasound images signified a girl:

It's a girl! I'm sure it's a girl. They said it was too early to tell, but the baby was so tiny and delicate. I know it's a girl. (Suzanne, 27, secretary)

Nirmala, who in her post-scan account of the fetus barely referred to what she had seen, came away certain she was having a girl:

I think it was a little girl. Baby was tiny, just a little thing. Boy is bigger, stronger. My baby was skinny, little, like me. (Nirmala, 30, homemaker)

For some women, beginning to think about the fetus in terms of its gender meant feeling 'differently about the baby.' Several women said they felt 'different' or 'closer' to the baby 'when you know it's not an it.'[4]

Not all women accepted the sonographer's claim that ultrasound was painless and safe. At the time of the research, women having ultrasound at the Met were required to drink four glasses of water about one hour prior to the time of their appointment.[5] Given that they often had to wait an hour or more for their appointment, many of them felt very full and uncomfortable by the time the scan started. As Esther explained:

I was thrilled to go to the bathroom [after the exam was over]. To tell you the truth, the scan could not have been done fast enough for me, 'cause I was just dying. It's really too bad. I would have liked to have enjoyed it, but my mind was just not on it at all.

'Seeing' the fetus wave, pose, and respond to the ultrasound brought out anxieties about how the fetus 'felt' during the scan. A few women, and the husbands of two others, were concerned that the fetus was being hurt or made uncomfortable by the ultrasound 'waves' or 'light' or by the pressure of the probe. But only one man expressed his concern to the sonographer.

The baby didn't like the scan. He kept moving away and putting his hand up. I really wanted her to hurry up and finish so he wouldn't be bothered by it anymore. I was thinking the whole time, 'I hope this isn't hurting him.' (Gillian, 30, financial adviser)

I couldn't believe how much it didn't like the ultrasound. The whole time she was doing the scan, it was moving and ducking and trying to get away. You know, like, 'Get out of my face.' It objected to being disturbed like that. (Cheryl, 33, office manager)

Well, because it was moving a lot and the way it was moving, I got an idea of what it liked and didn't like about the ultrasound. It seemed to be bothered by it and just wanted to be left alone. (Annabella, 25, office clerk)

The process of disciplining women through ultrasound is uneven. This was especially apparent in women's narratives after the second ultrasound and post-partum.

Seeing Less, Feeling More: The Second Routine Ultrasound

A second ultrasound at about thirty-two weeks is routine for women at the Metropolitan Hospital. Clinicians rationalize this second scan as essential for screening for delays in fetal growth and potential complications in childbirth.

Julie

I couldn't recognize anything! She [the sonographer] said everything was all right, so I was relieved. The head is down. But I already suspected that just from the way it moves. And we know it's a girl.

Does it make a difference now that you know it's a girl?
Yeah. It's our daughter, not just our baby ... I know who it is now. Before it was just a baby. I think about it as a girl. She has a name. It's not an 'it' ... We haven't told our family what it is. It'll be a surprise for them ...

Do you have any worries about the pregnancy now?
They come and go. I was fine right after the last ultrasound. Then after a day, I was worrying again. I had this awful nightmare that the baby had no legs. So I asked her at this scan: 'Does the baby have legs?' I felt like an idiot, but after the nightmare I had to ask.

Rosa

MARIO. The first time we see the whole baby. It hit me, like I told her, that looks like a boy! But now, we didn't see nothing.

ROSA. Yeh, only bits. It didn't feel like we saw our baby.

MARIO. Yeh, we were watching nothing ...

ROSA. We didn't want to know [the fetal sex]. And he [Mario] kept saying, 'Let's do it the old-fashioned way. And it'll be a surprise.' So we said okay, I'm not gonna ask. And I had to force myself to say you're not gonna know. And then as soon as the doctor came, she checked me, and she said, 'Oh, I see what it is.' And just knowing that she knew what my baby was ... We just looked at each other. She said, 'if you want to find out.' But I went and changed, and then I went after to say, 'Tell me what it is.' She said, 'Are you sure you want to know?' I said, 'Yeah.' So she said, 'You're having a boy.' Then he [Mario] came out and said, 'Give me a few hints.' What kinda hint, you know. Then he said, 'Just come straight out and let me know what it is.' But I'm not telling anybody [else] what it is. My family don't know. [To Mario.] But your sister asked, 'How's the baby?' I said, 'He's doing fine.' Right from the start I have the habit of saying 'he.' She goes, 'Hmm, you're saying "he."' I said, 'I don't know what it is. What do you want me to say? I'm not gonna say, "she!"'

Tamara

It was so hard to see. And I found the microphone [transducer] pushing too hard and I got that feeling that it was disturbing the baby.

Why?
Because it kept moving away. She was pushing and it seemed like the baby was moving so that it would be away from it. It would go somewhere else and then ... do you know what I mean? It was disturbed. And my bladder. I didn't think I would be able to last. And I kept thinking, as she was pushing, 'Oh God! I hope she's not hurting it.' Not that she was being rough, but that the whole procedure is not very pleasant for the baby.

What did you find out?
The weight. That it was perfect and average in everything and there were no surprises. I think I saw the sex, but I'm not sure ... I didn't ask

to know. Well, I asked specifically not to know ... I think I saw a penis. I think it's a boy ... From the minute I conceived I thought it was a boy. And then a lot of people have been telling me it's a girl, it's a girl. So I still have my gut feeling. But these people have given birth; they must know! I wasn't really sure, but after the second one I'm almost certain. Also, it's rough. It kicks a lot and it seems mischievous.

How did you feel after the scan?
Nothing different. Except that for the first few hours after I thought I saw the sex, I was relating to it differently. Like thinking, oh for sure it's that. Then after I discussed it with John, he said, 'You can't be sure. You don't know what you are looking at.' He's right ... So I've changed my mind from thinking that it's definitely a boy. So I'm not sure ... It just made me feel closer to it again, and I was looking forward to seeing it. I felt like I was actually just saying 'hello' to the baby. Like a strong bond to it.

Marie-Claude

The first one, you could see the whole baby. And you could tell more. This one was harder.

What did you find out?
The baby is okay and everything looks good ... We didn't want to know [the fetal sex]. And she said she couldn't tell because of the position the baby was in ... It's still breech and the face is inward. I can feel the head is high and all the kicking is down low ... It's definitely a boy. I have no idea why I think that, but ... Well, I knew the minute I got pregnant that I was pregnant, and I was right about that. And I've been positive from the beginning that it is a boy. Everyone says it's a girl. I call it 'Max' ... It moves a lot. It's active, but I think it has a nervous nature 'cause it moves all the time.

Do you have any worries about the pregnancy now?
No. Not really. It's just the anticipation now. And I hope I don't scream during the labour and scare the other women! ...

The women generally perceived this second routine scan as less important than the first for learning about the health, character, appearance, and behaviour of the fetus. The second ultrasound did prom-

ise to determine fetal gender and to provide information in prepara-
tion for labour and delivery ('exact due date,' estimated weight at
delivery, fetal position, whether the fetal head was 'too large' or the
woman's pelvis 'too small' to permit a vaginal delivery). The women
felt much less anxious about fetal health by this time in their pregnancy, and often described the later scan as 'more for the doctor' or
'just a double-check.' Some wondered why a second scan was necessary if the first had found no problems.

After the second scan,[6] over half of the women remarked, 'I didn't
see the baby,' and their subsequent accounts included relatively little
from the fetal image:

> I felt cheated, I guess. I didn't see anything this time. Last time we
> had an image but not this time. It seemed to go so fast, too. From
> what I saw, it's hard to say 'this is my baby.' I felt she could have
> given me more information. (Louisa, 28, counsellor)

As before, women recalled seeing the head, heart, and spine, and a
few said they'd seen the fetal face, hands, and feet. Yet most women
left the second ultrasound with relatively little new knowledge about
the fetus. As I mentioned in the previous chapter, sonographers tend
to preface these thirty-two-week scans by telling women that 'it's
harder to see.' While women welcomed the news that the fetus was
growing properly and 'looked fine,' their fears of fetal anomalies and
miscarriage had largely been alleviated by the first scan, by regular
prenatal visits, and by the fact that they could feel fetal movement.
By this time, too, women were more familiar with the ultrasound
protocol and thus less often alarmed by the presence of a physician during the ultrasound or by the sonographer's periods of quiet
concentration.

More women expressed doubts to me about the accuracy of the
clinical information after the second scan than after the first. Following the second scan, roughly two-fifths of the women questioned
whether ultrasounds were able to detect impairments, see the fetal
genitalia, estimate fetal size, or predict the due date. To give one example, although the women accepted the ultrasound-based fetal age
and due date at the time of the first scan, by the time of the second
scan, several of them had rejected or were questioning these estimates.
Nevertheless, women were still sensitive about how the sonographer
described the fetus. On being told that the fetus was 'small' or 'large,'

several women became alarmed that this meant 'too small' or 'larger than normal.' Others grew worried if the sonographer said the fetus was not moving much.

By the end of the second scan, over half the women had been told whether they were having a boy or a girl:

> [After we found out it's a boy] it became the name we chose for it. It became, it just sort of became more of a self as opposed to a part of me. More of an identity. When it's a non-sex, it's just an extension of me. Then I started thinking of it more as a child. (Tamara, 26, physiotherapist)

> I felt like it was more real. Now it's not an 'it.' It is different. It's a 'he,' not just a baby. Before it had no identity ... Now I think about it as a boy ... Now I use his name. (Maria, 28, counsellor)

Marie-Claude was among the one-third of the group who opted for what Rosa's husband Mario called 'the old-fashioned way'; she told the sonographer she did not want to know 'what it is.' Of the women who *were* told, one-third said that they and their husbands did not intend to disclose the information to anyone else. In each of four other couples, one spouse knew the fetal sex and the other did not want to know. Although only one woman openly expressed disappointment about the sex of her fetus, learning the fetal sex prior to delivery was often 'a mixed blessing.' On the one hand, knowing was enjoyable, because the couples could 'imagine it better' and think about it as 'our daughter, not just our baby.' On the other hand, finding out meant 'there was no surprise left' and 'nothing to look forward to at the end of labour.' In unanticipated ways, knowing whether the fetus was a boy or a girl troubled the social and linguistic terrain of being pregnant. Although these women had wanted to know the fetal sex in order to prepare rooms and clothes in gender-specific colours, they found themselves unable to do so. Knowing the fetus's sex when others did not required vigilance to avoid accidental disclosure; it also revealed the tendency in both English and French to use masculine pronouns for the fetus:

> God! Why did I ever say I wanted to know what it was! Now I have to force myself to say 'he' and 'it' when I know it's a little girl. I feel totally weird doing this. (Julie, 29, secretary)

[*Whispering.*] Well, I guess [things have changed] because I know the sex. I feel kinda bad for them [her in-laws who are in the next room]. Like my mother-in-law and them, they were hoping for a boy. They have ten grandchildren and only two boys. (Rita, 23, university student)

After the second ultrasound, over four-fifths of the women did not refer to the ultrasound image in their descriptions of fetal character, behaviour, or appearance, except in reference to whatever they learned about the fetus's sex and normality. In fact, women often answered my questions about the second fetal image by saying, 'I didn't learn anything,' or 'I didn't see anything.' The first scan had convinced the women of the reality of the fetus; this time, what became real for about one-third of the women was their own changing identity and role. Several women, having seen 'how big the baby was,' said that they 'felt like a mother' or that they suddenly realized they had a lot to do to prepare for the infant's arrival:

I saw her [the technician] putting on the gel and I saw how big my belly is and then she figured out that it weighs four pounds and I went – oh my God! It's here! It's happening! I'm a mother! ... Ever since, I've been, like, we've got to get ready. We've got to buy stuff, set up the crib, get diapers. (Karen, 26, university student)

I'm, like, super calm on the outside, but inside I'm running around thinking there's so much to do. The baby is coming soon. I mean, the size of it really struck us, you know. It weighs more than four pounds, and babies are born weighing that much. I'm supposed to be resting more, and he [her husband] doesn't want me doing too much, but I'm starting to panic about all that we have to do. (Laura, 27, dentist)

By the second ultrasound, the women were no longer relying so much on ultrasound, guide books, and other women for knowledge of their pregnancy. Their main source of information now was the fetal movement they felt (as opposed to visualizing). This movement reassured many women that the fetus was alive and healthy. Fetal movement was also interpreted as a sign of fetal awareness, thought, preference, character, and mood.

The baby moves a lot these days and it gives me a good feeling. I know he's okay, and everything is all right. When he moves, I can sort of tell what he's thinking, like if he's in a good mood today, or feeling sleepy, or if he really wants to party. (Pattie, 25, waitress)

It's like she [the fetus] say's 'I'm here.' Like she's telling me, 'You're too quiet. Move!' I can tell what music she likes and doesn't like. If I put some on, she'll start kicking and moving all over ... She'll get all excited when she doesn't like it. (Michelle, 27, data systems analyst)

I feel her all the time. It's great! I know what she's doing and what she's thinking. She's definitely not a morning person. She doesn't get up until later than me, and she stays up when I want to be asleep. I'm pretty sure she's going to be slender and athletic, too. The way she moves her body, like a dancer almost. (Jennifer, 31, counsellor)

I'm fascinated by it. I don't know! Ever since I've been pregnant, I just get so sucky! I have this little person who's inside of me, she eats, she wakes up, she sleeps. And Tom played with her fist one night. Yeah! One evening for about half an hour she'd poke out her fist and he'd touch it and then she'd pull away. It was great! (Julie, 29, secretary)

The women continued to talk to the fetus, as they had earlier in the pregnancy, to soothe and calm it, to apologize for loud noises, and to describe for it events and people outside the uterus. One woman was attempting to teach the fetus simple words, explaining, 'It can't hurt to see if it really works.' Two couples continued to play tape recordings to the fetus. As the fetus took on more and more of a social presence in their lives, one-quarter of the women told me that the fetus responded differently to their voice than to their husbands' voice:

We both talk to her. When I feel her move I think, 'Oh you're awake,' and then I'll say something to her ... [My husband] talks to her, too. Usually when he does, she gets scared and then she doesn't move. (Kate, 24, bookkeeper)

Ron plays music to it. The baby moves to the reggae beat. And he gives certain kicks to Ron's voice and mine, and he gives certain kicks when Ron or I rub my tummy. When Ron says 'Kick for me,' he does – the baby kicks! (Norma, 24, fast food restaurant worker)

I talk a lot, especially when I feel the baby move. I wonder what it's going through, like, why is it moving? I talk to it and I say, 'I'm sorry if you don't have enough room' ... I know it can hear whenever I talk to it or my husband talks to it. It can tell our voices ... I'm sure it can tell our voices because when my husband talks to it, it moves differently than when I do. (Annabella, 25, office clerk)

By the eighth month of pregnancy, women are more openly and unambiguously defined as mothers by themselves and by others.[7] Many of the women I interviewed were well-travelled in what Davis-Floyd (1992: 4) calls 'a year-long initiatory rite of passage' into motherhood. They looked pregnant, described the fetus as a 'skinny newborn,' and referred to it without hesitation as 'the baby.' Many were also tired of being differently shaped and sized, and complained about feeling 'gigantic,' 'slow,' and 'occupied.' Moreover, as Esther's complaint reveals, their bodies were increasingly read by others as signs of 'the baby' rather than of themselves:

I think I'm starting to get kind of fed up. If one more person touches my stomach, I think I'll break their head! I'm getting tired of people saying 'Hi!' and looking down at my stomach. Like, hey! There's a face up here. I'm glad I didn't get my hair done today, you know! It would have been wasted. (Esther, 27, office manager)

Reflecting: Post-Partum Thoughts on Fetal Imaging

Julie

Before we sit down to talk, Julie proudly shows me her tiny daughter, who is sleeping soundly in her crib. Julie was generally satisfied with the labour and delivery ('I thought it would be much harder'), but she regrets that she is not breastfeeding: 'I got discouraged and the nurses at the hospital just handed me a bottle.' I ask her to describe the 'best moment of the pregnancy':

Oh. Easy! Feeling her move the first time. I wanted to call somebody, but nobody was around, so I was jumping up and down by myself. I remember thinking, 'This is it! She's in there!' ... At the first ultrasound we could see her moving, but I thought it was weird, 'cause I couldn't feel it. It was like it was happening to someone else ... The ultrasound was kind of fun, too. I mean, you get to see the baby, well, sort of ... I knew they were wrong about the due date. Remember when they said I was two weeks later [meaning her due date]? Well, I knew I was right, and she was born almost on the day I predicted.

Rosa

While she feeds four-week-old Antonio from a bottle and rocks him to sleep, Rosa recounts her painful labour and her struggles to breast feed. With Mario at her side 'to remind them I didn't want nothing [for pain],' she struggled through thirty hours of labour. She has concluded that the labour took such a long time because the baby was 'in a wrong position.' Although she tried breast feeding, the 'final straw' came a week ago, when Mario was laid off. Since then, she has been a 'nervous wreck, crying and whining all the time':

He's [Antonio] not like I thought. I pictured a calmer baby. He seemed so calm when we saw him the first time.

On the ultrasound?
Yeah. But he's not like that. He's the opposite. He's nervous. He was really nervous with breast feeding, and now that he's on the bottle, he's better. But he still really gets upset ... I'm glad I had the ultrasound. It was nice, you know. Like I was looking at him, seeing him made him more real. It doesn't really tell you that much, like if you are coming right. I thought they were gonna be able to tell me how he was gonna come, but they didn't. Or maybe they can't. Anyway, when I was at the hospital it was like they didn't know he was gonna take so long ... You'd think all that ultrasound could'a told them he was in the wrong position.

Tamara

Looking rested and relaxed, Tamara hands her month-old son to her mother-in-law as we begin to talk. Tamara recounts that 'several days after her second routine scan, her physician told her 'the baby was a little small and one of his kidneys needed watching.' She had an additional two ultrasounds to follow fetal growth:

I never got a clear sense of just how small he was. They measured him and looked at the kidney each time. I was pretty stressed out by the time we got to delivery. Now they say he is perfectly normal and it was probably 'clinically insignificant.' Well, maybe to them! ... I hope it was all worry for nothing.

How did the labour and delivery go?
Great! Textbook case! I had contractions in the middle of the night, ... they broke my waters to speed things up ... Then later, I had some oxytocin. Then there were these huge contractions. I was begging them to give me an epidural [an analgesic administered in the lower back]. It didn't work the first time, so they did it again ... I finally made it to 10 centimetres, and they let me push. Pushing felt great! ... Thirty-nine minutes later, Samuel was born!

Marie-Claude

Marie-Claude and I peek in on her sleeping infant daughter and then settle down on the couch to talk. As she describes her labour and delivery, Marie-Claude bursts into tears, saying that she 'lost control' after the doctor broke her waters to speed up her contractions. Determined to give birth without an epidural and anxious about the effects of the drug on the fetus, Marie-Claude had used breathing to ease the discomfort of her labour for nearly twenty-four hours. Then, as she explained, after her waters were broken and the pain increased, the case room nurses urged her to have an epidural. Marie-Claude 'gave in' after the nurses told her it was her 'last chance' to have an epidural. While they were trying to insert the needle, Marie-Claude began to feel the urge to push. The nurses told her that she must not push, since she was not fully dilated. After several hours, told that dilation had ceased and that the 'baby must come out,' Marie-Claude had a caesarean delivery. Now, six weeks later, she is still angry, but 'enjoying every minute of the baby.' She is not planning to return to paid employment until her kids are all in school.

Tell me about your daughter.
She's the spitting image of her dad. Extremely curious. Very strong and tense. I thought it was a boy! The nurses thought I was disappointed, but I was just surprised ... On the last ultrasound, I could see her profile so clearly – she had my forehead and his nose. But I

thought it was a boy. Just the way it moved on the screen, I thought it was a boy. But I knew it was gonna be like my husband in one way. They both have the same character.

Hearing the heartbeat really meant the most to me. A heart beating is something really special. A life in there! She's alive! ... The scan was reassuring, but it was a medical procedure. If I hadn't had the complications [the early bleeding], it wouldn't have meant much. But after the bleeding, I wanted to know that it was okay.

Considering their excited and enthusiastic responses to the first scan, I was surprised to find that following childbirth, fewer than one-fifth of the women in this study ranked the ultrasound as the 'most important' or 'most meaningful' event when I asked them to compare seeing the fetal image, hearing the heartbeat, and feeling quickening. As part of their routine care, all but two of the women heard the fetal heartbeat prior to the first routine ultrasound, and three-quarters saw the fetal image prior to quickening. After delivery, however, the fetal image was the 'most important' or 'most meaningful' of these three events for fewer than one-fifth of the women. Far more women – almost half – said that hearing the heartbeat was the most important; about another third said this of quickening. Nonetheless, two-thirds of the women assessed ultrasound as a positive experience, and remembered the fetal image as 'reassuring,' 'enjoyable,' or 'exciting.' Only 6 of the 44 women (14 per cent) felt that having ultrasound had made their pregnancy less enjoyable or more stressful.

Those women who chose seeing the fetal image as the most important emphasized the reassurance it offered that the fetus was normally developed, and the ability to know the fetal sex:

For me, seeing her on the ultrasound was incredible! It was like, 'Oh my God! There really is a baby.' I felt so protective after that. It's just this little thing inside you. I wanted to be very careful, crossing the street, eating properly, not drinking ... I never really saw myself as a mother before. The ultrasound really helped me to prepare for that. When you see, you believe it's true. I mean, when I first felt her, it could've been gas ... Seeing her and finding out that it was girl. It was really important for me to use her name and talk to her like that. I hate it when people say 'it.' (Michelle, 27, data systems analyst)

I guess seeing it was more important because I knew he was really there. When you have an ultrasound, you think, 'It's real.' You actually see it. It's not just an idea. You know he's developed okay and you see all the physical things, seeing all his parts. (Francesca, 30, bank teller)

Those women who said the heartbeat or quickening was especially meaningful for their experience of pregnancy found the ultrasound 'exciting' and 'reassuring,' but hard to understand without assistance. Unlike fetal imaging, which required specialized equipment and expert interpretation, fetal movement was a continual bodily reminder that 'everything was okay.'

The movement was way more important to me than anything else. Because when you are seeing it on the ultrasound you don't know what you are seeing. Someone else is seeing for you: 'This is the arm. Here is the head.' But the movement – I felt it. No one had to tell me what it was. I felt it. (Térèse, 29, accountant)

The ultrasound was too hard to see. I couldn't understand anything until it was pointed out. It was great to know he had all his parts, but that's about it ... Hearing the heartbeat was very exciting. It was so early and I knew my baby was alive, everything was fine. That's what I liked. (Adelena, 29, office manager)

Women who said the fetal heartbeat was especially meaningful often described it as 'the first sign' of the pregnancy or commented on how early in the pregnancy they had heard it. In fact, their postpartum descriptions of hearing the heartbeat were strikingly similar to their earlier narratives on the fetal image:

It [hearing the heartbeat] was my first realization that I was going to have a baby. It told me the baby was well. That there was a baby in there! A little human being. (Angela, 27, secretary)

The heartbeat was the most reassuring. It was great! There is a living being in there. There is life! It's real! (Sophia, 31, graphic artist)

By post-partum, the distinctiveness and reliability of ultrasound's vision have eroded considerably for about one-third of the women, each of whom expressed disappointment and frustration with ultrasound's failure to accurately predict fetal size, a long and difficult labour, or a caesarean delivery. Especially strong criticism of ultrasound was expressed by those women who were sent for additional predelivery scans and then were told that the fetus was either 'too large' or 'too small,' or that the level of amniotic fluid was 'low.' Now believing that these assessments were wrong, these women felt that the additional ultrasounds had caused them unnecessary worry. Women who had difficult or premature deliveries wondered why the ultrasound hadn't been able to predict or detect problems. They had understood that the ultrasound – especially the second routine scan – was done to predict labour complications:

I'm lying there pushing and grunting and thinking, 'What the f— do these guys know?' My doctor told me the second scan would show the position of the baby and if there were any problems for the delivery. Now here I am, and this same guy is standing there telling me I'm too small, and the baby can't come out. Too small? They couldn't see that on the ultrasound? Come on. (Kate, 24, bookkeeper)

I realize now that the ultrasound cannot be that accurate. I think it depends on the technician. Like, they said he was big and when I told my doctor, it didn't jive with what the doctor thought. So the ultrasound was very misleading. He wasn't too big, but I was worrying about it right through the whole labour ... I was scared. What if they induce? What if he's too big? What if I have to have a caesarean? (Louisa, 28, counsellor)

They did another ultrasound [at about thirty-four weeks], because the doctor thought I was growing too fast. That doctor at the clinic really scared me. He started talking about diabetes. I thought I'd be diabetic, or he [the baby] would be diabetic, or something was mentally wrong ... And my doctor said for sure it'll be an operation [caesarean] because he's so big ... I don't understand why I had to go through all that labour if he knew I needed a caesarean ... I wanted the operation. I wanted them to take him out ... [After twelve hours] they gave me the epidural. I knew it could slow the labour, but I didn't know it could stop the labour. Then they tried to bring the labour back [by administering oxytocin]. But no go. So there's this big crisis. Like, your labour stopped – hurry, hurry we have to do a caesarean! ... I couldn't believe it. They knew they had to do a caesarean. They knew that from the ultrasound. (Francesca, 30, bank teller)

More light is shed on this kind of frustration when we consider the gap between some women's expectations for childbirth and their experiences of the birth. Nearly all of the women I interviewed had decided early in pregnancy that they wanted a 'natural' childbirth. The meanings of this term varied widely, but in general, women spoke of using non-medicinal pain relief (breathing, relaxation) for as long as possible, walking during early labour, pushing the infant out (rather than resorting to forceps), and being able to make their own decisions throughout the labour and delivery. Only a minority of women had that kind of childbirth.

The experiences of childbirth among the women in this study were not atypical of those of other women delivering their first child at the Metropolitan.[8] Although around four-fifths of the women in this study began labour spontaneously, over three-quarters of the forty-one women who did not have a prelabour caesarean section had labour accelerated with intravenously administered hormones or by having their amniotic membrane ruptured. In accordance with hospital policy, all of the women were attached to an intravenous glucose drip, and all were continuously attached to an external electronic fetal heart monitor. Many women also had an electrode introduced vaginally and implanted in the fetal scalp. Almost four-fifths of the women had an 'epidural,' and endured a painful period of forced immobility while the drug was dispensed slowly by automatic pump into their lower spine. Some of those who did said that nurses had pressured them to have one 'before it was too late.' Despite women's earlier intentions to walk during labour and find a comfortable position on their own, the artificially ruptured membranes and the use of monitors, electrodes, and needles effectively confined them to bed for the duration of labour and delivery. In the end, about two-thirds of the women had a vaginal delivery, and one-third a caesarean section.[9]

By post-partum, ultrasound's claims to 'see the baby' had become suspect, especially among the women whose birthing experiences left them feeling angry, disappointed, and disempowered. No longer as dependent on the ultrasound, and now immersed in the physicality and immediacy of caring for a newborn, the women were more open to criticizing the ultrasound and downplaying its significance to their experience of pregnancy.

Chapter Seven

Reconnections: Women, Ultrasound, and Reproductive Politics

> There is no single fetal subject, but rather a multitude of contingent, situated, and ever-shifting contexts within which fetuses are invoked.
> Michaels and Morgan (1999: 11)

In this chapter I move the analysis outward from the lives of women and the routines of sonographers to return to the issues raised in the opening chapter: how ultrasound mediates the experience of pregnancy, and how the ultrasound fetus can be 'denaturalized' so that we can see its social and cultural constitution. This discussion follows three converging paths. *First*, I revisit women's experiences of ultrasound fetal imaging in the context of the impacts of ultrasound and the social control of women. *Second*, in order to underscore how ultrasound fetal imaging is both socially and culturally shaped, I examine the diversity of the accounts of the Montreal women, and compare my own Canadian material with ethnographic accounts of ultrasound in the United States, Ecuador, the Philippines, and Greece. *Third*, I situate routine fetal imaging within the context of Canadian abortion politics, with the goal of highlighting the links between the technologically mediated reality of fetal ultrasound and the politics of gender and reproduction.

The Impact of Ultrasound: Benefit or Burden?

From the perspective of sonographers and many others, translating ultrasound's echoes (and other technologically produced signs such as blood pressure readings and fetal heart monitor blips) is equivalent to uncovering the natural and true 'facts' of the body. Ultrasound, then, lets us discover nature (i.e., the developing fetus) and makes intervention possible when nature goes awry (e.g., through emergency caesarean delivery, restriction of women's activities, or termination of the pregnancy. Moreover, when we render the contents of a woman's bodily interior into a pictorial real-time fetus through ultrasound, we not only gain rich and necessary clinical data but also provide the women with a 'more "naturally" human' fetus (Casper 1995: 195), one that moves, waves, and engages its viewers. This opportunity to see the fetus 'live,' as if on television, and to witness its normality and its 'natural' displays of agency and subjectivity, is a compelling and powerful moment. Seen in this light, the impacts of routine ultrasound are beneficial: maternal and fetal outcomes are improved, maternal anxiety is reduced, and the woman enjoys herself bonding with the fetus.

Despite the nearly hegemonic status of this perspective in biomedicine and in popular culture, ultrasound has not escaped criticism entirely. Questions have been raised about the clinical and psychological 'benefits' of routine ultrasound; there are also concerns about its social impacts. To a large extent, these concerns are embedded in a larger set of concerns about medical intervention into childbearing and the ethics of 'choosing our children' through prenatal screening. Ultrasound has not received nearly as much critical attention as amniocentesis and other forms of prenatal genetic diagnosis; even so, feminists, alternative birth advocates, and others have decried its role in heightening the social and moral status of the fetus and in diminishing women's rights.[1]

Several authors have traced the current debate over maternal versus fetal rights back to the consolidation of biomedical authority and control over childbearing women since the Second World War. For example, William Arney (1982: 54, 123) and Ann Oakley (1986a) have pointed out that technologies such as ultrasound, X-rays, fetoscopy, and fetal heart monitoring have been instrumental in legitimating claims made by modern medicine, and especially by obstetricians, to expertise in managing pregnancy. As it redefined pregnancy as a time of potential risk and pathology, obstetrics transformed itself from a profession that focussed on interventions during childbirth into one that monitored the woman throughout her pregnancy. Under this new obstetrical gaze, in which 'subjects must be separated, individualized, subjected to constant and total visibility' (Arney 1982: 89), the social relationships of pregnancy have been transformed. The fetus is now viewed as conceptually distinct from the pregnant woman; it has emerged as a new patient with its own unique signs of normality (growth rates, heart rate) and abnormality ('fetal distress,' fetal pathology). This reconceptualization of pregnancy as the 'interpretation of fetal signs,' and of the fetus as 'a little person lying in the womb' (Rothman 1989: 114) defines contemporary biomedicine's fetocentric view of reproduction. In this new approach, pregnancy is thought about and acted on from the perspective of the endangered, vulnerable, personified, fetal patient, with profound implications for the agency of pregnant women. As Ann Oakley first pointed out, ultrasound and other fetocentric technologies (e.g., fetal heart monitoring and amniocentesis) are 'revolutionary because, for the first time, they enable obstetricians to dispense with mothers as intermediaries, as necessary informants of fetal status and life-style.' Knowledge of the fetus based on the woman's own contact with that fetus – a contact independent of technology – can be marginalized and devalued (Oakley 1986a: 155). Women's bodily experiential knowledge of the fetus can be redefined as 'beliefs,' 'anecdotes,' and 'impressions,' and the woman's presence can be reduced to 'echogenic tissue' or 'maternal environments.' In the new environment of obstetrics, physicians and other health care providers are subject to increasing scrutiny as both fetal experts and advocates.

This critique rings true when we view ultrasound from the vantage point of broad historical and social trends in the medical and technological management of childbearing. Yet the social realities of ultrasound, and the lived experiences of pregnant women, their partners, and sonographers, merit a more detailed reading, one that restores agency to those who have and use this technology. In the opening chapter of this book I suggested that a critical and feminist anthropological accounting of ultrasound forces us to examine how ultrasound shapes women's embodied perceptions, how it reproduces and transforms meanings of pregnancy and fetality, and how it subjects women, fetuses, and others to particular kinds of surveillance and social control. In the following section I suggest how that sort of reading alerts us to the powerful dominant meanings that ultrasound mobilizes; and to the variable meanings articulated in the context of particular life circumstances, personal histories, and desires; and to the ways in which women can and do intervene in this technology. Women's accounts of fetal imaging also reveal how women engage, negotiate, and rework the woman–fetus relationship in the context of contemporary Canadian reproductive practice and politics, and how they reclaim (to some extent) maternal agency.

Separation and Reconnection

Ultrasound fetal imaging is an undeniably fetocentric technology that powerfully shapes the way women experience pregnancy. As American and British researchers have observed, and as I observed independently in Montreal, ultrasound mobilizes an influential narrative of separation and reconnection, risk and bonding. Below, I revisit women's experiences of this narrative to show the extent to which women accept and reproduce it, but also to suggest that ultrasound's effects are uneven, transitory, and open to critique. Women are not passive recipients or 'victims' of ultrasound; they can and do intervene in ultrasound's constructions of both fetality and maternalism.

As I have described, sonographers translate ultrasound's echoes into 'facts' about two distinct persons – the fetus and the pregnant woman. The ultrasound echoes reflect off flesh, fluid, and bone – all of which are within the woman's body – yet only some of these echoes are regarded as 'maternal anatomy'; the rest are regarded as 'the baby.' By rendering women's bodies permeable (Franklin 1991) and by relocating the fetus to an external monitor, this process conceptually separates woman from fetus. It also sends a clear message that ultrasound is *about* the fetus. Any examination of 'maternal anatomy' is dispensed with quickly at the beginning of the ultrasound; most of the scan is about examining, measuring, recording, and describing 'the baby.' Echoes from maternal anatomy are read mainly for evidence of the woman's capacity to sustain the pregnancy and of possible risks to the fetus. Meanwhile, fetal echoes are evaluated and personified as sonographers carefully select those elements of fetal anatomy – brain, fingers, toes, beating heart – that convey life, animation, normality, and a sentimentalized 'baby.'

How did the women I interviewed experience and respond to being made permeable and transparent, and to being 'separated' from the fetus?[2] Remarkably, most of them do not think of the ultrasound as seeing 'inside' their bodies. Few asked whether their own anatomy was visible on screen. Rather, ultrasound was a way to 'see the baby.' Their excitement about the 'chance to see,' their conviction that 'seeing is believing,' and their fascination with the print-out of the fetal image – the 'baby's photo' – were testimony to this singular preoccupation with the baby.

This loss of bodily boundaries and bodily knowledge often passed unnoticed or without comment, as the women were captivated by the fetal image or distracted by the discomfort of a full bladder (which is still required at the Met and many other hospitals). During a scan, everyone is focused on the fetal image on the monitor, and very little attention is paid to the fetus *inside* the woman's belly or to the woman's bodily knowledge. None of the women talked explicitly about feeling invaded, disturbed, intruded on, or opened up by ultrasound. Even so, some of their comments about the fetal movement they saw suggest that ultrasound changed how they perceived both their body and the fetus *in* their body. While this 'technological quickening' strengthened the notion that ultrasound was providing them with authoritative and distinctive information, and while it imparted a 'tactile quality' to the fetus (Georges 1997: 99), some women found it unsettling:[3]

It was like it [the fetus] moved for her [the sonographer], but not for me. (Christina, 25, secretary)

It was neat and all that, you know, to see the baby moving. But I don't know, I guess I thought the mother was supposed to feel it. Like that's when you know it's there. (Tina, 28, child care worker)

Some of the women yielded to the authoritative knowledge of the sonographer:

We could see it moving and I told her [the sonographer] I had felt it when I was taking the Metro [the subway]. She said that wasn't it, that I couldn't feel it until a few more weeks. I thought for sure it was the baby moving, but I guess not. (Teresa, 27, small business owner)

I heard only a few other comments suggesting that becoming transparent is not always desirable:

I found it was hard to get a whole picture. To tell you the truth, like, it was very interesting and I'm glad to find out that everything is

okay and developing normally, but it just felt like I was looking at ...
I don't know. Like I wasn't even sure that it was inside me. (Sylvie,
25, chef)

Ultrasound does more than separate the pregnant woman from what
lies within her body; it also reconnects the two in specific ways. This
process is a clear example of what Joe Dumit and Robbie Davis-Floyd
(1998) call the One-Two Punch of Technocracy: first, ultrasound conceptually separates woman and fetus; then it comes to be seen as
vital to the process of reconnecting the two, and as a site for instruct-
ing women about their 'proper' relationship to this new individual.
Throughout this process of translation, separation, and reconnection,
women are subjected to increased surveillance. As sonographers carry
out the scan, they mediate not only the bodily and physical connections between woman and fetus, but also the emotional attachment
between the two, and their social relationship.

This relationship is strongly affected by pervasive notions of risk
and potential pathology. As I discussed earlier, the idea that the fetus
is at risk from genetic disorders, from maternal age, from environmental hazards, from poor maternal diet, and so on, is central to both
medical-scientific and popular discourses on pregnancy in Canada.
The notion of risk during pregnancy constructs 'objective conditions
of danger' and at the same time offers means for preventing or mini-
mizing that danger (Quéniart 1992: 164). Risk is what has justified the
routinization of ultrasound fetal imaging, and the insecurity that risk
creates is what has long compelled women to undergo ultrasound.
The need to do routine scans is confirmed when impairments and
complications are 'caught' through ultrasound.

At the same time, the reconnection of woman and fetus through
ultrasound crystallizes a set of ideas about the relationship mothers
should have with their offspring. Simply by having an ultrasound, the
woman is demonstrating that she is a 'good mother' – responsible,
altruistic, and willing to reduce risks to the fetus. While examining the
fetus, the sonographer assesses the pregnant woman's connection to
it. Does she show the 'right' amount of interest in the fetus? Does she
seem too interested in knowing fetal sex? Does she seem to be a suit-
able parent? In most cases this evaluation is unconscious; the sonographer interprets her statements, behaviour, and appearance in the
context of a tacit set of ideas about 'good' mothers. The notion of 'risk'
intensifies the moral and emotional dimensions of this social relationship between woman and fetus. For the women in this study, the

pleasure of hearing that 'everything is okay' confirmed the value of ultrasound and the need to see inside the black box of pregnancy. At the same time, when fetal imaging 'revealed' a low-risk fetus, and when the sonographer perceived a 'nice' woman, the woman was more likely to be 'shown' the baby in some detail. This is not to contend that ultrasound produces a fetal subject, which is then accepted or resisted by the woman. Rather, women, their companions, and sonographers produce the fetal subject through their interaction. 'Showing the baby' engages them all in a dialogue that may or may not improve a woman's comprehension of the image, but that usually alleviates her anxiety, pleases her and her partner, and offers a site for her to publically demonstrate her worthiness as a good mother.

Women who are 'different' – that is, who are regarded by sonographers as unemotional, too emotional, disinterested, or interested in the 'wrong' things – may provoke a different kind of narrative. In some cases, sonographers respond to such women with relative silence, offering brief, unelaborated descriptions of the image that constrain the pleasures of 'seeing' the baby. The ultrasound image is sometimes used as a window onto an endangered fetal self or onto a woman whose body or behaviour must be corrected. Ultrasound images of the placenta and a smaller-than-average fetus may be utilized to show the woman the effects of her smoking habits. A grainy, hard-to-see image may be used to reveal to the woman the effect on the fetus of her obese body or of multiple pregnancies. Fetal size ('intrauterine growth retardation') and the risk of miscarriage 'show' the woman she must constrain her activities and rest in bed. The ultrasound image may also be used to 'prove' to her the need for a caesarean delivery. In the United States, this proof has occasionally been used to justify court-ordered caesareans against the wishes of the woman (Irwin and Jordan 1987).

In short, for many of the women in this study, the fetus encountered during the ritualized, technological, and public quickening of ultrasound transformed both the lived sensation of pregnancy and its social reality. Clearly, for these women, ultrasound's greatest power lay in its ability to 'show' them their baby at around eighteen weeks into the pregnancy. These women perceived the experience generally as empowering – as enabling them to wear maternity clothes, announce the pregnancy, and otherwise 'be pregnant' both publicly and physically. Through ultrasound, the fetus was personified, made into a distinctive individual; it was no longer simply a generalized object of scientific imagery or maternal desire.

Yet ultrasound images do not by themselves make women into mothers, or fetuses into babies. Ultrasound is only one of the many practices through which pregnant women mobilize notions of fetality and motherhood. The shift from 'being pregnant' to 'having a baby' begins before the first ultrasound and involves multiple signifiers, including quickening, hearing the fetal heart beat, and bodily changes. That being said, the power of the ultrasound arises from the specific cultural and social contexts in which it is used, and from the specific life experiences of individuals. Some of those specifics can be discerned by considering the similarities in women's accounts.

Common Visions

Accounts of pregnancy and fetal imaging were strikingly similar among the women I interviewed. This point deserves further discussion, since it underscores the extent to which ultrasound's vision of the fetus and of themselves made sense and seemed 'natural' to them. As is likely true for many women in Canada, they were accustomed to thinking they needed expert medico-scientific knowledge and technological help to understand, diagnose, and treat their own bodies. Unable to entirely trust their own bodily sensations and imaginings, they sought out that other knowledge to 'meet' or 'experience' their developing fetus. Universal and comprehensive health insurance in Canada now includes at least one prenatal scan, and many Canadian women now expect this technologically mediated introduction to the fetus. In Montreal, ultrasound has been part of prenatal care for at least a generation, and at 'English hospitals' like the Met, multiple ultrasounds are the norm. Through the experiences of women friends and kin, knowledge of what ultrasound is supposed to show has seeped deep into the popular consciousness. For example, some guidebooks not only tell women why ultrasound is done, but how to experience the scan:

> Bring your partner with you, so you can share the special moment when you 'see' your baby for the first time. (Corporation professionnelle des médecins du Québec 1990: 10)

> If the apparatus used has a TV-like viewing screen, it provides a unique opportunity to 'see' your baby – and maybe even get a sonogram photo

to show to friends and family – though it may take an expert to make out
a head or buttocks in the blurry image. (Eisenberg et al. 1991: 45)[4]

The similarities among the women's accounts also underscored the
extent to which they relied on the sonographer to 'find' their baby for
them in the confusing mass of echoes. Undoubtedly, the accounts offered by the women in this study were similar partly because their
ultrasounds were all conducted at the same hospital. The sonographers
at the Met were proud of what they called 'knowing how to talk to
patients' and of their ability to personalize and make pleasurable what
might otherwise be a dry and unexciting routine clinical procedure.
The obstetricians' claims to authority over radiologists in producing
and interpreting fetal images also played a significant role here, as did
the sonographers' conviction that 'showing the baby' was good for
women – that it reduced their anxiety and helped them to accept the
pregnancy.

The similarities between the women's narratives and those of the
sonographers highlighted the deep interconnections between popular
and medical-scientific views of pregnancy, the fetus, and ultrasound
in Canada. As Lindenbaum and Lock (1993: 147) remind us, 'forms of
knowledge that are not widely shared are difficult to incorporate into
the diagnostic and therapeutic practices of biomedicine.' Notwithstand-
ing differences in terminology and in how knowledge was expressed,
the sonographers and pregnant women at the Met were members of
the same broad culture and shared many assumptions about the fetus
and about pregnancy in general. This was, perhaps, especially true of
relations between the women and the technicians, since they were
often of similar age and life status, and since the sonographers tended
to be women. Well before the first routine ultrasound, as they read
about the fetus and changed their diets and activities, the women
envisioned the fetus as active, sentient, and susceptible to their actions
and moods. For many women the ultrasound image, with its strong
suggestions of fetal agency and subjectivity, was exactly what 'common sense' told them to expect.

Few of the women expressed negative feelings or were critical of
ultrasound while they were pregnant. Only a handful of them expressed any dissatisfaction with the accounts sonographers offered
them. The cultural apparatus of ultrasound was accepted by the women
as the 'natural' way to understand the fetus, and rarely intruded on or

competed with their own bodily (but no less cultural) sensations or their own ideas and fantasies of the fetus. After listening to the sonographer lay claim to the fetus, some women – like Teresa, who had felt fetal movement while she was riding on the subway – tried to (re)assert the importance of their own bodily awareness in detecting fetal movement and determining fetal age and gender. But the women rarely won these contests over knowledge about the fetus. For example, estimates of fetal age based upon ultrasound measurements nearly always took precedence in physicians' reports over the estimates the women gave. The women might voice their disagreement with the ultrasound evidence about fetal age or size to their family and friends, but few expressed their opinions to physicians.

It is possible that very few of the women were critical of ultrasound while they were pregnant because they felt so dependent on the technology. For many of the women, the first few months of pregnancy brought about a heightened sense of the possibilities of their own body. They talked at length about the subtle changes in its shape and appearance, and they worried openly about whether it was normal, and whether it would fail. Anxious about miscarriage and fetal abnormalities, many of the women hesitated to tell friends and extended family about the pregnancy or to signal their changing status by wearing more comfortable maternity clothing; in effect, they were putting the pregnancy 'on hold' until after they had 'passed' the first ultrasound exam (see Browner and Press 1995 for this point in connection with another form of prenatal diagnosis – the alpha-fetoprotein or AFP blood test.) Paradoxically, as Quéniart (1992: 167) has pointed out, 'the need for reassurance at all costs ... means ... taking risks.' Although many of the women I interviewed were unsure of the long-term effects of ultrasound on the fetus, they were willing to undergo ultrasound in order to 'avoid' the risk of an abnormal newborn.

Reworking, Resisting, and Reflecting

While the accounts of these women showed strong similarities, there were also variations which suggest that they engaged this conventionalized discourse of fetal subjectivity, risk, and bonding from within the possibilities and constraints of their own particular subject positions.

Variations in women's 'commitment,' as Rayna Rapp (1990) calls it, to medical discourse explains some of these variations. The strongest criticisms of ultrasound, and the sharpest disagreements with its findings, were expressed mainly by nine women (18 per cent of those interviewed). These nine, like most of the women in the study, read avidly during pregnancy. However, they were more likely than the others to invoke the language of science and medicine in describing the fetus and ultrasound. They also tried to model their pregnancies on the idealized versions in their guidebooks; they then expressed anxiety and frustration when the 'facts' in the books seemed to bear little relationship to their felt experiences:

> I thought I'd feel different, more maternal, more pregnant. I keep looking in the book, but nothing's happening! (Sylvie, 25, chef)

> Once again it's like I've heard the heart beat and I've seen it. But I still don't feel it and I still don't feel pregnant. So, no. It's almost weirder. One more piece of evidence seeing that there is something there, but I don't feel it. (Elaine, 28, social worker)

Keenly attuned to the discourse on risks, and embodying the self-disciplining woman encountered in their advice books, Tamara and the other women in this group 'worked' at being pregnant. During my early conversations with them, these women described their efforts to prepare their lives (saving money, accomplishing certain career goals) and their bodies (dieting, charting ovulation, letting their 'system clean out' after years on the Pill) for pregnancy. They also recounted their attempts to avoid or manage the nausea, fatigue, and early weight gain of pregnancy. Several women in this group kept detailed diaries to record their prenatal experiences. Typically, their descriptions of fetal development were detailed, and included specific and discrete events (e.g., the end of the embryonic and beginning of the fetal stage) and specific body parts (e.g., describing individual internal organs rather than saying 'the insides of the baby'). Many tried to reproduce the vocabulary of their guidebooks and to recount the developmental events in what they perceived to be the correct sequence. Intent as they were on memorizing the stages of fetal development, their accounts often sounded synoptic and abstract, like a summary of 'how a baby develops' without reference to themselves or to their own bodies. Some found the fetal images in their guidebooks alienating and hard to reconcile with their 'imagined baby':

> When I was first pregnant, I wanted to know every day what stage the baby was at, what feet were growing, and what toenails were

happening. But it's like I know that it's in there, but it's hard. Maybe when I see the ultrasound ... but it's hard to put the two together, to know that everything that is in the book is in your stomach. (Karen, 26, university student)

The women who adopted the 'medical-scientific' perspective as they encountered it in their guidebooks tended to regard the ultrasound images – and those same guidebooks – as simultaneously empowering and frustrating, authoritative and alien. (See Rapp 1990: 40 for a similar observation among white middle-class women in New York City.) Like Tamara, they were eager to 'bond' yet found the ultrasound 'technical.' Eager to read and know 'everything' about pregnancy and fetal development, they found themselves increasingly anxious after reading and often complained of 'knowing too much about what could go wrong.' Not insignificantly, the four women whose backgrounds included biological sciences were in this group. Paradoxically, those women who were most familiar with the discourses of biomedicine, and most attentive to the advice in their pregnancy manuals, may have been the least reassured by ultrasound. Their anxiety about fetal abnormality heightened their desire to see the fetus and rendered them especially dependent on the sonographer's assessment of fetal normality. At the same time, their anxiety about the limitations of ultrasound, and their assumptions about the pervasiveness of risks, meant that they left the ultrasound still craving that reassurance or, like Tamara, reassured only briefly.

Ten of the women (roughly 20 per cent) read the advice books somewhat differently, and were somewhat less likely to swallow whole the medical-scientific discourse in those books, or the findings of their ultrasound. Generally, the women in this group were less intent on managing the physical and emotional changes of pregnancy, and did not view pregnancy as an event they had to do something about. Although they accepted the importance of 'eating properly' and 'avoiding stress,' they did not manage and monitor their bodies to the same extent as the women in the first group. While conversant in the language of risks during pregnancy, several women in this group talked about the outcome of the pregnancy as ultimately not in their control. For some, like Rosa, the health of the infant was going to be a matter of 'fate' or 'destiny' and not mainly the result of their own efforts. In addition, the healthy offspring of female kin offered persuasive evidence of their own ability to have a healthy baby. In general, the women in this group used the medical-scientific narrative in their guidebooks as a background reference point, not as a protocol they needed to reproduce *verbatim* or 'get right.' For these women, the order, timing, and scientific vocabulary of fetal development were less important than what they were imagining, desiring, and experiencing. They tended to personalize what they read, referring to *their* baby and *their* stage of pregnancy. Unlike the women who regarded the popularized medical models as standards against which to measure themselves, the women in this second group perceived ultrasound images as alternative or additional sources of information about the fetus, not as the definitive source. Physicians, sonographers, and guidebooks might have something useful and instructive to say about pregnancy and the fetus, but so did mothers, friends, and the clerk at the local *depanneur* [corner store].

Some studies suggest there is a relationship between social class and 'commitment' or 'resistance' to biomedical discourses (Lazarus 1988, 1994; Martin 1987; Rapp 1993; Georges 1997). Yet the relationship between social class (i.e., education, income, and employment) and commitment to the narratives of medical science is variable. Most of the women I interviewed were 'middle class,' yet the sample also included women who were clearly 'working class,' and a few who might be called 'upper class.' Among the interviewed Canadian women generally, perceptions of pregnancy and fetal imaging are by no means a simple reflection of social class differences. The women in this study who adhered closely to medical-scientific narratives tended to be university educated and working in 'white collar' professions. Those who expressed less commitment tended to have lower incomes and less education and to work in service sector jobs. Based on her research among women in Boston, Emily Martin (1987) concluded that low-income, less-educated, working-class women were more likely to resist dominant medical-scientific narratives of the body because of their socially marginalized position. However, the variable 'effect' of social class in my own research is indicated by the presence of educated, professional, financially secure women in the 'less committed' group. Thus, a weaker commitment to the dominant obstetrical discourse may stem from being socially marginalized, or from being socially empowered to pick and choose from within that discourse and to draw from additional sources of authority (e.g., family, friends, midwifery, intuition).[5] A stronger tie to biomedical discourses may derive, in part, from feelings of insecurity about one's ability to cope with pregnancy and childbirth, and from anxiety about fetal impairments and miscarriage. Clearly, the narratives and experiences of several of the women, including Tamara and Marie-Claude, exemplified this sense of vulnerability, which was engendered and perpetuated by biomedical models of childbearing.

'Commitment,' then, to the dominant biomedically organized narratives in which ultrasound is embedded is not absolute and fixed. This point is particularly noteworthy, since the women I interviewed began their pregnancies convinced that pregnancy and childbirth required the expert care of an obstetrician, not a general practitioner, and certainly not a midwife. However, within their particular life contexts, they did not follow biomedical advice by rote, but rather by accommodation, interpretation, and negotiation.[6] When I followed these women's experiences through the second routine scan and on through childbirth, I found that their stories pointed to a more complex and uneven effect. By the second scan, around thirty weeks into pregnancy, nearly all the women regarded fetal movements – felt directly rather than seen through ultrasound – as meaningful signs of fetal health, sentience, character, emotion, and behaviour. By post-partum, the ultrasound has become, for many women, just another medical procedure. Their ambivalence, complaints, resistance, and multiple interpretations complicate both the notion of medicalization and their commitment to dominant discourses.

Not unexpectedly, women's self-definition as either 'pro-life' or 'pro-choice' explains some of the variation in their ideas about fetality. Of the thirty-seven women in the study who were willing to articulate their stance on abortion, over one-third (13) were 'pro-life' and just under two-thirds (24) were 'pro-choice.' As I discussed in chapter 4, most of the women I interviewed held notions of the fetus that mirrored the highly personified narratives on fetal development in their advice books. Thus, nearly all of the women spoke of the 'baby' inside them as active, aware, and sensitive to their moods. In contrast to 'pro-choice' women, those who were 'pro-life' were convinced and willing to state that the fetus was a person. The 'pro-life' women also tended to say that the fetus was sentient and conscious from conception, resembled a newborn from very early in the pregnancy, and was capable of intentional thought prior to delivery. Roughly one-third of the 'pro-life' women also said that decisions on abortion belonged, ultimately, to the woman.

While two different subject positions are discernible here, they are not without overlap. Women who described themselves as 'pro-choice' might still refer to the fetus in their own body as unconditionally a person. Moreover, as I noted in chapter 4, among the entire group, women's notions of the fetus were not neatly articulated, but emerged in brief utterances, casual references, and off-hand remarks. In response to my requests that they elaborate on their statements about fetality, women usually said, 'I can't explain it,' or 'I haven't really thought about it.'

The fetus is a recent arrival in our cultural landscape, and many of us are still stumbling to put our images of and thoughts about the fetus into words. There is, however, a more significant dimension to the indefinite answers given by the women in this study. Attributing a kind of agency and sentience to the fetus, but not articulating either the specifics of those attributes or their implications, makes it possible for a woman to 'bond' and then later, if need be, to 'disengage.' In a society that simultaneously valorizes women and blames them for the outcome of their children, that constructs pregnancy as 'natural' yet in need of constant technological and medical monitoring, and that expects women to love their fetus unconditionally while undergoing tests to determine its viability, women's notions of fetality are indeterminate and contingent for solidly pragmatic reasons. That women's notions of fetality are malleable does not mean they are insincere, opportunistic, or false. Nor does it mean that women's notions of fetality are intrinsically 'natural,' or a kind of biologized intuition. Rather, women's notions of fetality accommodate the complex social demands and personal meanings surrounding pregnancy. The dichotomous language of self versus other, of a separate person lying inside the body of a woman, does not adequately reflect women's diverse experiences of pregnancy and fetality. Neither does the assumption that women, having ultrasound and reading advice books, will passively accept being controlled by dominant fetocentric messages. On the contrary, being pregnant at this particular historical moment requires women to be tremendously socially adept. Their statements and practices of fetality reveal their agility in negotiating the complex demands as well as the pleasures, and absurdities, of growing another human inside their bodies. In this context, it is clear that women may seek out the apparent immediacy and veracity of the ultrasound fetus in order to legitimate their bodily changes, verify that they have made the 'right' choices, and experience and enjoy 'their baby.'

For women and couples who are told that 'something is wrong with the baby,' the experience of ultrasound is markedly different. My current research on diagnoses of fetal impairment, and the experiences of several of the women in my Montreal study are worth noting. Their stories graphically illustrate the contingency and specificity of fetality; they also complicate our assumptions regarding medical control and sharpen our understanding of how experience is mediated through technology.

Not unexpectedly, learning that the fetus has a problem plunges women and their partners into a pool of anxiety, frustration, uncertainty, and sadness. Nearly all of the more than eighty individuals I have interviewed about this experience have made comments like this one, from a woman whose fetus was found to have a potentially lethal impairment: 'I feel as if everything is on hold.' This sense of disruption, and the anger and grief associated with that disruption, are broadly common to other stories of loss and suffering. We know that life crises such as the death of a family member and the diagnosis of a potentially life-threatening illness are characterized by a liminal period during which the sufferer feels 'out of' or separated from the everyday world (Turner 1969). In particular, the diagnosis of fetal impairment calls into question assumptions about the natural course of reproduction, the inevitable development from conception to bouncing baby, and the social transformation from 'expecting' parent to parent. That most couples terminate the pregnancy after a serious fetal anomaly is detected does not mean that their notion of fetality has changed fundamentally. Rather, what becomes key are the specifics of the impairment – its seriousness, degree of disfigurement, extent of paralysis, and so on – within the context of the couple's life circumstances (i.e., life stage, reproductive history, family support, coping ability, and so on). Also, the decision to terminate a pregnancy does not silence the discourse on 'bonding.' An increasingly common practice at Canadian hospitals encourages women and men to look at and hold the dead fetus delivered after the pregnancy is terminated. 'Bonding' at this point is articulated by social workers, nurses, and physicians, as well as by the involved women and men, as desirable to provide 'closure' and help along the grieving process.[7]

The narratives I am hearing from women and men following a diagnosis of fetal impairment are not dissimilar from those which follow a positive amniocentesis result.[8] Reactions to the prenatal detection of fetal impairment through either ultrasound or amniocentesis include grief over the loss of the hoped-for child, feelings of stigma, anger, and isolation, and uncertainty about one's ability to parent a child with a disability. Yet the technology of ultrasound may shape these experi-

ences in particular ways. One of the most commonly voiced senti-
ments among the women and men with whom I talked was that they
hadn't thought about the ultrasound in terms of its potential to detect
anomalies. One woman in my current research, whose routine ultrasound detected a lethal fetal impairment, bitterly expressed her un-
preparedness this way: 'We were so naïve. We thought we were going
to see the baby and get a nice photo.'

Informed consent must be given for amniocentesis; there is no such
requirement for ultrasound. This means there is no specific point at
which women can ask: 'Do I want to have ultrasound?' 'What information will it provide?' 'What will I do with this information?' While
amniocentesis is linked firmly in the public mind to images of clinical
tests and needles, and even to specific types of impairment (especially
'Down syndrome'), routine ultrasound's social meaning is very different. Ultrasound's association with pleasure, entertainment, and memorabilia can heighten feelings of loss and anger when the pregnancy
goes wrong.

Different Visions, Different Voices

During my research, I glimpsed other meanings of ultrasound and of
fetality in the narratives of immigrant women, and in considering
ultrasound fetal imaging in other cultural contexts.

Four of the women in my study were recent arrivals in Montreal.
They saw ultrasound mainly as a diagnostic test rather than as a means
of elaborating the social identity of the fetus. While they came from
different cultures (Sri Lankan Hindu, Armenian Christian, Lebanese
Muslim) and different social worlds (refugee, factory worker, student),
each of these women was a recent immigrant to Canada, and each was
unfamiliar with North American obstetrical traditions, including ultrasound and the discourse of maternal–fetal bonding. Their own alternative models of the doctor–patient relationship were suggested by
how they confirmed pregnancy. Most of the women in the study missed
a period, conducted a home pregnancy test, and *then* went to a physician for confirmation that they were 'really pregnant'; in contrast, the
four immigrant women missed a period and then waited a further
four to six weeks in order to 'be sure' they were pregnant before
seeing a physician. From the perspective of all four women, who were
unacquainted with North American obstetrical narratives on reproduction and fetal development, pregnancy was not about the fetus.

They said very little about the fetus and believed that it could not see, hear, or feel anything, nor could it sense the woman's emotional state until near delivery. Believing the sixteen-week fetus to be 'unformed' and without any human form, and unfamiliar with *in utero* fetal images, they were surprised to hear the sonographer describing fetal limbs, digits, and facial features during the first ultrasound. After her first ultrasound, one of these women repeated several times that she had thought the baby 'was just a blob.' Linguistic interference during either the interview or the ultrasound was only one factor at work here. Perhaps a significant factor was that each of these women received a relatively unadorned description of the fetal image. All four believed the test to be 'for the doctor,' and none had been socialized into proper 'ultrasound etiquette'; thus, to the sonographers, they seemed relatively disinterested in the image. That, as well as their lack of fluency in French or English, signalled their difference to the sonographers, and this difference in turn largely silenced the sonographer's descriptions of the fetal image. While the group was so small that I cannot generalize from their accounts to any particular patterns of cultural variability, or even describe 'the immigrant experience' of obstetrical ultrasound in Montreal, the distinctiveness of their accounts suggest that important cultural differences exist, and that women vary across cultures in how they relate to the sites and sources of authoritative knowledge. Given Canada's socially and culturally diverse population, the different possibilities that ultrasound holds for women of different medical traditions – and for disabled women, lone-parent women, very young or older women, lesbians, and women planning midwife-assisted home births – is fertile ground for future research.

Ultrasound in the United States, Ecuador, the Philippines, and Greece

The different metaphors and assumptions that framed the accounts given by the women I interviewed signal that links exist between the meaning of fetal images, the gatekeeper role of sonographers, and women's life experiences and cultural and social worlds. But what do we know about how body, power, and ultrasound technology intersect outside of Canada, and beyond North America?

It is tempting to claim that wherever obstetrical ultrasound diffused from its origin in Glasgow, a common set of assumptions followed regarding pregnancy, women, and fetuses: that ultrasound is by definition a patriarchal and repressive instrument of 'technodocs' (Arditti et al. 1984; Corea 1985; Corea et al. 1987; Spallone 1989); that it is an 'obstetrical fantasy' about men controlling women's bodies (Petchesky 1987: 68–71); or that it is one of many 'strategies for educating women to be good mothers' (Oakley 1984: 185). Another assumption is that fetal images always show an autonomous fetal subject. While these interpretations of ultrasound, and of reproductive technology in general, alert us to the close connections and hegemonic relations between technology, capitalism, and the politics of reproduction (Rothman 1989), they are based on assumptions that are problematic in the context of both feminist and contemporary cross-cultural thinking. Specifically, these readings presume not only some stable meaning inherent in fetal images, but also a universal notion of personhood, an essentialized, naturalized Woman, and polarized oppositional relations between men and women, and between medicine and everyday life. Rapp (1997: 33) astutely describes the problems this claim creates for feminist anthropologists:

> It is an enduring irony of contemporary feminist thought that 'we' who are most likely to benefit from the technologies of modernity often count ourselves amongst their strongest critics. Our discourse too often mirrors a familiar conundrum: either we march in lockstep with obstetric-technologists with whom we share a worldview of interventionist cultural control over nature (Davis-Floyd 1992), or we are aligned with an anti-technological romanticism to which we often attach a feminine label (cf. Corea 1985; Rothman 1989).

The end result, Rapp concludes, is to silence and marginalize 'all other experiences and their interpretation.'

The experiences of American women with ultrasound parallel closely those of the women in my study (Morton 1993; Taylor 1993, 1998; Rapp 1997, 1999). In the United States, during routine ultrasound, women and their partners get some clinical information about the fetus and pregnancy. Also, they are expected to be interested in and to enjoy ultrasound, and they are encouraged to bond with the image. Sonographers and many women understand these fetal images to be pictures of an autonomous fetal agent possessing an individual appearance, character, and subjectivity. Based on her fieldwork in an American hospital, Janelle Taylor (1993: 8) suggests that 'the ultrasound exam may convey the message that "birth" is not something

that only women can do – babies are brought into the world by medical experts, technologies, and institutions.' Given the shared medical
models of pregnancy and childbirth management, this claim could
also be made for ultrasound in Canada. Like the Canadian women I
interviewed, the women in Christina Morton's California study (1993)
regarded ultrasound as an especially compelling version of the fetus;
however, they also constructed the fetus by engaging in a variety of
other 'interactional practices,' including monitoring bodily changes,
reading pregnancy guides, and observing fetal movement.

The fact that collections of echoes pass easily for 'baby's first picture' in both Canada and the United States is not surprising. Yet the
similarities in interpretation are not evidence of ultrasound's 'objective' meaning; rather, they make sense given the broad similarities in
Canadian and American culture and social organization. Both countries are 'federally organized, industrialized liberal democratic states'
whose major institutions are founded on assumptions of liberal individualism (Teghtsoonian 1996: 119; Rothman 1989). Many Canadians
balk at some of the individual rights enshrined in the U.S. Constitution (most notably, the right of individuals to own firearms). Also,
many Canadians may be dismayed by recently rejected proposals to
change the privatized American health care system to one more like
Canada's state-administered system. Nonetheless, the cultural and social connections run deep. Despite public and private sector attempts
to bolster 'Canadian content,' everyday life north of the 49th parallel
is saturated with American goods, services, images, and ideas.

Nonetheless, there are significant differences between the Canadian
and American situations, particularly where race, class, politics, and
health care intersect, and these differences raise interesting questions
for further research. Does the widespread availability of ultrasound in
private clinics in the United States foster the 'entertainment' and 'commodity' aspects of fetal imaging such as purchasing videos? In the
same vein, does it encourage having a scan 'just to see' or specifically
to determine the sex of the fetus (Taylor 1998)? How does the experience of pregnancy, fetality, and 'bonding' vary between wealthy American women and those who are poor, or of colour, or who are disen-
franchised in other ways? To what extent is ultrasound in the United
States shaped by the powerful American version of neoconservativism,
which promotes 'traditional' family forms and values, restrictive roles
for women, and anti-choice politics?

Outside the North American context, ethnographic accounts of ultrasound fetal imaging are beginning to emerge. Evidence of other practices and interpretations can be glimpsed in reports of ultrasound for sex selection in India and China (Hartmann 1995; Patel 1989). Harnessed to local cultural preferences for sons, ultrasound images (and amniocentesis) skew the demographics of gender and offer a site for controlling pregnant women. But are they also empowering? What 'benefits' come to a woman whose ultrasound shows she is carrying a son? Do images of daughters offer some women a pathway for resistance? How does the rhetoric of 'family planning,' differently articulated in China and in India, intersect with the meaning of fetal images? What do fetal images in these political economies say about persons – fetal, female, maternal, and other persons? Questions like these are stimulating researchers to look closely at ultrasound from a political and cross-cultural perspective.

On ultrasounds in Quito, Ecuador, Lynn Morgan (1994: 12) writes:

> The ultrasound monitor was oriented to face the physician, rather than the patient (as has become routine in the United States). The physician said little during the exam, nor did he 'read' the image to the woman by pointing out sex or body parts or size or activity levels of the fetus. He took pictures to include in the woman's medical chart; she did not ask for or expect to be given a 'fetal photo' for her refrigerator. She was apparently schooled to accept medical authority, so she deferred to the doctor's obscure and specialized knowledge. During the exam she watched the physician's face rather than the monitor, and she rarely asked a question. (The doctor explained to me that women are beginning to hear that ultrasound can determine sex, so they ask him about that more often now than a few years ago.) There is an air of anxiety in the room, as she waits to be told whether her pregnancy is at risk ... The purpose of the ultrasound, in other words, is not to introduce the mother/parents to their fetus, but to determine whether the pregnancy is advancing normally.

Women in Quito do not have ultrasound routinely, but rather, only if there is a suspected problem, and even then only if they can afford to pay. Yet Morgan's description of those scans, read against the experience of fetal imaging in the United States, strongly suggests that other cultural scripts are at work. The absence of a fetal subject in Ecuadorian ultrasounds makes sense, given the belief that the 'unborn are liminal, unripe and unfinished creatures' who may slip in and out of personhood (Morgan 1997: 329). For instance, a man who is unfaithful to his pregnant wife or a woman who continues to breastfeed during pregnancy 'may "undo" the nascent personhood of the unborn' (Morgan 1997: 346; 1994: 8). Furthermore, although both the Catholic Church and the government condemn abortion and many Ecuadorians regard abortion 'as a sin ... it is a sin of self-mutilation rather than murder. At issue is the mutilation of the pregnant woman's own body, not the personhood of the fetus' (Morgan 1997: 330).

Recently, as part of preliminary fieldwork, I watched prenatal ultrasounds in an urban area on the island of Negros in the central Philippines. Some government hospitals have ultrasound, which, if it happens to be operational, may be used for obstetrical emergencies and 'complex cases.' Ultrasound is also provided for those who can afford it at private clinics owned and operated by obstetricians. Some of the women at these clinics have been referred by their physicians, but many are 'walk-ins' in their last month or two of pregnancy. In the private clinics, as the scan begins the woman is asked what she wants to know. All of the women I observed, and 'nearly all' according to the obstetricians I spoke to, said they wanted to know if the baby was a boy or a girl. Besides determining fetal sex, the obstetrician examines fetal anatomy and turns the screen to point out some parts of the fetal image to the woman, but the entire examination lasts well under ten minutes. Little or no information about fetal health is reported to the woman, even if fetal demise or impairment is seen. A copy of the ultrasound report is sent to the woman's physician, but women are generally not told of any problems until after delivery. That women use the ultrasound to know the fetal sex is intriguing, but few probably intend to terminate a pregnancy based on the results. Not only is abortion illegal in the Philippines and repugnant to many Catholic women, but among Christian Filipinos, daughters as well as sons are desired.[9] Moreover, with an average family size of four children, the odds are that parents will have at least one son and one daughter. The question of why Filipinas want to have ultrasound will be explored in my upcoming research.

Abortion, personhood, religion, and ultrasound intersect differently again in a public hospital in Greece. Below, I draw extensively from Nia Georges's analyses of fetal imaging in Greece, including our previously published comparison of ultrasound in Greece and Canada

(Mitchell and Georges 1997). When juxtaposed, the Greek and Canadian accounts make very clear that what is 'seen' during ultrasound is not inherent in the technology; rather, it emerges out of particular configurations of culture, history, technology, and power.

In Greece as in Canada, fetal ultrasound is a routine procedure, with most women undergoing multiple scans over the course of a normal pregnancy. It is common for Greek women to have four or five scans during pregnancy, each lasting about five minutes.

> The [ultrasound] screen is generally turned toward the doctor. The woman can view it by craning her neck, but her eyes are often directed toward the doctor's face. Quickly and silently, the doctor scans the entire fetal image, then focuses on the genital area for a while. At this point, he may break his silence to announce 'girl' or 'boy' – unless the woman has already jumped in to tell him she doesn't want to know the sex. (This rarely happened, however.) Or he may tell the woman that the position or age of the fetus doesn't permit him to see the sex at this time and that he will look again next month. Finally, the doctor scans to the skull and freezes the image to measure the biparietal diameter (skull width). He checks a chart over the bed on which the woman is lying and announces the age of the fetus, in weeks and days. If the doctor himself does not tell the woman at this point that 'the baby is all right' (no anomaly was ever detected in the more than eighty sessions I observed), she will ask him. Most often, this is the only time she speaks. Finally the doctor wipes the gel from the woman's abdomen with a paper towel, and leaves. After pulling up her clothes, the woman follows the doctor back to the office. If her husband is with her, as was the case with about one-third of the women, they may exchange a few quick comments in the corridor, usually about the fetus's announced sex. (Georges 1997: 97)

The similarities with Canadian ultrasounds are striking. In Greece just as in Montreal, fetal ultrasound provides women with relatively little clinical diagnostic information, but considerable reassurance and pleasure. These parallels remind us that however it is locally configured, ultrasound is part of a package of biomedical knowledge that has diffused widely. That both Canadian and Greek women 'see' their baby in the blurry echoes may also index, as Georges and I have argued elsewhere (1997: 18), codes and conventions of visual realism that ultrasound shares with other technologies – television in particular. As members of the television generation, women in both locations are 'relatively flexible readers of images' (Condit 1990: 85); thus, they easily transform the recomposed echoes, pixels, and grey-scale shadows of the ultrasound's television-like monitor into 'a picture of my baby.'

Yet there are also striking differences. In Greece, women watch the sonographer, not the screen; physicians reveal only fetal age and sex, and expectant couples do not think of the ultrasound as an opportunity to 'meet their baby.' Significantly, the Greek women Georges interviewed 'never spoke of the fetus as an autonomous *in utero* subject' (Mitchell and Georges 1997: 391). Even though they looked to the ultrasound for confirmation that a fetus was present, Greek women did not see subjectivity, agency, and potentiality in the fetal image.

At the root of these differences between Greek and Canadian ultrasound are differing conceptions of personhood. The 'separate little person' visible to women in Montreal is grounded in a liberal philosophical tradition of society as a collection of 'isolated, atomistic individuals' (Rothman 1989: 89; 115). This conception informs statements by both women and sonographers that the fetus has its own personality, routines, and likes and dislikes. In Greece, however, 'fetal persons, like persons generally, are constituted processionally, across time, and relationally, through their connection with others, most importantly with family members, and not as autonomous and separate units' (Mitchell and Georges 1997: 19). This relational aspect of Greek fetal personhood is well illustrated by widely expressed concerns that individuals who are envious of a pregnant woman and those who are inattentive to her desires (especially her food cravings) may cause harm to the fetus (20–1).

Furthermore, ultrasound, risk, and bonding do not intersect in Greece in the same way as in Canada. In Canada, maternal–fetal bonding derives considerable emotional force from its rhetorical location as a 'natural' process. Yet this bonding is also conceptualized as a process that requires monitoring and sometimes instruction if the woman is to undertake it properly. In Greece, woman and fetus are physically and socially inseparable until delivery, so there is no ontological gap that needs to be bridged through bonding. Like women in Canada, Greek women are concerned about risks to the fetus. Some of these risks sound particularly 'Greek' (risk of infection or cold from bathing in the sea, harm brought about by the evil eye); others do not (risk from medication, poor diet, and genetic disorders) (Georges 1997: 96). In

Greek medical and lay narratives, just as in Canadian ones, some risks to the fetus are positioned in the activities of women; however, the 'problem' of Greek women is different. Whereas Canadian women need surveillance and instruction to deal with the unruliness of their personal habits and with the occasional persistent 'old wives' tale,' the problem in Greece is scientific illiteracy. Pregnant women in Greece are admonished by their physicians and guidebooks to be 'civilized,' and 'up to date' and to reject superstitions, and are thus encouraged to be 'modern' and 'progressive':

> Part of an ongoing and longstanding debate over national identity, these terms are ... part of a concatenated set of binaries such as traditional/ modern, East/West, Europe/Other, conservative/progressive and the like which have become 'paradigms of analysis of the modern Greek condition' (Panouryia, 1996: 28). Within this set, 'Europe' and 'European' are tropes that carry particular rhetorical force. Today, as in the preceding century, the idea of 'Europe' is closely related to what has been called a 'perennial crisis' in Greeks' sense of identity (is Greece part of the East/ Orient or of the West/Europe?) ... [In] practice, Greece is often regarded by the more powerful [Economic Union] states as a marginal, unruly and 'semi-Oriental' junior partner, whose capability of applying such Western values and institutions as rationality and efficiency remains an open question. (Mitchell and Georges 1997: 11–12)

In this context, Greek physicians who use ultrasound routinely and often during pregnancy, and women who desire ultrasound, are actively constituting themselves as modern. Modernity is not at stake for Canadian women and thus is nearly absent as a concept from their guidebooks and from their own reflections on prenatal care, ultrasound, and reproduction. What *is* at stake, as I have already noted, is their ability to negotiate the complex and often contradictory meanings of fetal personhood.

Many Canadians, like most of the pregnant women and their partners in my research, envision and engage with the fetus from early in pregnancy as if it were a separate individual, a sentient and rights-bearing subject. For them, the notion of the fetus as an active participant in pregnancy and even in the everyday social world of the pregnant woman seems 'natural' and common sense. Moreover, this construction of fetality is reinforced at each prenatal visit and amplified in advice books on pregnancy. At the same time, being pregnant is experienced as a process of conditions, evaluations, and uncertainties, rather than a state of absolutes and definitives.

Reproductive Politics in Canada

Around the time I began to study ultrasound, the battle over fetal persons and abortion rights was reaching a fever pitch. The old abortion law had been struck down in 1988 (see chapter 2) and politicians were debating proposed legislation, Bill C-43, that would redefine abortion as a medical procedure and amend the Criminal Code to allow abortion *only* if the woman's doctor determined that her health (physical, mental, psychological) or life would likely be threatened by the pregnancy. Alarmed by its ambiguous wording ('psychological health,' 'likely to be threatened') and by the possibility that the new legislation would allow criminal prosecution for abortion, physicians in many areas of the country withdrew their abortion services (Brodie 1992: 111). In July 1989, people in Montreal and across Canada opened their newspapers to read that the U.S. Supreme Court had upheld a Missouri law which declared that life began at conception, and which prohibited government employees from counselling about or providing abortions. Other pro-life states would follow suit. As the summer dragged on, Canadians followed media accounts of two pregnant women, Barbara Dodd in Ontario and Chantal Daigle in Quebec. Each of these women was faced with a belligerent ex-boyfriend who had managed to get a provincial court injunction to block her abortion (Morton 1992: 275). As the courts, the media, politicians, and pro-choice and anti-choice groups wrangled over the fate of Dodd and Daigle, the subject of fetal personhood and fetal rights became the centre of national attention. In its November 1989 ruling on Daigle's case, the Supreme Court of Canada overturned the injunction, ruling that male partners do not have the right to prevent a woman from having an abortion.[10] In 1991, in a case involving two midwives charged in a death during childbirth, the Supreme Court ruled that the fetus is not a person according to the Criminal Code (Fraser 1991). Although it passed in the House of Commons, Bill C-43 was defeated in the Senate; as a result, Canada has no federal abortion law.

In the intervening years, the fetal subject has gained considerable rhetorical and emotional force, even though fetal personhood is not recognized in Canadian law. By turns amplified and subdued in interpretations of ultrasound images, glossed in the language of medical science, and comically enlarged in films, the 'fetal baby' has become increasingly visible in the Canadian social landscape. Stories about fetal risks, diagnosis, and therapy and about the ongoing struggle over abortion rights appear regularly in the Canadian media. Warnings about dangers to the fetus are visible on cigarette packages, in liquor stores, and on stickers placed on the walls and in the toilet stalls of restaurants and bars. These warnings, in conjunction with the admonishments of advice books, physicians, friends and relatives, and the occasional stranger on the street, remind women that the fetus is in danger and that they are not only responsible for its well-being, but also under scrutiny. Refusing prenatal diagnosis, giving birth at home, and even drinking coffee may be interpreted as signs that a woman has made the 'wrong' choices or lacks the 'right' information and has put her own desires and pleasures ahead of the safety and well- being of the fetus. Women who are unwilling or unable to give up cigarettes, alcohol, illicit drugs, and all but essential medications during pregnancy are considered selfish. Those who engage in these taboo activities risk being excluded from the category of 'good mothers' and may be subject to increased surveillance, restriction, and instruction.[11]

In the summer of 1996, Ms G, a pregnant woman and the mother of three children – two of whom were brain damaged and in government care – was ordered into drug treatment by a Manitoba court (Gee 1996: D1). Although few acknowledged it, her fundamental rights over her own body were being interfered with. Her case was not the first instance in Canada of a state intervention in pregnancy being contested (see Ginn 1999 and Gavigan 1992), but the enormous amount of attention her case attracted, and the knee-jerk reactions of blame in the media and among the public, are disquieting.[12] Even though she had sought assistance for her drug problem and had been turned away by social services, this woman, in the public glare of the media and the courts, stood for what Cynthia Daniels (1997: 583) refers to as the symbolic 'anti-mother.' As in the American iconography of 'crack mothers' and 'welfare mothers' discussed by Daniels (1997), Ms G was demonized as the embodiment of the selfish, undisciplined pregnant woman. For some Canadians, that Ms G is an aboriginal woman further 'explained' her addiction and/or the state's attempt to force her into treatment (i.e., to prevent yet another aboriginal child from becoming a burden to society).

Many voices have been raised in Canada about Ms G, but only a handful have addressed the fact that 'fetal protection' often amounts to state surveillance of disadvantaged women under the guise of 'rescuing' 'endangered babies' from 'bad mothers.' Evidence from the United States and (to a lesser extent) Canada has shown that women of colour and low-income women are overrepresented in instances of state intervention during pregnancy (RCNRT 1993: 953; Whiteford 1995). Canadian lawyer Diana Ginn (1999: 128) sums up the ongoing problem: fetal protection measures 'fail to place responsibility where it belongs – on the state's failure to provide adequate resources for addiction treatment and the alleviation of poverty' – and, I would add, on unhealthy working conditions.

Canadian courts have been more resistant than American ones to the language of fetal persons and fetal rights. In the United States, pregnant women have often been forced into treatment (e.g., caesarean section) (Whiteford 1996; Irwin and Jordan 1987). The Supreme Court of Canada eventually ruled in Ms G's case that pregnant women cannot be forced into treatment under existing laws (Makin 1997). In some American states, homicide laws extend to the fetus (Brown 1999: A18; Perreaux and Wattie 2001). At least one Canadian woman has been charged with the attempted murder of her fetus; however, the judge dismissed that case since the fetus has no legal status (Tibbetts 1997: A8).[13] In almost two-thirds of American states, parents are permitted to bring a wrongful death suit when a fetus is killed – for example, in a car accident. However, in 1999 the Supreme Court of Canada ruled that a child cannot sue its mother for harm caused in the womb (Anderssen 1999: A3). In Canada, legal personhood begins at birth.

These rulings must not be read as a broad or enduring commitment by the Canadian judicial system to safeguard women's fundamental rights to basic health care and reproductive autonomy. A 1998 poll found that 79 per cent of Canadians believe that abortion decisions should rest with a woman and her doctor (CARAL 1998: 6); yet access to safe, legal abortion services varies widely from province to province, and one province, Prince Edward Island, has no abortion services at all. Women living outside the major urban centres must travel long distances at their own expense to obtain an abortion. Half of the country's provincial health care plans do not provide full payment for abortions – a violation of the Canada Health Act (CARAL 1999).[14] More and more hospitals are eliminating or reducing their abortion services, and fewer medical students in Canada are learning abortion procedures. Since 1994, three Canadian doctors have been shot or stabbed by anti-abortion activists (Luton 1998: 4); the most recent physical attack – the stabbing of Vancouver physician Garson Romalis – was in July 2000.[15] The harassment, threats, and violence directed at abortion clinics and providers continues to undermine Canadian women's access to safe, legal abortions.

The Supreme Court of Canada has ruled repeatedly that changing the laws to grant legal personhood to the fetus, to allow a fetus to sue a woman, or to grant the state increased powers to intervene in pregnancy is a matter for legislatures and not the courts. The prospect of turning these matters over to politicians is unsettling. As noted earlier, after the 1988 SCC decision the federal government tried unsuccessfully to pass new legislation on abortion. Bill C-43 not only recycled the discourse of medicalization but would have recriminalized abortion except where a physician determined the woman's health was threatened by the pregnancy. Since then, and similar to the recent trend in the United States, Canada has witnessed the rise of neoconservative, right-wing Christian politics, with its restrictive roles for women and openly anti-choice stance. Stockwell Day, the leader of the current federal opposition party, the Canadian Alliance (formerly the Reform Party), has stated that he is in favour of recriminalizing abortion and that public money should be used only to pay for abortions required to save a woman's life (CARAL 2000). Two proposals introduced recently into the House of Commons – one that would make most abortions ineligible for health care funding, and another that would amend the Criminal Code to recognize the fetus as a person – highlight the continued efforts of the religious right to have their minority views on the fetus, women, and family made into law. To date, although the Canada Health Act states that abortion is 'a medically necessary procedure that must receive full funding through provincial health care plans' (Anderson 1999: 4), provinces that restrict abortion funding have not been penalized by the federal government.

Since the courts have turned the question of fetal personhood over to elected politicians, the notions of fetality held by Canadians will be pivotal to the ongoing debate over abortion. Ideas about the fetus and pregnant women are powerfully intertwined with the practices of ultrasound. Is the use of routine ultrasound fetal images converting people to an anti-choice position? Where and how do ultrasound images of the fetus intersect with the increasingly entrenched and institutionalized controversies about abortion, fetal personhood, and state intervention in pregnancy, and with other reproductive issues?

From my perspective, what is troubling about ultrasound fetal imaging is not that it may suddenly and dramatically 'convert' individual parents to an anti-choice perspective. Some women's and men's ideas about the fetus, and possibly their views on abortion, may change based on what they see during ultrasound. However, pregnant women and their partners are often heavily invested, socially and emotionally, in their own particular fetus long before they see their first ultrasound image. Furthermore, despite the anti-choice rhetoric that 'if there were a window on a pregnant woman's stomach, there would be no more abortions' (Ginsburg 1989: 104), fetality is unstable and contingent. Most of the women I interviewed in Montreal continued to support a pro-choice position even while perceiving the fetus *they were carrying* as a person. Studies have shown that most women/couples facing a diagnosis of fetal impairment terminate the pregnancy even when they may deeply desire a child and be actively engaged in constructing the fetus as a member of their family. A clear majority of Canadians continue to support women's access to safe and legal abortion despite the routinization of obstetrical ultrasound imaging, the popularity of fetocentric advice books, and the sentimentalization of the fetus.

Nevertheless, Canadians who are concerned about the erosion of women's reproductive autonomy need to pay close attention to how ultrasound fetal imaging is used and talked about. Ultrasound is a powerful technology in large part because it transforms our embodied knowledge and, at the same time, normalizes experiences of pregnancy and fetality. Ultrasound is now deeply entrenched in prenatal care. It has become routine even though there is no compelling evidence that it positively affects the health of pregnant women or newborns. Having an ultrasound is now equated with 'responsible' behaviour on the part of pregnant women. That the women I interviewed equated ultrasound with 'looking at the baby,' rather than looking at their own bodily interiors or even 'at what's going on inside,' dramatically expresses our cultural preoccupation with the fetus as the central concern during pregnancy. Watching digitalized echoes on a monitor is widely perceived as a normal, direct way to experience – see, feel, appraise, communicate with – *in utero* 'babies.' 'Seeing' these 'babies' heightens women's and men's sense that the fetus is socially present, and strengthens the idea of the fetus as a subject and agent in their lives.

In short, we have come to think of ultrasound mainly as a site for experiencing the fetus and for producing fetal memorabilia. When we consume fetal images in this way, as 'baby pictures,' we diminish the possibility of seeing those images in other ways – as mobile and developing parts of a woman's body, as machine-generated representations of a fetus, or as specialized diagnostic tests. In approaching ultrasound images as if they were 'baby's first picture,' we are letting our attention be drawn toward individual women, fetuses, and families as sites of vulnerability and endangerment, and away from the social sources of anxiety, distress, risk, and loss during pregnancy. It is as if the ultrasound images seen each year in Canada by tens of thousands of pregnant women, spouses, kin, and co-workers have only personal significance, and none that is cultural or political.

So long as we continue to view images in this way, we will be masking the disquieting parallels between the images of the fetus deployed by anti-choice groups and those encountered in routine prenatal ultrasound.[16] Both anti-choice fetal images and routine prenatal ultrasound images are powerfully constructed of the apparati and discourses of medical science. Both types engage the viewer to 'witness' the fetus as natural, self-evident, and more relevant to pregnancy than the woman. Both highlight the minutiae of fetal bodies, as well as fetal agency, potentiality, and subjectivity. In both, the fetus is carefully constructed and focused, through image and language, to appear unambiguously human, equivalent to a 'baby,' and in need of protection (Petchesky 1990: 339; Condit 1990). Both types of images are embedded in emotional discourses about 'vulnerable babies' and particular kinds of women – 'good mothers' or irresponsible, self-interested ones. Significantly, both not only encourage the viewer to connect emotionally with the fetus, but also emphasize visualization rather than either corporeal sensation ('quickening') or the social relationship between woman and fetus, as the basis of that bond (Taylor 1998). 'Seeing the baby' during a routine ultrasound encourages the viewer to form an emotional and social tie with that particular, individualized fetus. In contrast, in anti-choice imagery, as Janelle Taylor (1998) argues, 'spectatorial kinship' is deployed to encourage the public to bond with and protect *all* fetuses. Through routine ultrasound imaging, the technologically generated experience of the fetus becomes risk-free, desirable, and even pleasurable. The political and social consequences of this are expressed by Janelle Taylor (1998: 38–9):

> The conditions have been established for arguing that the public may form a relationship with the fetus that is equally emotionally profound as that of the pregnant women – or indeed more profound, if the viewers have 'succeeded' in bonding with the fetus and the pregnant woman has, for whatever reason, 'failed.' In other words, the notion of ultrasound 'bonding' lays the groundwork for arguing that a relationship with an abstract image or idea of 'the fetus' can be just as deep and valid as, or indeed more profound than, an actual concrete specific relationship of a particular woman and her particular pregnancy.

I have argued in this book that what collections of echoes say about the fetus (if anything) emerges out of culturally shaped and historically shifting combinations of assumptions, representational styles, social relationships, technologies, and institutional agendas, as well as the multifaceted webs of beliefs, relationships, experiences and emotions in which individuals suspend those echoes. Identifying fetality as contingent and unstable is a vital step toward countering the powerful anti-choice rhetoric on fetality and reproduction. It is equally important to disrupt the conventional readings of fetal images and to harness the compelling 'reality' of ultrasound to agendas that support women's reproductive autonomy. In the concluding chapter, I suggest what might be involved in transforming ultrasound images into something other than 'baby's first picture.'

Chapter Eight

Re-Visions: Other Ways of Seeing

> By now, the curled-up profile, with its enlarged head and finlike arms, suspended in its balloon of amniotic fluid has become so familiar that not even most feminists question its authenticity (as opposed to its relevance).
>
> Petchesky (1990: xiv)

In this concluding chapter, I suggest how prenatal ultrasound might be used and interpreted in ways other than as 'baby's first picture.' My inspiration for this exercise came initially from Monica Casper's feminist ethnographic analysis of fetal surgery. At the end of her book, Casper (1998: 220) outlines 'what needs to be in place – clinically, socially, culturally, economically, ethically, and legally – to enable women to undergo fetal surgery safely, effectively, and autonomously.' The changes she outlines are wide-ranging, and include making fetal surgery safer and accessible to all women, while at the same time working 'to ensure that all pregnant women have access to good nutrition, regular physician or midwife visits, and clean, safe places to live' (224). She also advocates developing fetal surgery and abortion as options within a reproductive rights framework that both supports pregnant women's autonomy and agency and works to increase social support for women who are raising a child with disabilities. While Casper is writing mainly about the United States, her suggestions are vital to the broader social project of restoring women's agency to reproductive issues in Canada and elsewhere.

My own agenda in this chapter is somewhat more modest. I want to consider what kinds of changes could be made so that prenatal ultrasound highlights female subjects rather than fetal ones. Like Casper, I

consider it unlikely that fetocentric technologies and practices like ultrasound will be eliminated. Even though the routine use of this technology does not improve pregnancy outcomes, ultrasound will be difficult to dislodge. Ultrasound will continue to be widely regarded as
an essential means of managing even low-risk pregnancies. Several
other screening and diagnostic techniques now rely on seeing the fetus *in utero*. Amniocentesis, if it is going to be done, should be done
with ultrasound so as to avoid injury to the woman and to the fetus.
Screening maternal blood for biochemical indicators of Down syndrome, for other chromosomal changes, and for neural tube disorders
might once have been considered an alternative to ultrasound. Yet the
accuracy of this procedure seems to be dependent on ultrasound-
determined fetal age and visually assessed fetal markers. In short,
health care providers, pregnant women, and families now rely heavily
on and are emotionally wedded to the idea that ultrasound offers
'choice' and 'control' in childbearing.

If prenatal ultrasound is here to stay, then we need to think creatively and concretely about how ultrasound fetal images can be produced, talked about, and used in ways that acknowledge the culturally valued notion of 'choice,' but that highlight female rather than
fetal autonomy and agency.

Feminist and pro-choice interventions in the representational politics of fetality and abortion have taken a number of different forms.
One has been to de-emphasize the fetus and to avoid both fetal subjectivity and the use of fetal imagery. As Meredith Michaels (1999: 117)
describes this approach, 'in order to ... establish the *significance* of
women as persons, it was left to feminism to establish the relative
insignificance of fetuses. Hence, the feminist fetus was nothing more
than a blob of protoplasm, and pregnancy nothing more than a condition of woman's body, the fetus akin to a tumor.' Representing fetality
as nothing more than tissue, or representing pregnancy as being only
about the interests of women, runs the risk of denying and ostracizing
the lived experiences of many women. It also inadvertently supports
the construction of the woman-fetus relationship in terms of incom-
patible interests. That framework of antagonism is vital to the anti-
choice position.[1]

Other pro-choice approaches have been similarly concerned with
restoring women's bodies to the visual and textual accounts of pregnancy and reproduction, and with restoring women as central agents
in the abortion issue. Some arguments have tended to emphasize, on

the one hand, the personhood, autonomy, and individuality of women, and on the other hand, the relationality of woman and fetus. Thus, it is a woman's relationship to the fetus, as she chooses to construct it, that counts. In contrast to the female and fetal essentialism and individualism that is so common to anti-choice narratives, the notion of relationality acknowledges that there are 'different fetuses in specific women's bodies at different stages in women's lives' (Oaks 1999: 193).

My research with women in Quebec and British Columbia strongly suggests that it makes sense to approach fetality as necessarily emergent, contingent, and intimately grounded in the specific life world of the pregnant woman. Yet relationality can also place an undesirable emphasis on the biological connection between a women and a fetus at the same time that it presumes two distinct corporeal beings.[2] In addition, the idea of a *relationship* has been harnessed with great affectiveness to the notion of 'fetal risk' and maternal responsibility, and underlies the notion that the fetus must be protected and the mother closely monitored. Any acknowledgment that fetality is constructed and contingent rather than inherent and absolute must be supported legally, politically, and socially by mechanisms that accord women both the right and the opportunity to wield that interpretive power. At the same time, as Laurie Oaks (1999: 194) cautions, we as 'feminists need to be prepared for what we might hear when women's private experiences enter public debate.' Women do not present a uniform voice on fetality, pregnancy, or abortion. Relationality does not mean eliminating fetal subjects from the debates around reproductive health and freedoms. Rather, it means opening up a space to include rather than assume or enforce the possibilities of fetal agents.

A number of visual artists, film makers, feminist theorists, and reproductive rights advocates have produced works that are intentionally disruptive of the anti-choice narrative.[3] For some, the point of departure is that visually arresting anti-choice fetal imagery must be countered by something more than absent fetuses or the now conventionalized 'coat hook' images of illegal abortion. In other words, rather than arguing that women's deaths are the only antidote to fetal life, we need images that attach new meanings to pregnancy, fetality, and abortion and that significantly reframe reproductive rights in terms other than maternal versus fetal rights. One example of an attempt to recover the terrain of reproduction is video artist Sherry Millner's 'Womb with a View' (1999). Millner chronicles pregnancy from the embodied perspective of a pregnant woman (herself). Although not often visualized, the fetus is not absent. Rather, fetality emerges in the ambiguities, discomforts, and humour of Millner's bodily expansion ('self-inflation'), her pleasure in her increased sensuality, her dialogue with her partner, and their encounters with conventionalized discourses of childbirth and infant care. Another set of images – this time intentionally non-realist ones – is offered by feminist philosopher Laurie Shrage. Shrage (forthcoming: 32) employs Barbie as the vehicle for a series of 'parodic images that draw critical attention to what the pro-life movement is doing with its imagery': '*Post-Porn Reproductive Barbie* would come with a non-detachable *Fetal Barbie* inside her. To view *Fetal Barbie*, owners would press the internal flashlight mechanism to make *Fetal Barbie* visible inside big Barbie's womb ... *Breeder Barbie* would feature the proverbial leaf over crotch image. The instructions read, "pull back the leaf and you'll see that Barbie is *really* two Barbies, not one"' (forthcoming: 28).

Shrage (28) suggests that 'such images may encourage viewers to reflect on how the ... "pro-life" ... fetus is better groomed for sentimental value and stardom or, in other words, how the "pro-life" fetus is what Duden calls a managed image.' It may be that women who are unfamiliar with postmodern and feminist codes and conventions of interpretation and social commentary will dismiss Shrage's and Millner's unconventional representations as undecipherable, élitist, or irrelevant. More widely accessible representations are envisioned when Shrage (forthcoming: 19) asks: 'Can we change the social meaning of abortion so that it becomes associated with delayed, planned, and responsible reproduction, rather than the wrongful destruction of human life? Can we represent the evils of involuntary pregnancy, without representing the fetus as an evil doer or the pregnant woman as desperate enough to use a coat hanger? For, even if women do not resort to bad abortions, policies leading to involuntary pregnancies are bad and we need some way to show this.'

Shrage also suggests how fetal imagery might be used in the service of progressive social reforms such as universal health care in the United States. Given the current crisis in Canada's health care system, similar messages supporting increased health care funding and opposing the development of a two-tiered health care system could be usefully applied here. Fetal images could also be used creatively to focus our attention not on the bodies and behaviour of pregnant women, but rather on the myriad ways that corporations and governments inflict harm on reproducing women and men, as well as fetuses (Daniels

1999). Fetal images or, even better, images of pregnant women could be deployed effectively against cigarette manufacturers to highlight the close connections between smoking, poverty, and the widening gaps in the Canadian network of social assistance, or to advocate for a long overdue national child care program.

What concrete possibilities do these alternatives suggest for the practices of ultrasound fetal imaging? The list that follows is meant to be practical and concrete; it is also just a beginning. Undoubtedly, other ways to practice and narrate prenatal ultrasound will be proposed, and I look forward to hearing about them.

1. *Using ultrasound selectively rather than routinely*
Given the evidence now offered by several review panels (see chapter 2), the practice of using ultrasound routinely for all or most pregnant women seems unwarranted. From the perspective of health care economics, prenatal care, and women's health, ultrasound imaging should be used selectively. Which criteria will be used for determining that ultrasound is necessary is a matter for discussion among local health boards, whose members should include consumers, physicians, women's health advocates, policy makers, disability rights advocates, and technology assessment experts. That being said, I would argue that the most important criterion for doing ultrasound is not medical, but social – a woman's informed choice.

2. *Informed choice*
An effort needs to be made to ensure that all women who are offered ultrasound have the opportunity and the resources to make an informed decision about whether they want the procedure. Here I am specifically using the term 'informed choice' rather than 'informed consent.' Too often, informed consent simply involves asking the woman, 'Do you understand the reason for doing this test?' 'Are you aware of the risks?' and 'Do you have any questions?' Sometimes the woman is provided with a pamphlet to read on her own while she waits in an anteroom for her already scheduled ultrasound, amniocentesis, or maternal serum screening. Informed *choice* is about being given the support to take responsibility for one's own health and one's decisions, and for the outcomes of those decisions.[4] Informed choice, while it may be aided by written materials, calls for something more. It involves a different set of questions: 'Why do I want to see the fetus before it is born?' 'What difference will having an ultrasound make to

my pregnancy?' 'Would I have an abortion if the ultrasound showed something was wrong?'

A study done in England and published recently in the *British Medical Journal* speaks directly to both possibilities and also to the politics of an informed choice approach for ultrasound. Two pamphlets about ultrasound were designed – one for pregnant women, and the other for midwives and sonographers (radiologists, for the most part) (Oliver et al. 1996). The pamphlets were intended to summarize 'the best available evidence' about both the safety of ultrasound and the effectiveness of its routine use for estimating gestational age and detecting fetal impairments. The leaflet for women encouraged them to participate in decisions about maternity care. The leaflet for health professionals concluded that 'ultrasound scanning should not be presented as routine but rather as one possible course of action' (Oliver et al. 1996).

How were the pamphlets received? The midwives viewed the pamphlets as a positive contribution to informed choice and evidence-based care. The response of the sonographers was rather different. At one hospital, the sonographers withdrew from the study, saying they were concerned about the credibility of the evidence in the pamphlet, its potential effects on women's anxiety, and the way it presented ultrasound's dubious safety record. At the other hospital, the sonographers 'were generally reluctant to raise the subject of the leaflet with women,' saying it was better not to create anxiety among them (Oliver et al. 1996). The women who received the pamphlets were surprised and even shocked by what they learned, but they saw the information as important and useful. It did not particularly raise their level of anxiety. And 'even under conditions of informed choice, ... uptake of ultrasound ... is markedly above that which would be expected for other prenatal screening tests' (Baillie and Hewison 1999: 805).

At a minimum, informed choice for ultrasound would involve a face-to-face discussion between the woman and the care giver that touches on the following points:

- What ultrasound can specifically detect, and what it cannot.
- The likelihood of false positives and false negatives.
- Safety.
- The social and psychological consequences of seeing the fetus through ultrasound.

In conversations among obstetricians, geneticists, family physicians, midwives, and other care providers, this question is often raised: 'Why do women have amniocentesis or maternal serum screening if they would not consider terminating the pregnancy?' The argument being made here is that the consequences of such tests must be discussed with women *before* they undergo them. Precisely the same approach should be applied to ultrasound, especially since it is seen more and more as a technique for detecting fetal impairments rather than for determining fetal age, size, and sex. An informed choice discussion could be a valuable way to make the entire premise of ultrasound less fetocentric. What needs to be discussed is not just 'seeing the baby,' but whether the woman wants to have ultrasound, and what the implications might be of having it.

3. Producing and talking about ultrasound images
What kinds of changes might be implemented where ultrasound is used? It is worth noting that many ultrasound clinics in Canada are modifying their protocols and policies in response to concerns that ultrasound is becoming too 'commercial' and too 'frivolous' and is moving too far from the clinical rationale of screening fetal health. Concerns are also being raised about the cost of prenatal ultrasound – in particular, that its use as a form of psychological reassurance is simply too expensive. In part due to concerns that ultrasound was contributing to sex selection, some clinics now refuse to reveal fetal sex. Also, some clinics no longer provide or sell copies of the fetal image to women.

One option might be to conduct the exam in near silence, with little or no discussion about the image. While this might curtail the extent to which the fetal image is 'personified' and made available as a site for 'bonding,' a sonographer's silence is often interpreted by women as a sign that 'something is wrong.' So how can we talk about the fetus without raising women's anxiety unnecessarily, thereby invoking 'the biologistic two-person model of pregnancy' (Shrage forthcoming: 26), and without impinging on women's reproductive autonomy?

At a minimum, ultrasound should be about fetuses *as part of* women's bodies rather than about babies, or even about babies *in* women's bodies. Rather than saying, 'Here is your baby,' the sonographer could describe the image as follows: 'Fetal development inside you has reached the stage where you can see arms, legs, torso and head.' The image should be described in terms of anatomy and development rather than activity, agency, and subjectivity. This would mean identifying 'fetal fingers' and 'the fetal legs' rather than 'baby's little fingers' or 'cute thighs.' Comments about the completeness and minuteness of anatomy should be replaced with or balanced by comments about fetal parts and functions that are as yet incomplete or rudimentary. For example, the sonographer could point out that the fetal eyelids are fused until well past the time of the first routine scan, instead of saying 'He's posing for the camera.' Fetal movement should be described as involuntary and reflex rather than as 'behaviour' or 'activity.' The changes I am suggesting are not about switching to a 'more scientific' vocabulary. Rather, they acknowledge that fetuses look increasingly more like human infants as they develop, but also that the social characteristics of a newborn should not be attributed to the fetus.[5]

In the late 1990s, in the wake of the Royal Commission on New Reproductive Technologies, a number of Canadian hospitals changed a part of their ultrasound protocol. Signs were now posted saying, 'Ultrasound is conducted to assess your baby's health. Please don't ask about the sex of your baby.' Nonetheless, fetal sex was still determined as part of the routine examination. I propose that unless there are compelling medical reasons, fetal sex should not be determined routinely.

It should be explained clearly to women why ultrasound is being used, what the sonographer is doing during the examination, and what ultrasound's limitations are. This need not entail a lengthy list of anatomical parts, impairments, or measurements with unfamiliar names. 'I am looking at the fetal spine to see how it is developing' tells women what is appearing on the screen and why. 'We look at fetal movement' reassures the woman that there is movement without imputing intentionality or personality to the fetus. Summarizing statements about the results of the ultrasound, and responses to women's question, 'Is everything okay?' should be concrete: 'We cannot see and do not look for all the possible problems. Based on what we can see, there is no reason for concern.'

Sonographers should not approach ultrasound as an opportunity to assess women's behaviour or statements for evidence of maternalism. Women's marital status, weight, age, smoking habits, and preference for knowing the sex of the infant are not relevant to ultrasound and should not generate commentary.

Moreover, when fetal ultrasound is conducted, it should be done in such a way as to minimize the idea of the fetal image as entertainment. This would mean no separate viewing screen for the women and her partner, no take-home picture, no fancy 3-D effects, no 'comment bubbles' on the printed image, and no fetal 'voice' saying 'Hi, Mum!' or 'Having fun in here!'

4. *Training of sonographers*
During their training, ultrasound technicians should be encouraged to adopt language that does not personify or sentimentalize the fetal image. They should be made aware of the links between the discourse and images they use to talk about prenatal ultrasound, and the social and political realities of pregnancy. Sonographers should be encouraged to think critically and reflexively about how their own assumptions about fetality and family influence their descriptions of ultrasound images and their attitude toward pregnant women.

5. *Other changes*
Some changes should be made outside the clinics to foster and support the uses and interpretations of ultrasound that I am advocating.

We need to do away with the guidebooks to pregnancy as they exist today. In their place, we need books and pamphlets that do not reduce women's agency during pregnancy to self-monitoring. We need care guides in which women narrate a range of sensations, emotions, and experiences about their pregnancies and about the fetus. Instead of romanticizing pregnancy and highlighting its uncertainties, books on pregnancy should discuss some of the social and political realities of being pregnant and affirm the diversity of life and family circumstances.

We need to support and make accessible approaches to reproduction and birthing that encourage women's agency and decision making and that are less driven by technology. In this respect, the return of midwifery to Canada is encouraging. Yet as I learned recently, ultrasound as part of a midwifery model of care is not a simple calculus of 'more midwives means fewer ultrasounds.' Following an address I gave to the B.C. College of Midwifery, one midwife commented that in the context of all the other interventions and tests (amniocentesis, maternal serum screening) that constitute contemporary pregnancy care, 'getting away with just an ultrasound' can seem desirable. Ironically, then, ultrasound can actually make it easier for a woman to have a 'low tech' pregnancy or birth.

Produced, refracted, and glimpsed through multiple lenses – medicine, entertainment, politics, law, social science, feminism, and religious belief, among others – fetuses appear and disappear, coalesce and dissolve from view. In descriptions and images in guidebooks to pregnancy, the fetus appears abstract and alien, yet something pregnant women should know about. Glimpsed during a routine ultrasound, the on-screen grey fetus emerges as intensely real and reassuringly normal. Over time, the embodied fetus, sensed through women's bodies and minds, grows more convincing to women as the 'real' fetus. In labs, the fetus may be depersonalized – an object of scientific inquiry, mere tissue for experimentation, evidence of the advance of knowledge, a 'disembodied tool' for therapy and research (Casper 1998, 1994). When *in vitro* fertilization and the techniques of egg retrieval and zygote implantation are used, the resulting fetus may be imbued with heroic agency as a survivor, a fighter, or as 'failed pregnancy' and a reflection of one's own failed self (see Franklin 1997; Modell 1989). In pro-life rallies, the fetus may be both a full person and an angel. During an abortion or miscarriage, the fetus is part of the 'products of conception' that are expelled or extracted. Where 'selective reduction' is carried out, the number of fetuses may determine to what extent they are persons (Berkowitz et al. 1988). With a velcrotummy 'Mommy Doll,' the fetus becomes an object of socialization and play, a kind of practice for the medicalized fetocentric pregnancy that so many women experience (Erickson 1996). Portable ultrasound that enables us to see the fetus 'live' on our home computers, and home-use fetal heart monitors, transform the fetus into an object of continual 'self-monitoring,' entertainment, and interaction.

The existence of these diverse perspectives and practices underscores the point that fetuses are not natural entities, but dynamic cultural constructions crafted to suit certain agendas. Only partially of woman born, fetuses are made through the intersections of culture, body, technology, and power. Therein lies both the danger and the pleasure for women's experiences and agency.

Appendix

Profiles of the Women

The following list of the women I interviewed includes pseudonym, age, self-described identity, and (generalized) occupation.

Julie	29, 'anglophone,' secretary
Tamara	26, 'anglophone,' dentist
Marie-Claude	27, 'Québècoise,' part-time sales clerk
Rosa	22, 'Italian,' garment factory worker
Sara	27, 'Jewish,' office manager
Lena	28, 'Greek Canadian,' accountant
Michelle	27, 'Québècoise,' data systems analyst
Marie-Louise	31, 'Québècoise,' sales clerk
Olivia	28, 'Italian Canadian,' shipping manager
Claudette	27, 'French,' secretary
Rita	23, 'anglophone,' university student
Sandy	27, 'anglophone,' secretary
Dorothea	28, 'Greek Canadian,' office administrator
Alison	28, 'Canadian,' data systems analyst
Vicki	25, 'Jewish,' dental assistant
Sylvie	25, 'Québècoise,' chef
Jennifer	31, 'Canadian,' counsellor
Annabella	25, 'Italian Canadian,' office clerk
Norma	24, 'Canadian,' cashier
Sophia	31, 'Italian Canadian,' graphic artist
Naomi	31, 'Moroccan Jewish,' accountant
Suzanne	27, 'Québècoise,' secretary
Natalie	27, 'Greek Canadian,' office clerk
Cheryl	33, 'Canadian,' office manager

Kate	24, 'American Canadian,' bookkeeper
Clara	30, 'Colombian,' university student
Elaine	28, 'anglophone,' social worker
Karen	26, 'Canadian,' university student
Christina	25, 'Italian Canadian,' secretary
Nicole	28, 'Québècoise,' esthetician
Louisa	28, 'Italian Canadian,' counsellor
Esther	27, 'anglophone,' office manager
Adriana	26, 'Greek,' data systems manager
Cathy	33, 'Canadian,' office manager
Térèse	29, 'Canadian,' accountant
Angela	27, 'Italian Canadian,' secretary
Laura	27, 'Canadian,' dentist
Gillian	30, 'Canadian,' financial advisor
Erika	24, 'Greek Canadian,' small business owner
Nirmala	30, 'Sri Lankan,' homemaker
Maria	28, 'Italian Canadian,' counsellor
Pattie	25, 'Guyanese,' waitress
Francesca	30, 'Italian Canadian,' bank teller
Adelena	29, 'Italian Canadian,' office manager
Layla	27, 'Lebanese,' accountant
Rachel	22, 'Israeli,' university student
Nadya	26, 'Armenian,' garment worker
Teresa	27, 'Italian,' small business owner

Notes

1: Introducing Ultrasound Fetal Imaging

1 Four main types of ultrasound are used in North American obstetrics: (1) Doppler ultrasound, used in electronic fetal monitors to listen to and assess fetal heart rate; (2) colour Doppler, which is used to produce a coloured image of blood flow – for example, in the umbilical cord or fetal heart; (3) 'real-time' imaging, which produces a grey-scaled moving image of the fetus in two-dimensional sections or planes; and (4) 3D ultrasound, not yet widely used, but an increasingly popular add-on for real-time machines. My research is concerned with real-time imaging. For descriptions and images of the different types of ultrasound, see the website at www.ob-ultrasound.net/joewoo2.html.

2 There are many references investigating the psychological and behavioural 'effects' of seeing the fetus through ultrasound, including Bralow 1983, Dewsbury 1980, Field et al. 1985, Hyde 1986, Lerum and LoBiondo-Wood 1989, Reading and Cox 1982, Reading, Cox, and Campbell 1988, Reading, Campbell, Cox, and Sledmere 1982, and Thorpe et al. 1993.

3 Thus, Lippman (1986: 442) refers to ultrasound as 'the first non-voluntary application of prenatal diagnosis.'

4 For the United States, see Morgan 1989: 102.

5 For an analysis of the different visions of the fetus in the Canadian Royal Commission on Reproductive Technologies, see MacDonald 1994. See also Valverde and Weir 1997.

6 See, for example, Carrithers et al. 1985, Daniel 1984, Kondo 1990, Lee 1959, Marsella, DeVos, and Hsu 1985, Rosaldo 1980, Schweder and Bourne 1982, and Turner 1985.

7 See Gaines 1982, 1985 for one of the earliest challenges to the assumption of a uniform construction of the Western self; see also Spiro 1993.

8 Among the many works on the ways in which technology, body, and knowledge are co-constituted, see in particular Downey 1998, Downey and Dumit 1997, Haraway 1997, Hess 1995, Latour and Woolgar 1979, Oudshoorn 1994, and Wajcman 1991.

9 See, for example, Butler 1990, Duden 1991, Epstein and Straub 1991, Foucault 1979, Gallagher and Laqueur 1987, Gilman 1991, Haraway 1991, 1997, Horn 1994, Jordanova 1989, Martin 1987, 1994, and Turner 1985.

2: Opening the Black Box: The Ontology of Fetal Ultrasound Images

1 A number of scholars now argue that 'improvements in sanitation, pre-natal care, pasteurization of milk, refrigeration, and ... immunization' rather than hospitalization, were the key factors responsible for more mothers and infants surviving (Pierson et al. 1990: xvii; see also Oakley 1986a; Strong-Boag and McPherson 1990; Tew 1990).

2 See Oakley 1986a for this story in Great Britain.

3 Vertical blips represent the strength of the signal, and the horizontal baseline is a measure of the distance from the ultrasound probe.

4 Apparently Ian Donald had met John Wild in the early 1950s, but did not meet Howry until after 1960 (McNay and Fleming 1999).

5 New words – 'sonoembryology' and 'sonopathology' – have been coined to describe this hybrid fetus (Nimrod and Ash 1993: 425, 427).

6 See Pasveer 1989: 364 on this point in the history of X-rays.

7 These scans are also called Level II or III scans. The Society of Obstetricians and Gynaecologists of Canada (1997b) now uses the terms 'complete' for the routine scan, and 'comprehensive' for those performed in the case of suspected 'complex fetal conditions/anomalies.'

8 The Danish Health Ministry (Beech et al. 1985; Jackson 1985), the U.S. Food and Drug Administration (Thompson 1983), and the World Health Organization (Beech et al. 1985; The Lancet 1984a: 361) all took a firm stand against routine ultrasound scanning during pregnancy. The American College of Radiology (Thompson 1983), the American College of Obstetricians and Gynecologists (1981), and the National Institutes of Health (1984) did not recommend routine scanning, but their reviews are not especially critical of ultrasound. The British Ministry of Health advised physicians not to advocate routine screening (The Lancet 1984b: 995). However, both the Medical Ultrasound Society and the Royal College of Obstetricians and Gynaecologists in Britain disagreed with the Ministry and stated that there was no reason not to continue routine scanning (Jackson 1985). A

worthwhile reference is *Ultrasound? Unsound* (1994), written by one of the most vocal critics of routine ultrasound, Beverley Beech.

9 For a more detailed commentary on the NIH Consensus statement and other reviews of obstetrical ultrasound imaging, see Beech et al. 1985; Gold 1984; Shearer 1984.

10 For example, in Ontario and British Columbia the rate of ultrasound use doubled between 1981–82 and 1989–90. In both provinces, only slightly more than 10 per cent of the increase is due to a rise in the number of pregnancies (Anderson 1992).

11 BCOHTA evaluated clinical practice guidelines from the Royal Commission for New Reproductive Technologies (1993), the Canadian Task Force on the Periodic Health Examination (1994), the Saskatchewan Health Services Utilization and Research Commission (1996), and the United States Preventive Services Task Force (1996). They also evaluated two meta-analyses – Bucher and Schmidt (1993), and the Cochrane Collaboration (see, for example, Neilson 1995).

12 In the United States, malpractice suits concerning missed fetal anomalies are the most common type of litigation involving ultrasound (Saunders 1998).

13 See the articles and references in Diony Young 1982, as well as Marieskind 1989.

14 For example, during the period of research, I was often referred to a list of approved indications for ultrasound issued as part of a Consensus Statement on Routine Ultrasound by the National Institutes of Health. Among the twenty-eight indications in that list are such broad categories as estimates of gestational age, evaluation of fetal growth, vaginal bleeding, and suspected multiple fetuses (U.S. Department of Health and Human Services 1984).

15 The assumption of ultrasound's veracity and objectivity, which Borowski hoped would sway Canadian judges, is central to the 1984 film *The Silent Scream*, produced by Dr Bernard Nathanson and the U.S. National Right-to-Life Committee. *The Silent Scream* claims to show, through real-time ultrasound, the 'pain' and 'fear' of a twelve-week-old fetus being aborted (see Petchesky 1987).

3: The View from the Field

1 After some discussion, the hospital, the obstetricians, and I agreed that I could to recruit 'low risk' women who met the following criteria:
• No objection from the woman's obstetrician regarding her participation in the study, although physicians did not know which of their patients elected to participate.

- Nulliparous (had not had a live born infant).
- No previous obstetrical ultrasound. This criteria was eventually relaxed, since so many women had had an ultrasound because of first trimester bleeding. Five women in this study had had an 'early' scan before ten gestational weeks. .
- No known family history of genetic disease or other indication for prenatal genetic diagnosis.
- Between eighteen and thirty-four years of age at the time of recruitment.
- No past or concurrent significant medical disease (e.g., hypertension, diabetes).
- Singleton pregnancies (no twins or triplets).
- No history of three or more miscarriages.
- French or English speakers (but not limited to women whose maternal language is either French or English).

   Of 275 pregnant women I contacted at the hospital and at physician offices, 118 were eligible by the above criteria to participate. Of that group, 49 decided to participate in the research and were interviewed.

2 Health policy reforms, in conjunction with government control over language use, brought about major changes in the administration and cultural character of Quebec hospitals. Subsequent to recent legislative reforms, hospitals that were once exclusively for English speakers must now offer services in French. All health professionals, regardless of where they work in Quebec, must now pass French-language competency tests (Schachter 1982). The hospitals are permitted to use bilingual signs only if a majority of their patient population speaks a language other than French (Thompson 1990). Despite these reforms, the terms 'English' and 'French' are still used to distinguish among some hospitals in Montreal, and to some extent these labels reflect continuing differences (or perceived differences) in styles of patient care, religious orientation of hospitals, and the linguistic, economic, and cultural characteristics of medical staff and patients.

3 For example, in a 1993 national survey, responding Quebec hospitals had the highest rates (46 per cent) of routine administration of intravenous fluids (mean of all Canadian hospitals responding was 14 per cent) and of women delivering in the lithotomy position with stirrups (61 per cent) (Canada 37 per cent) (Levitt et al. 1995: 46, 159). Episiotomy (64 per cent of Quebec women, Canada 63 per cent) was used routinely. There is evidence that interventions such as forcep use and episiotomy are falling out of use in Quebec (Ministère de Santé et Services Sociales 1999). In

comparison, routine maternity care practices in British Columbia tend to be less interventionist, and Maritime provinces tend to be slightly more interventionist (Levitt et al. 1995). All of that being said, there is considerable variation from hospital to hospital in each province.

4 Barley (1988) has written about the temporal organization of ultrasound work among radiologists and radiology technicians.

5 Notably, francophone physicians in Quebec seem to be more like their anglophone colleagues than physicians in France. In fact, women in France have on average 3 or more routine ultrasounds per pregnancy (Renaud et al. 1993: 246).

6 Faced with reductions in government financing, hospitals have turned to additional sources of funding, including private donors and facility and equipment grants. Requests for funds for ultrasound equipment are not uncommon in hospital newsletters. With outpatient services, such as ultrasound fetal imaging, hospitals can bill directly to the Quebec Health Insurance Board (le Regie de l'Assurance Maladie du Québec), thereby securing additional funds for medical services (Rodwin 1984: 135).

7 The national survey of Canadian physicians found that '76 per cent of obstetrical ultrasound scans were carried out by radiologists, 18 per cent by obstetricians, and the remaining 6 per cent by other specialists. Radiologists in the study said they averaged 969 obstetrical scans per year, obstetricians 402' (Renaud et al. 1993: 276).

8 See Janelle Taylor's (1998) analysis of ultrasound, the notion of bonding, and the differences between mother–infant and mother–fetal bonding.

9 Many studies have been carried out to test whether visualizing the fetus through ultrasound influences maternal–fetal bonding; the results have been inconsistent (Kemp and Page 1987; Lerum and LoBiondo-Wood 1989; Sparling et al. 1988). Several studies support physicians' impressions that ultrasound imaging has a positive impact on women's feelings toward the fetus (Garel and Franc 1980; Kohn et al. 1980; Milne and Rich 1981; Villeneuve et al. 1988), but other studies do not support these findings (Cranley 1985; Grace 1983; Kemp and Page 1987; Sparling et al. 1988). One study suggests that the positive effects may be neither long-lasting nor particularly important to women (Reading et al. 1984). In another study, women said that fetal movement or 'quickening' was a more important source of 'bonding' for them than seeing the fetal image through ultrasound (Villeneuve et al. 1988). (Garel and Franc 1980; Grace 1983; Kemp and Page 1987; Kohn, Nelson, and Weiner 1980; Milne and Rich 1981; Sparling, Seeds, and Farran 1988; Villeneuve et al. 1988).

4: Being Pregnant and Coming to Know the Fetus

1 I have used pseudonyms for the women and staff. I have also generalized the occupations and life history information of the women and their partners. I have also refrained from providing demographic details concerning the obstetricians and the technicians in order to preserve both their own and the hospital's anonymity. Given the small number of sonographers in my research, I also felt that any conclusions I might draw about how sonographers' gender, religion, or cultural background shaped their interpretations of ultrasound would be extremely tentative.

2 See Martha McMahon (1995) for a symbolic interactionist study of childbearing and Canadian women's identity.

3 Somatization has been discussed with reference to a number of bodily experiences including *nevra* among Greek Canadians (Lock and Wakewich-Dunk 1990), *nerves* among women in outport Newfoundland (Davis 1989), and menopause and PMS among American women. See also Lock 1993: 142–3 and Low 1994.

4 My analysis of the guide by Eisenberg and colleagues is based on a more recent edition (1991) than that read by the women. However, the descriptions of the fetus and the advice given are only slightly changed in the later edition.

5 See Michie's commentary (1998) on the strategic deployment of autonomy and choice in her analysis of *What to Expect*.

6 Elsewhere, with Nia Georges, I have compared two of these Canadian guides to manuals on pregnancy read by women in Greece (Georges and Mitchell 2000).

7 See Cynthia Daniels 1997, 1999 on the social construction of male and female risks to the fetus in the United States.

8 A notable exception is Sheila Kitzinger's 1991 book, with its many illustrations of women and its women-centric text.

9 Bruce Willis, the voice of the fetus, is familiar to North American audiences as the star of several dramatic action films. His presence in the film confirms that this is a take-charge fetus who makes things happen.

10 There were six women who did not want to draw or describe in detail their image of the fetus to me. See also Lumley 1980.

11 The chronology of events – hearing the fetal heart and seeing the fetal image – was remembered differently at different interviews. At the first interview, 75 per cent of the women said they had already heard the fetal heart. In the post-partum interview, 96 per cent said that hearing the fetal heart had preceded seeing the image.

5: 'Showing the Baby:' Sonographers' Accounts of Fetal Images

1 A variety of terms are used to distinguish scans in which there is no suspected impairment ('basic,' 'Level 1') from scans that are made when there is reason to suspect some fetal impairment ('detailed,' 'targeted' or 'Level 2') (Society of Obstetricians and Gynaecologists of Canada 1981, 1999; the American College of Obstetricians and Gynecologists 1991.

2 The language of the ultrasound – English or French – is usually determined by the woman's language of choice, and is ascertained by the sonographers when they first meet the woman in the waiting room. The translations of the French text are my own.

3 During the research period, one of the older machines at the Met still required sonographers to manually compare ultrasound measurements with photocopied growth charts.

4 Note that I am talking about routine ultrasounds. During scans that involve a suspected or diagnosed fetal anomaly, more specific diagnostic information may be provided to parents.

5 Although sonographers dislike finding any kind of serious fetal pathology, anomalies of the head and brain are especially shunned. Fetuses with anencephaly, microcephaly, or hydrocephaly – serious cranial and cerebral anomalies – are regarded by sonographers as taboo subjects, awful to look at on-screen and worse to imagine at delivery.

6 This couple was bilingual, so the language of conversation changed throughout the explanation.

7 Sunera Thobani (1993) discusses how the opening of a sex selection clinic in the United States directed at South Asian women in western Canada reinforced racist and patriarchal assumptions about South Asian culture.

6: 'Seeing the Baby': Women's Perspectives on Ultrasound

1 Rosa is referring to the fact that in many ultrasound clinics the screen is positioned awkwardly to the right and slightly behind the woman's head.

2 Since the advent of high-resolution ultrasound in the early 1990s and the increasing familiarity of ultrasound fetal images, 'seeing' has probably become less dependent on the sonographer's explanations. Women I have interviewed since 1997 say confidently that they have seen the shape of the fetus, as well as its facial features, and have counted its fingers and toes, and so on.

3 My thanks to an anonymous reviewer for pointing this out.

4 Sometimes fetal sex is disclosed accidentally. One physician walked into the room and, not realizing the woman did not want to know the sex, referred to the image as 'une belle fille.' In the post-scan interview, the woman confided to me that while she didn't mind finding out, her husband was upset that the 'surprise had been ruined.'

5 Not all hospitals follow this practice, but many do. Sonographers at the Met told me that the water improved visibility, particularly of a woman's cervix, because the enlarged bladder pushed the uterus up.

6 I interviewed forty-four women after observing their later scans. By the time of the interview after the second ultrasound, five women had left the study for a variety of reasons: two women miscarried, one woman switched to a different hospital, one woman dropped out after a fetal anomaly was diagnosed during the second scan, and one woman chose to end her participation just prior to the second scan.

7 Davis-Floyd (1992: 4) comes to a similar conclusion in her analysis of pregnancy and birth in the United States 'as a year-long initiatory rite of passage' into motherhood. She writes (27) that 'by the seventh or eighth month [the pregnant woman] has adapted to her new symbolic status and the social rituals that accompany it.'

8 I compared the reports of women in my study to statistics gathered by the hospital's Department of Obstetrics.

9 The provincial caesarean section rate during the research period was between 18.5 and 17.7 per cent. By 1998–99, that rate had declined only slightly, to 17.3 per cent (Ministère de la Santé et Services Sociales 1999 website).

7: Reconnections: Women, Ultrasound, and Reproductive Politics

1 See for example, Petchesky 1987, Duden 1993, Stabile 1992, Hartouni 1993, and Taylor 1998.

2 Barbara Duden (1993: 78) refers to women's desire to see the fetal image as 'becoming a participant in her own skinning, in the dissolution of the historical frontier between inside and outside.'

3 See Duden 1992 for a historical analysis of quickening and its changing meanings.

4 Interestingly, in both of these passages the text is written as '"see" your baby.' While the inclusion of quotation marks acknowledges that ultrasound does not in fact allow one to see the fetus directly, the guides nonetheless continue to perpetuate the idea that the fetus has in fact been seen directly.

5 See Abby Lippman 1999 on women's embodied knowledge and amniocentesis.

6 See Markens, Browner, and Press 1997 for a discussion of factors such as
costs, time, and beliefs about self-care that influenced American women's
negotiation of biomedical advice on diet during pregnancy.

7 See Linda Layne's writings (1992, 1999) on the construction of fetal personhood among couples who have experienced stillbirth or miscarriage.

8 See Rapp 1999.

9 I have not had the opportunity to observe ultrasounds among Muslim
Filipinas.

10 In *Dodd* the injunction was overturned. Dodd had the abortion and then
reappeared in the media 'wearing a pro-life T-shirt, [saying] that she
regretted her choice of abortion and had acted under pressure of her
family and pro-choice activists' (Morton 1992: 275–6). In *Daigle*, a provincial Superior Court judge had supported the injunction saying that 'a
conceived child not yet born is a human being under Article 1 of the
Quebec Charter of Rights and Freedoms' (Moore 1989: A1). One month
later, as the Supreme Court was hearing her case, Daigle ignored the
injunction and had an abortion. Almost immediately after, the Supreme
Court of Canada overturned the Quebec decision (Paquin 1989: A1).

11 Canadian advocates of fetal protection include Edward Keyserlingk; see,
for example, his 1983 article, 'The Unborn Child's Right to Prenatal Care,'
Parts I & II, *Health Law in Canada* 3: 10–21, 30–41. See also the Law Reform
commission of Canada (1989). 'Crimes Against the Foetus,' Working
Paper no. 58. Ottawa: Supply and Services.

12 Headlines announcing the Supreme Court decision in *Ms G* included,
'*Le foetus n'a pas de droits*' (*Le Devoir*, 2 novembre 1997: A1), 'Court puts
mothers before fetuses,' (*The Globe and Mail*, 1 November 1997: A1), and
'Supreme court won't recognize rights of fetus' (*Victoria Times-Colonist*,
1 November 1997: A8). These headlines both perpetuate the notion of
maternal–fetal conflict and seem to suggest that the fetus has rights – the
court just won't privilege or recognize them.

13 In December 1996, police charged Brenda Drummond of Ontario with
attempted murder after it was discovered that her newborn had a pellet
in his brain. Drummond had fired a pellet gun into her vagina two days
before the delivery. Murder charges were dismissed by a provincial court
judge. Drummond pleaded guilty to failing to provide the necessities of
life to her son (Kondro 1997).

14 The provincial medicare plans of Prince Edward Island, Nova Scotia, New
Brunswick, Quebec, and Manitoba do not provide full coverage.

15 In fact, Dr Romalis was almost killed in 1994 when he was shot by an anti-abortion sniper.
16 Nor has the idea of using ultrasound images to convert viewers been lost on anti-choice advocates. See ch. 2, note 14.

8: Re-Visions: Other Ways of Seeing

1 See in particular the collection of articles in *Fetal Subjects, Feminist Positions* (Morgan and Michaels 1999).
2 We speak of a woman's 'relationship with the fetus,' that is, with that part of her interior which is conceptualized as the fetus, but we do not speak of her 'relationship' with her liver, or her (non-pregnant) uterus. While Canadian and American ethnophysiology attributes agency, autonomy, and sentience to those body parts labelled as 'embryo' and 'fetus,' our pounding hearts, gurgling intestines, and shedding uteruses languish without 'bonds' or social identity.
3 In addition to the works mentioned in the text, see Sara Franklin's discussion (1999) of feminist artist Helen Chadwick, Valerie Hartouni's analysis (1993) of Aline Mare's video *S'Aline's Solution*, and Kathy High's images published throughout *Feminist Studies* 23 (2).
4 As an example of this approach to informed choice, see the website of the College of Midwifery in British Columbia: www.cmbc.ca.
5 An example of the kind of language and imagery that might be used is contained in a pamphlet, 'Pre-natal Development: Pregnancy ... Miscarriage ... Abortion ... Childbirth,' produced by the Childbirth by Choice Trust. This pamphlet can be viewed on the website of the Canadian Abortion Rights Action League (CARAL), the largest pro-choice activist group in the country: www.caral.ca. Because this representation is uncommon, I quote at some length from this pamphlet. Unlike some pro-choice narratives, it neither shies away from the fetus nor prioritizes the woman. Women are not present as the self-disciplining woman 'bonding' with her baby from its earliest moments, nor are they present as the whole-bodied reproductive agent of the relational arguments. In this narrative, fetal subjectivity, agency, and sociality all begin at birth.

At 2 Weeks' Gestation (from Conception):
... Pregnancy (with its hormonal changes) begins when and if the zygote implants in the woman's uterus. Because of abnormalities, nature has aborted about 55% of all fertilized eggs by this point. Another 12% or more will spontaneously abort sometime after.

At 8 Weeks' Gestation (from Conception):
The embryo is now called a fetus. It has the primitive beginnings of most of the major body organs. Organ functions have not yet developed. The heart is beginning to form the typical four-chambered structure of mammals. The fetus moves by reflex. No brain waves (regular electrical patterns) yet exist ... The fetus has begun to look human, with a rudimentary face, limbs, hands, and feet (webbing disappears). It is structurally immature and functionally quite limited.

At 16 Weeks' Gestation:
The body of the fetus grows dramatically. It weighs about 6 ounces. Its organs continue to grow and differentiate. It has no awareness (including no awareness of pain), because the part of tle brain that deals with thought and perception, called the neocortex, has not yet begun to develop the necessary interconnections ... The pregnant woman will soon begin to feel the fetus' movements for the first time.

At 20 Weeks' Gestation:
The rate of fetal growth is slower. Its internal organs continue to mature. The lungs remain immature. The eyelids are completely fused. In the fetal brain, the first few synapses or connections begin to form among the nerve cells in the neocortex, with the greatest part of the process of interconnection yet to follow.

References

Abbott, Maude. 1931. *History of medicine in the province of Quebec*. Montreal: McGill University Press.

Abdulla, U., Stuart Campbell, C.J. Dewhurst, and David Talbert. 1971. Effect of diagnostic ultrasound on maternal and fetal chromosomes. *The Lancet*. 16 October: 829–83.

Acheson, Louise, and Lisa M. Mitchell. 1993. The routine antenatal diagnostic imaging with ultrasound study: The challenge to practice evidence based obstetrics. *Archives of Family Medicine* 2: 1229–30.

American College of Obstetricians and Gynecologists. 1981. Diagnostic ultrasound in obstetrics and gynaecology. Technical Bulletin no. 63. *Women and Health* 7: 55–63.

– 1987. *Antepartum fetal surveillance*. Technical Bulletin no. 107. Washington, D.C.: American College of Obstetricians and Gynecologists.

– 1988. *Ultrasound in pregnancy*. Technical Bulletin no. 116. Washington, D.C.: American College of Obstetricians and Gynecologists.

– 1991. Ultrasound Imaging in Pregnancy. ACOG Committee Opinion, No. 96. Washington, D.C.: American College of Obstetricians and Gynecologists.

Anderson, Geoffrey. 1994. Routine prenatal ultrasound screening. In *The Canadian guide to clinical preventive health care*. 4–14. Ottawa: Minister of Supply and Services Canada.

Anderson, G.M. 1992. *An analysis of temporal and regional trends in the use of prenatal ultrasonography*. Ottawa: Royal Commission on New Reproductive Technologies.

Anderson, Melanie. 1999. Canada's abortion law. *Pro-choice Forum*. Canadian Abortion Rights Action League. May 1999, p. 5.

Anderssen, Erin. 1999. Child harmed in womb can't sue mom, top court rules. *The Globe and Mail*. 10 July: A3.

Angles, J.M., et al. 1990. Effects of pulsed ultrasound and temperature on the development of rat embryos in culture. *Teratology*. 42: 285–93.

Arditti, Rita, Renate Duell Klein, and Shelley Minden, eds. 1984. *Test-tube women: What future for motherhood?* London: Pandora Press.

Armstrong, David. 1983. *The Political Economy of the Body: Medical Knowledge in Britain in the Twentieth Century*. Cambridge: Cambridge University Press.

– 1993. Public health spaces and the fabrication of identity. Sociology 27(3) (August): 393–411.

Arney, William R. 1982. *Power and the profession of obstetrics*. Chicago: University of Chicago Press.

Arnup, Katherine. 1994. *Education for motherhood: Advice for mothers in the twentieth century*. Toronto: University of Toronto Press.

Arnup, K., A. Lévesque, R. Pierson, and Margaret Brennan, eds. 1990. *Delivering motherhood: Maternal ideologies and practices in the 19th and 20th centuries*. New York: Routledge.

Baillie, Catherine, and Jenny Hewison. 1999. Obtaining selective consent to scanning, rather than screening, is possible [letter]. *British Medical Journal* 318 (20 March): 805.

Bakketeig, L.S., et al. 1984. Randomised controlled trial of ultrasonographic screening in pregnancy. *Lancet* 2(8396) 207–11.

Balakrishnan, T.R., and John Kralt. 1987. Segregation of visible minorities in Montreal, Toronto, and Vancouver. In *Ethnic Canada. Identities and inequalities*, ed. Leo Driedger. Toronto: Copp Clark Pitman.

Barad, Karen. 1998. Getting real: Technoscientific practices and the materialization of reality. *Differences: A Journal of Feminist Cultural Studies* 10(2): 87–128.

Barley, Stephen, R. 1988. On technology, time, and social order: Technically induced change in the temporal organization of radiological work. In *Making Time: Ethnographies of high technology organizations*, ed. Frank A. Dubinskas. 123–96. Philadelphia: Temple University Press.

Basen, Gwynne, Margrit Eichler, and Abby Lippman, eds. 1994. *Misconceptions: The Social Construction of Choice and the New Reproductive and Genetic Technologies*. Prescott, Ont.: Voyager Publishing.

Becker, Anne. 1994. Nurturing and negligence: Working on others' bodies in Fiji. In Thomas Csordas, ed. *Embodiment and experience: The existential ground of culture and self*. 100–15. Cambridge: Cambridge University Press.

Beech, Beverly. 1999. Ultrasound: Weighing the propaganda against the facts. *Midwifery Today* 51: 31–3.

Beech, Beverly, Marilyn Green, Christine Rodgers, and Johann Squire. 1985. *A commentary on the report of the Royal College of Obstetricians and Gynaecologists working party on routine ultrasound examination in Pregnancy.* London: Association for Improvements in the Maternity Services.

Beech, Beverly, and Jean Robinson. 1994. *Ultrasound? Unsound.* London: Association for Improvements in the Maternity Services.

Bennett, M.J., Gillian Little, Sir John Dewhurst, and Geoffrey Chamberlain. 1982. Predictive value of ultrasound measurements in early pregnancy: A randomised controlled trial. *British Journal of Obstetrics and Gynaecology* 89: 338–41.

Benoit, Cecilia. 1991. *Midwives in passage: The modernization of maternity care.* St John's, NF: Institute of Social and Economic Research.

Berkowitz, Richard, Lauren Lynch, Usha Chitkara, Isabelle Wilkins, Karen E. Mehalek, and Emanuel Alvarez. 1988. Selective reduction of multifetal pregnancies in the first trimester. *New England Journal of Medicine* 318: 1043–7.

Berlant, Lauren. 1997. *The Queen of America goes to Washington City: Essays on sex and citizenship.* Durham: Duke University Press.

Berwick, Donald, and Milton Weinstein. 1985. What do patients value? Willingness to pay for ultrasound in normal pregnancy. *Medical Care* 23: 881–93.

Bigwood, Carol. 1991. Renaturalizing the body (with the help of Merleau-Ponty). *Hypatia* 6(3) (Fall): 54–73.

Birnholz, Jason. 1988. On observing the human fetus. In *Behaviour of the Fetus*, ed. William Smotherman and Scott Robinson. 47–60. Caldwell, NJ: Teleford Press.

Black, Rita Beck. 1992. 'Seeing the Baby: The Impact of Ultrasound Technology.' *Journal of Genetic Counselling* 1: 45–54.

Blondel, Béatrice. 1986. Antenatal care in the countries of the European community over the last twenty years. In *Perinatal care delivery systems: Description and evaluation in European Community countries,* eds. Monique Kaminski, Gérard Bréart, Pierre Buekens, Henk Huisjes, Gillian McIlwaine, and Hans-Konrad Selbmann. 3–15. Oxford: Oxford University Press.

Blu, Karen. 1980. *The Lumbee problem: The making of an American Indian people.* Cambridge: Cambridge University Press.

Bolsen, Barbara. 1982. Question of risk still hovers over routine prenatal use of ultrasound. *Journal of the American Medical Association* 247: 2195–7.

Bordo, Susan. 1993. *Unbearable weight: Feminism, western culture, and the body.* Berkeley: University of California Press.

Bouchard, Louise, Marc Renaud, Odile Kremp, and Louis Daillare. 1995. Selective abortion: A new moral order: Consensus and debate in the medical community. *International Journal of Health Services* 25: 65–84.

Bourdieu, Pierre. 1977. *Outline of a theory of practice*, trans. Richard Nice. Cambridge: Cambridge University Press.

- 1984. *Distinctions: A social critique of the judgement of taste*. Cambridge: Harvard University Press.

Bralow, Lisette. 1983. Maternal bonding in early fetal ultrasound examinations [letter]. *New England Journal of Medicine* 309: 114.

Braun, Francoise, and Hélène Valentini. 1984. Échographie: un examen au-dessus de tout soupçon? *Naissance-Renaissance* 1: 7–16.

Brent, Robert L., R.P. Jensh, and D.A. Beckman. 1991. Medical sonography: reproductive effects and risks. *Teratology* 44: 123–46.

Breton, Raymond. 1987. Symbolic dimensions of linguistic and ethno-cultural realities. In *Ethnic Canada: Identities and inequalities*, ed. Leo Driedger. 44–64. Toronto: Copp Clark Pitman.

Brodie, Janine. 1992. Choice and no choice in the house. In Janine Brodie, Shelley A.M. Gavigan, and Jane Jenson. 1992. *The politics of abortion*. 57–116. Toronto: Oxford University Press.

Brown, Brian. 1999. All too human. *National Post*. 30 June: A18.

Browne, J.C. McLure, and Geoffery Dixon. 1978. *Browne's antenatal care*. 11th edition. Edinburgh: Churchill Livingstone.

Browner, Carole H., and Nancy Ann Press. 1995. The normalization of prenatal diagnostic screening. In *Conceiving the new world order: The global politics of reproduction*, ed. Faye Ginsburg and Rayna Rapp. 307–22. Berkeley: University of California Press.

- 1997. The production of authoritative knowledge in American prenatal care. In *Childbirth and authoritative knowledge: Cross-cultural perspectives*, ed. Robbie Davis-Floyd and Carolyn F. Sargent. 113–31. Berkeley: University of California Press.

Bucher, H.C., and J.G. Schmidt. 1993. Does routine ultrasound scanning improve outcome? *British Medical Journal* 307 (6895): 13–17.

Buckley, Suzanne. 1979. Ladies or midwives? Efforts to reduce infant and maternal mortality. In *A not unreasonable claim: Women and reform in Canada, 1880s–1920s*. 131–49. Toronto: The Women's Press.

Butler, Judith. 1990. *Gender Trouble: Feminism and the Subversion of Identity*. New York: Routledge.

Bynum, Caroline Walker. 1991. *Fragmentation and redemption: Essays on gender and the human body in medieval religion*. New York: Zone.

Cable News Network (CNN). 1982. Fetal effects of ultrasound. CNN transcript for program televised 16 and 17 April, 1982.

Campbell, J.D., R.W. Elford, and R.F. Brant. 1993. Case-control study of prenatal ultrasonography exposure in children with delayed speech. *Canadian Medical Association Journal* 149: 1435–40.

Campbell, Stuart. 1971. The accuracy of ultrasonic measurement of the fetal biparietal diameter during the second trimester. In *Recent advances in diagnostic ultrasound*, ed. Elias Rand. 97–108. Springfield, MA: Charles C. Thomas.

Canadian Abortion Rights Action League (CARAL). 1998. Did you know ...? *Pro-choice Forum* (December): 6.

– 1999. Across Canada. *Pro-choice Forum* (July): 7. P. 7.

– 2000. Abortion rights hang by a thread. Op/Ed piece sent on bulletin list for CARAL [in newspapers on 14 June 2000].

Carrithers, M., S. Collins, and S. Lukes, eds. 1985. *The category of the person: Anthropology, philosophy and history.* Cambridge: Cambridge University Press.

Cartwright, Lisa. 1993. Gender artifacts in medical imaging: Ultrasound, sex identification, and interpretive ambiguity in fetal medicine. Paper presented at American Anthropological Association Annual Meeting, Washington, D.C.

Casper, Monica J. 1994. At the margins of humanity: Fetal positions in science and medicine. *Science, Technology and Human Values* 19: 307–23.

– 1995. Fetal cyborgs and technomoms on the reproductive frontier: Which way to the carnival? In Chris H. Gray, Heidi J. Figueroa-Sarreira, and Steven Mentor, *The cyborg handbook.* New York: Routledge.

– 1998. *The making of the unborn patient: A social anatomy of fetal surgery.* New Brunswick, NJ: Rutgers University Press.

Chitty, Lyn S. 1995. Ultrasound screening for fetal abnormalities. Prenatal Diagnosis 15: 1241–57.

Collins, Anne. 1985. *The big evasion: Abortion, the issue that won't go away.* Toronto: Lester and Orpen Dennys.

Comaroff, Jean. 1985. *Body of power, spirit of resistance: The culture and history of a South African people.* Chicago: University of Chicago Press.

Condit, Celeste M. 1990. *Decoding abortion rhetoric: Communicating social change.* Urbana: University of Illinois Press.

Conklin, Beth A., and Lynn M. Morgan. 1996. Babies, bodies, and the production of personhood in North American and a Native Amazonian society. *Ethos* 24: 657–94.

Corea, Gena. 1985. *The mother machine: Reproductive technologies from artificial insemination to artificial wombs.* New York: Harper and Row.

Corea, G., J. Hanmer, B. Hoskins, J. Raymond, R. Duelli Klein, H.B. Holmes, M. Kishwar, R. Rowland, and R. Steinbacher. 1987. *Man-made women: How new reproductive technologies affect women.* Bloomington: Indiana University Press.

Corporation professionnelle des médecins du Québec (CPMQ). 1987. *The practice of obstetrics: Patient care during pregnancy, obstetrical echography.* Montréal: CPMQ.

- 1990. *Nine months for life*. Montréal: CPMQ.

Cranley, M. 1985. Development of a tool for the measurement of maternal attachment during pregnancy. *Nursing Research*. 30: 281–4.

Crary, Jonothan. 1990. *Techniques of the Observer: On vision and modernity in the nineteenth century*. Cambridge: MIT Press.

Csordas, Thomas. 1990. Embodiment as a paradigm for anthropology. *Ethos* 18(1): 5–47.

- 1994. Introduction: The body as representation and being-in-the-world. In Thomas Csordas, ed., *Embodiment and experience: The existential ground of culture and self*. 1–24. Cambridge: Cambridge University Press.

Cunningham, F. Gary, Paul C. MacDonald, and Norman F. Gant. 1989. *Williams obstetrics*. 18th ed. Norwalk, CT: Appleton and Lange.

Daniel, E. Valentine. 1984. *Fluid signs: Being a person the Tamil way*. Berkeley: University of California Press.

Daniels, Cynthia. 1997. Between fathers and fetuses: The social construction of male reproduction and the politics of fetal harm. *Signs: Journal of Women in Culture and Society* 22: 579–616.

- 1999. Fathers, mothers, and fetal harm: Rethinking gender differences and reproductive responsibility. In *Fetal subjects, feminist positions*, ed. Lynn M. Morgan and Meredith W. Michaels. 83–100. Philadelphia: University of Pennsylvania Press.

Davis, Dona. 1989. The variable character of nerves in a Newfoundland fishing village. *Medical Anthropology* 11: 63–78.

- 1991. The cultural constructions of the premenstrual and menopause syndromes. In *Gender and health*, ed. C. Sargent and C. Brettel. 57–86. Englewood Cliffs, NJ: Prentice Hall.

Davis-Floyd, Robbie E. 1992. *Birth as an American rite of passage*. Berkeley: University of California Press.

Dewsbury, A. 1980. What the fetus feels [letter]. *British Medical Journal* (16 February): 481.

Donald, Ian. 1968a. Ultrasonics in obstetrics. *British Medical Bulletin* 24: 71–5.

- 1968b. Sonar in obstetrics and gynaecology. *Yearbook of Obstetrics and Gynaecology*, 1967–1968: 242–66.

- 1969. On launching a new diagnostic science. *American Journal of Obstetrics and Gynaecology* 103(5): 609–28.

- 1976a. The Utrasonic boom. *Journal of Clinical Ultrasound* 4(5): 323–8.

- 1976b. Sonar and X-ray in obstetrics and gynaecology. In *Combined textbook of obstetrics and gynaecology*, ed. James Walker, Ian MacGillivray, and Malcolm Macnaughton. 552–74. Edinburgh: Churchill Livingstone.

– 1980. Medical sonar – the first 25 years. In *Recent advances in ultrasound diagnosis*, Vol II. ed. Asim Kurjak. 4–20. Amsterdam: Excerpta Medica.

Donald, Ian, J. MacVicar, and T.G. Brown. 1958. Investigation of abdominal masses by pulsed ultrasound. *The Lancet* (June): 1188–95.

Douglas, Mary. 1973. *Natural symbols*. New York: Vintage.

Downey, Gary Lee. 1998. *The machine in me: an anthropologist sits among computer engineers*. New York: Routledge.

Downey, Gary Lee, and Dumit, Joseph, eds. 1997. *Cyborgs and citadels: Anthropological interventions in emerging sciences and technologies*. Santa Fe, NM: School of American Research Press.

Drugan, Arie, Anne Greb, and M.P. Johnson, 1990. Determinants of parental decisions to abort for chromosome abnormalities. *Prenatal Diagnosis* 10: 483–90.

Dubose, Terry J. 1996. *Fetal sonography*. Philadelphia: Saunders.

Duden, Barbara. 1991. *The woman beneath the skin: A doctor's patients in eighteenth-century Germany*. Cambridge: Harvard University Press.

– 1992. Quick with child: An experience that has lost its status. *Technology in Society* 14: 335–44.

– 1993. *Disembodying women: Perspectives on pregnancy and the unborn*. Cambridge: Harvard University Press.

Dumit, Joseph, and Robbie Davis-Floyd. 1998. Cyborg babies: Children of the third millenium. In *Cyborg babies: From techno-sex to techno-tots*, ed. Robbie Davis-Floyd and Joseph Dumit. 1–18. New York: Routledge.

Eastman, Nicholson J., Louis M. Hellman, and J.A. Pritchard. 1966. *Williams obstetrics*. 13th ed. New York: Apple Century Crofts.

Eik-Nes, Sturla H., O. Okland, J.C. Aure, and M. Ulstein. 1984. Ultrasound screening in pregnancy: A randomised controlled trial [Letter]. *The Lancet*. 1 (Jun 16): 1347–50.

Eisenberg, Arlene, Heidi E. Murkof, and Sandee E. Hathway. 1991. *What to expect when you're expecting*. 2nd ed. New York: Workman.

Epstein, Julia, and Kristina Straub. 1991. *Body guards: The cultural politics of gender ambiguity*. New York: Routledge, Chapman and Hall.

Erikson, Susan. 1996. Pregnancy pastiche: Ultrasound imagery as postmodern phenomenon. *PoMo Magazine* 2(1): 1–9.

Ewigman, Bernard. 1989. Should ultrasound be used routinely during pregnancy? An opposing view. *Journal of Family Practice* 29: 660–4.

Ewigman, Bernard, M. LeFevre, and J. Hesser. 1990. A randomized trial of routine ultrasound. *Obstetrics and Gynecology* 76(2): 189–94.

232   References

Ewigman, Bernard, et al. 1993. Effect of prenatal ultrasound screening on perinatal outcome. *New England Journal of Medicine* 329(12): 744–50.

Eyers, Diane E. 1992. *Mother-infant bonding: A scientific fiction.* New Haven: Yale University Press.

Field, Tiffany, David Sandberg, Thomas Quetel, Robert Garcia, and Marie Rosario. 1985. Effects of ultrasound feedback on pregnancy anxiety, fetal activity, and neonatal outcome. *Obstetrics and Gynaecology* 66: 525–8.

Flavell, Kay. 1994. Mapping faces: National physiognomies as cultural prediction. *Eighteenth-Century Life.* 18 (Nov): 8–22.

Fletcher, John, and Mark Evans. 1983. Maternal bonding in early fetal ultrasound examinations. *New England Journal of Medicine* 308: 392–3.

Foucault, Michel. 1975. *The birth of the clinic: An archeology of medical perception,* trans. A.M. Sheridan Smith. New York: Vintage.

– 1979. *Discipline and punish: The birth of the prison,* trans A.M. Sheridan Smith. New York: Vintage.

Franklin, Sarah. 1991. Fetal fascinations: New dimensions to the medical-scientific construction of fetal personhood. In *Off-centre: Feminism and cultural studies,* ed. Sarah Franklin, Celia Lury, and Jackie Stacey. 190–205. New York: Routledge.

– 1997. *Embodied progress: A cultural account of assisted conception.* New York: Routledge.

– 1999. Dead embryos: feminism in suspension. In *Fetal subjects, feminist positions,* ed. Lynn M. Morgan and Meredith W. Michaels. 61–82. Philadelphia: University of Pennsylvania Press.

Franklin, Ursula. 1999. *The real world of technology* [revised ed]. Toronto: Anansi Press.

Fraser, Graham. 1991. Fetus not person, top court reiterates. *The Globe and Mail.* 22 March: A1, A4.

Gabbe, Steven. 1988. Obstetric ultrasound update. *Clinical Obstetrics and Gynaecology* 31: 1–2.

Gadd, Jane. 1995. Where women stand now. *The Globe and Mail.* 12 August: A5.

Gaines, Atwood D. 1982. Cultural definitions, behaviour and the person in American psychiatry. In *Cultural conceptions of mental health and theory,* ed. A. Marsella and G. White. 167–92. Dordrecht: D. Reidel.

– 1985. The once- and the twice-born: Self and practice among psychiatrists and Christian psychiatrists. In *Physicians of western medicine.* ed. R. Hahn and A. Gaines. 223–43. Dordrecht: D. Reidel.

Gallagher, Catherine, and Thomas Laqueur. 1987. *The making of the modern body: Sexuality and society in the nineteenth society.* Berkeley: University of California Press.

Garel, M., and M. Franc. 1980. Réactions des femmes à l'échographie obstétricale. *Journal of Gynaecology, Obstetrics, Biology and Reproduction* 9: 347–54.

Gavigan, Shelley A.M. 1992. Beyond Morgantaler: the legal regulation of reproduction. In Janine Brodie, Shelley A.M. Gavigan, and Jane Jenson, *The politics of abortion*. 117–46. Toronto: Oxford University Press.

Gee, Marcus. 1996. The issue that won't go away. *The Globe and Mail.* 17 August: D1.

Geertz, Clifford. 1983. *Local knowledge: Further essays in interpretive anthropology*. New York: Basic Books.

Georges, Eugenia. 1997. Fetal ultrasound imaging and the production of authoritative knowledge in Greece. In *Childbirth and authoritative knowledge: Cross-cultural perspectives*, ed. Robbie Davis-Floyd and Carolyn F. Sargent. 91–112. Berkeley: University of California Press.

Georges, Eugenia, and Lisa Mitchell. 2000. Baby talk: The rhetorical production of maternal and fetal selves. In *Body talk: Rhetoric, technology, reproduction*, ed. Mary M. Lay, Laura Gurak, Clare Gravon, and Cynthia Myntti. 184–203. Madison: University of Wisconsin Press.

Gilman, Sander. 1991. *The Jew's body*. London: Routledge.

Ginn, Diana. 1999.The Supreme Court of Canada rules on coercive state intervention in pregnancy. *Canadian Woman Studies* 19(1, 2): 122–31.

Ginsburg, Faye D. 1989. *Contested lives: The abortion debate in an American community*. Berkeley: University of California Press.

Gold, Rachel Benson. 1984. Ultrasound imaging during pregnancy. *Family Planning Perspectives* 16: 240–43.

Gonzalez, Frederick. 1984. Ultrasound. *Journal of Nurse-Midwifery* 26: 391–4.

Good, Byron. 1984. *Medicine, rationality, and experience: An anthropological perspective*. Cambridge: Cambridge Univ. Press.

Gordon, Deborah. 1990. Embodying illness, embodying cancer. *Culture, medicine and psychiatry* 14: 275–97.

Gould, Stephen Jay. 1981. *The mismeasure of man*. New York: W.W. Norton.

Government of Canada. 1987. *The charter of rights and freedoms: A guide for Canadians*. Ottawa: Minister of Supply and Services Canada.

Grace, Jeanne. 1983. Prenatal ultrasound examinations and mother-infant bonding. *New England Journal of Medicine* 309: 561.

Graham, David. 1983. Ultrasound in clinical obstetrics. *Women and Health* 7: 39–54.

Green, Carolyn, David Hadorn, Ken Bassett, and Arminée Kazanjian. 1996. Routine ultrasound imaging in pregnancy: How evidence-based are the guidelines? B.C. Office of Health Technology Assessment discussion paper no. 96: 2D.

Greene, Gayle. 2000. *The woman who knew too much: Alice Stewart and the secrets of radiation*. Ann Arbor: University of Michigan Press.

Greenhill, J.P., ed. 1966. *Yearbook of Obstetrics and Gynaecology*, 1965–66. Chicago: Yearbook Medical Publishers.

Hacking, Ian. 1990. *The taming of chance*. Cambridge: Cambridge University Press.

Hahn, R. 1987. Perinatal ethics in anthropological perspective. In *Ethical issues at the outset of life*, ed. William Weil and Martin Benjamin. 213–38. Boston: Blackwell Scientific.

– 1995. *Sickness and healing: An anthropological perspective*. New Haven: Yale University Press.

Handler, Richard. 1988. *Nationalism and the politics of culture in Quebec*. Madison: University of Wisconsin Press.

Hanratty, Maria J. 1996. Canadian national health insurance and infant health. *American Economic Review* 86: 276–84.

Haraway, Donna. 1991. *Simians, cyborgs and nature: The reinvention of nature*. New York: Routledge.

– 1997. *Modest_Witness@Second_Millenium.FemaleMan© _Meets_OncoMouse™*. New York: Routledge.

– 1999. The persistence of vision. In *The visual culture reader*, ed. Nicholas Mirzoeff. 191–8. New York: Routledge Press.

Harris, Grace Gredys. 1989. Concepts of individual, self, and person in description and analysis. *American Anthropologist* 91: 599–612.

Harrison, Michael. 1982. Unborn: Historical perspective of the fetus as a patient. *The Pharos* (Winter): 19–24.

Harrison, Michael, Mitchell S. Golbus, and Roy A. Filly. 1984. *The unborn patient: Prenatal diagnosis and treatment*. Orlando: Grune and Stratton.

– 1990. *The unborn patient: Prenatal diagnosis and treatment*, 2nd ed. Philadelphia: Q.B. Saunders.

Hartmann, Betsy. 1995. *Reproductive rights and wrongs*. Boston: South End Press.

Hartouni, Valerie. 1991. Containing women: Reproductive discourse in the 1980s. In *Technoculture*, ed. Constance Penley and Andrew Ross. 39–47. Minneapolis: University of Minnesota Press.

– 1993. Fetal exposures: Abortion politics and the optics of allusion. *Camera Obscura* 29: 130–49.

– 1999. Reflections on abortion politics and the practices called person. In *Fetal subjects, feminist positions*, ed. Lynn M. Morgan and Meredith W. Michaels. 296–303. Philadelphia: University of Pennsylvania Press.

Hays, Sharon. 1996. *The cultural contradictions of motherhood*. New Haven: Yale University Press.

Health Services Utilization and Research Commission (Saskatchewan). 1996. *The use of ultrasound in pregnancy*. Saskatoon: Health Services Utilization and Research Commission.

Hess, David. 1995. *Science and technology in a multicultural world*. New York: Columbia University Press.

Hiddinga, Anja, and Stuart Blume. 1992. Technology, science, and obstetric practice: The origins and transformation of cephalopelvimetry. *Science, Technology, and Human Values* 17: 154–79.

High, Kathy. 1997. 'Instructions: Circle characteristics desired' [computer generated image] *Feminist Studies* 23(2): 322.

Himmelweit, Susan. 1988. More than 'a woman's right to choose'? *Feminist Review* 29: 38–56.

Horger, Edgar O., and Charles Tsai. 1989. Ultrasound and the prenatal diagnosis of congenital anomalies: A medico legal perspective. *Obstetrics and Gynaecology* 74: 617–19.

Horn, David. 1994. *Social bodies: Science, reproduction, and Italian modernity*. Princeton: New Jersey University Press.

Hotchner, Tracey. 1984. *Pregnancy and childbirth. The complete guide for a new life*. New York: Avon.

Huet, Marie-Hélène. 1993. *Monstrous imagination*. Cambridge: Harvard University Press.

Hyde, Beverley. 1986. An interview study of pregnant women's attitudes to ultrasound scanning. *Social Science and Medicine* 22: 587–92.

Irwin, Susan, and Brigitte Jordan. 1987. Knowledge, practice, and power: Court-ordered Cesarean sections. *Medical Anthropology Quarterly (n.s.)* 1: 319–34.

Jackson, R. 1985. The use of ultrasound in obstetrics. *Irish Medical Journal* 78: 149–50.

Jacoby, Miriam. 1995. Time, magic, and gynaecology: Contemporary Israeli practice. *Science in Context* 8: 231–48.

Jaffe, Richard, and The-Hung Bui, eds. 1999. *Textbook of fetal ultrasound*. New York: Parthenon.

James-Chetelat, Lois. 1990. The cultural roots of the Canadian birthing system. *Pre- and Peri-Psychology* 4: Summer 301–18.

Jenson, Jane. 1992. Getting to Morgentaler: From one representation to another. In Janine Brodie, Shelley A.M. Gavigan, and Jane Jenson. *The politics of abortion*. 15–55. Toronto: Oxford University Press.

Jimenez, Marina. 1999. Ultrasound imaging can change cells of mice. *National Post*. 10 June: A1.

Jordan, Brigitte, with Robbie Davis-Floyd. 1993. *Birth in four cultures: A cross-*

cultural investigation of childbirth in Yucatan, Holland, Sweden, and the United States, 4th ed. Prospect Heights, IL: Waveland Press.

Jordanova, Ludmilla. 1989. *Sexual visions: Images of gender in science and medicine between the eighteenth and twentieth centuries*. Madison: University of Wisconsin Press.

Kantrowitz, Barbara, Pat Wingert, and Mary Hager. 1988. 'Preemies.' *Newsweek*, 16 May: 62–7.

Kaplan, E. Ann. 1994. Look who's talking, indeed: Fetal images in recent North American visual culture. In *Mothering: Ideology, experience, and agency*, ed. Evelyn Nakano Glenn, Grace Chang, and Linda Rennie Forcey. 121–37. New York: Routledge.

Katz, Miriam, Israel Meizner, and Vaclav Insler, eds. 1990. *Fetal well being: Physiological basis and methods of clinical assessment*. Boca Raton, FL: CRC Press.

Keeling, Jean, ed. 1994. *Fetal pathology*. New York: Churchill Livingstone.

Kemp, Virginia, and Cecilia Page. 1987. Maternal prenatal attachment in normal and high-risk pregnancies. *Journal of Obstetrics, Gynaecology and Neonatology in Nursing* (May/June): 179–83.

Keyserlingk, Edward. 1983. The unborn child's right to prenatal care, parts I and II. *Health Law in Canada* 3: 10–21, 30–41.

Kirmayer, Laurence. 1988. Mind and body as metaphors. In *Biomedicine examined*, ed. M. Lock and D. Gordon. 57–94. Dordrecht: Kluwer Academic.

Kitzinger, Sheila. 1989. *The complete book of pregnancy and childbirth*. New York: Alfred A. Knopf.

Koch, Ellen B. 1993. In the image of science? Negotiating the development of diagnostic ultrasound in the cultures of surgery and radiology. *Technology and Culture* 34: 858–93.

Kohn, C.L., A. Nelson, and S. Weiner. 1980. Gravidas' responses to realtime ultrasound fetal image. *Journal of Obstetrics, Gynaecology and Neonatology in Nursing* 9 (March/April): 77–80.

Kolata, Gina. 1990. *The baby doctors: Probing the limits of fetal medicine*. New York: Delacorte.

Kondo, Dorinne. 1990. *Crafting selves: Power, gender, and discourses of identity in a Japanese workplace*. Chicago: University of Chicago Press.

Kondro, Wayne. 1997. Canadian fetal-rights case decided. *The Lancet* 349(9045) (11 November): 112.

Krasnegor, Norman. 1988. On fetal development: A behavioral perspective. In *Behaviour of the fetus*, ed. William Smotherman and Scott Robinson. 227–31. Caldwell, NJ: Teleford.

Kunisch, Judith R. 1989. Electronic fetal monitors: Marketing forces and the resulting controversy. In *Healing technology: Feminist perspectives*. Kathryn S. Ratcliff et al. 41–60. Ann Arbor: University of Michigan Press.

Lachapelle, Réjean. 1990. 'Changes in fertility among Canada's linguistic groups.' In *Canadian social trends*, ed. Craig McKie and Keith Thompson. 153–9. Toronto: Minister of Supply and Services Canada and Thompson Educational Publishing.

LaFleur, William. 1992. *Liquid life: Abortion and Buddhism in Japan*. Princeton: Princeton University Press.

Laforce, Helene. 1990. The different stages in the elimination of midwives in Quebec. In *Delivering motherhood: Maternal ideologies and practices in the 19th and 20th centuries*, ed. K. Arnup, A. Lévesque, R. Pierson, and M. Brennan. 36–50. New York: Routledge.

Lakoff, George, and Mark Johnson. 1980. *Metaphors we live by*. Chicago: University of Chicago Press.

Lancet. 1984a. Diagnostic ultrasound in pregnancy: WHO view on routine screening [editorial]. 11 August: 361.

– 1984b. Minister's warning about routine use of ultrasound in pregnancy [editorial]. 27 October: 995.

Latour, Bruno, and Woolgar, Steve. 1979. *Laboratory life: The construction of scientific facts*. Beverley Hills: Sage.

Laurendeau, France. 1987. La médicalisation de l'accouchement. In *Accoucher autrement*, ed. Francine Saillant et Michel O'Neill. 125–62. Montreal: Édition Saint-Martin.

Law Reform Commission of Canada. 1989. *Crimes against the foetus*. Working paper no. 58. Ottawa: Supply and Services.

Layne, Linda L. 1992. Of fetuses and angels: Fragmentation and integration in narratives of pregnancy loss. *Knowledge and Society: The Anthropology of Science and Technology* 9: 29–58.

– 1999. 'I remember the day I shopped for your layette': Consumer goods, fetuses, and feminism in the context of pregnancy loss. In *Fetal subjects, feminist positions*, eds. Lynn M. Morgan and Meredith W. Michaels. 251–78. Philadelphia: University of Pennsylvania Press.

Lazarus, Ellen. 1988. Poor women, poor outcomes: Social class and reproductive health. In *Childbirth in America: Anthropological perspectives*, ed. Karen Michaelson. 39–54. South Hadley, MA: Bergin and Garvey.

– 1994. What do women want? Issues of choice, control, and class in pregnancy and childbirth. *Medical Anthropology Quarterly* 8: 25–46.

Leavitt, Judith Walzer. 1986. *Brought to bed: Childbearing in America, 1750–1950*. New York: Oxford University Press.

Lee, Dorothy. 1959. View of the self in Greek culture. In *Freedom and culture*, ed. D. Lee. Englewood Cliffs, NJ: Prentice Hall.

Leopold, George. 1990. Seeing with sound. *Radiology*. 175: 23–7.

Lerum, Carolyn, and Geri LoBiondo-Wood. 1989. The relationship of maternal age, quickening, and physical symptoms of pregnancy to the development of maternal-fetal attachment. *Birth* 16: 13–17.

Levitt, Cheryl, Louise Harvey, Denise Avard, Graham Chance, and Janusc Kaczorowski. 1995. *Survey of routine maternity care and practices in Canadian hospitals*. Ottawa: Health Canada and Canadian Institute of Child Health.

Lindenbaum, Shirley, and Lock, Margaret. 1993. *Knowledge, power, and practice*. Berkeley: University of California Press.

Lippman, Abby. 1986. Access to prenatal screening services: Who decides. *Canadian Journal of Women and the Law* 1: 434–5.

– 1999. Embodied knowledge and making sense of prenatal diagnosis. *Journal of Genetic Counselling* 8: 255–74.

Lock, Margaret. 1980. *East Asian medicine in urban Japan*. Berkeley: University of California Press.

– 1993. Cultivating the body: Anthropology and epistemologies of bodily practice and knowledge. *Annual Review of Anthropology* 22: 133–55.

Lock, Margaret, and Patricia Kaufert. 1998. Introduction. In *Pragmatic women and body politics*, ed. Margaret Lock and Patricia Kaufert. 1–27. Cambridge: Cambridge University Press.

Lock, Margaret, and Pamela Wakewich-Dunk. 1990. Nerves and nostalgia: Expression of loss among Greek immigrants in Montreal. *Canadian Family Physician* 36 (February): 253–8.

Low, Setha. 1994. Embodied metaphors: Nerves as lived experience. In *Embodiment and experience: The existential ground of culture and self*, ed. Thomas Csordas. 139–62. Cambridge: Cambridge University Press.

Lumley, Judith. 1980. The image of the fetus in the first trimester. *Birth and the Family Journal* 7: 5–14.

Luton, Kim. 1998. Letter to Andy Scott, former Solicitor General of Canada. Pro-Choice Forum (Dec): 4.

Lyons, E. et al. 1988. In utero exposure to diagnostic ultrasound: A six year follow up. *Radiology* 166: 687–90.

MacDonald, Maggie. 1994. Procreation and the creation of meaning: Studying the new reproductive technologies. In *Misconceptions: The social construction of choice and the new reproductive and genetic technologies*, ed. Gwynne Basen, Margrit Eichler, and Abby Lippman. 86–98. Prescott, ON: Voyager.

MacKay, R. Stuart. 1984. *Medical images and displays: Comparisons of nuclear magnetic resonance, ultrasound, X-rays, and other modalities.* New York: John Wiley & Sons.

Mageo, Jeannette Marie. 1995. The reconfiguring self. *American Anthropologist* 97: 282–96.

Makin, Kirk. 1997. Court puts mothers before fetuses. *The Globe and Mail* (1 November): A1, A10.

Manning, Frank. 1995. Dynamic ultrasound-based fetal assessment: The fetal biophysical profile score. *Clinical Obstetrics and Gynaecology* 38(1): 26–44.

Manning, Frank, Lawrence Platt, and Louise Sipos. 1980. Antepartum fetal evaluation: Development of a fetal biophysical profile. *American Journal of Obstetrics and Gynaecology* 136 (March 15): 787–95.

Marieskind, Helen. 1989. Cesarean section in the United States: Has it changed since 1979? *Birth* 16: 196–202.

Markens, Susan, C.H. Browner, and Nancy Press. 1997. Feeding the fetus: On interrogating the notion of maternal-fetal conflict. *Feminist Studies* 23(2): 351–72.

Marsella, A.J., G. DeVos, and F. Hsu, eds. 1985. *Culture and self: Asian and western perspectives.* New York: Tavistock.

Martin, Emily. 1987. *The woman in the body: A cultural analysis of reproduction.* Boston: Beacon.

– 1994. *Flexible bodies.* Boston: Beacon.

Maser, Peter. 1991. Quebec wants more babies. *The Gazette* (Montreal). 5 January: B1.

McLaren, Angus, and Arlene Tigar McLaren. 1986. *The bedroom and the state.* Toronto: McClelland & Stewart.

McMahon, Martha. 1995. *Engendering motherhood: identity and self-transformation in women's lives.* New York: Guilford Press.

McNay, Margaret B., and John E.E. Fleming. 1999. Forty years of obstetric ultrasound, 1957–1997: From A-scope to three dimensions. *Ultrasound in Medicine and Biology* 25: 3–56.

Meire, H.B. 1987. The safety of diagnostic ultrasound [commentary]. *British Journal of Obstetrics and Gynaecology* 94: 1121–2.

Meizner, Israel. 1987. 'Sonographic Observation of in utero fetal masturbation.' *Journal of Ultrasound in Medicine* 6: 111.

Michaels, Meredith. 1999. Fetal galaxies: Some questions about what we see. In *Fetal subjects, feminist positions,* ed. Lynn M. Morgan and Meredith W. Michaels. 113–32. Philadelphia: University of Pennsylvania Press.

Michaels, Meredith, and Lynn M. Morgan. 1999. Introduction: The fetal imperative. In *Fetal subjects, feminist positions,* ed. Lynn M. Morgan and

Meredith W. Michaels. 1–9. Philadelphia: University of Pennsylvania Press.

Michie, Helena. 1998. Confinements: The domestic in the discourse of upper-middle-class pregnancy. In *Making worlds: gender, metaphor, materiality*, ed. Susan Hardy Aiken, Ann Brigham, Sallie Marston, and Penny Waterstone. 258–73. Tucson: University of Arizona Press.

Millner, Sherry. 1999. 'Womb with a View' script and stills. In *Fetal subjects, feminist positions*, ed. Lynn M. Morgan and Meredith W. Michaels. 201–35. Philadelphia: University of Pennsylvania Press.

Milne, L., and O. Rich. 1981. Cognitive and affective aspects of the responses of pregnant women to sonography. *Maternal-Child Nursing Journal* 10: 15–39.

Ministère de la Santé et Services Sociales. 1999. Évolution du taux de césarienne. Québec 1969 à 1998–1999. www.msss.gouv.gc.ca/f/statistiques/index.htm.

Mitchell, Lisa M. 1994. The routinization of the other: Ultrasound, women and the fetus. Vol. 2 of *Misconceptions: The social construction of choice and the new reproductive and genetic technologies*. 146–60. Hull, PQ: Voyager.

Mitchell, Lisa M., and Eugenia Georges. 1997. Cross-cultural cyborgs: Greek and Canadian women's discourses on fetal ultrasound. *Feminist Studies* 23: 373–401.

Mitchison, Wendy. 1991a. *The nature of their bodies: Women and their doctors in Victorian Canada*. Toronto: University of Toronto Press.

– 1991b. The medical treatment of women. In *Changing patterns: women in Canada*, ed. S. Burt et al. 237–63. Toronto: McClelland & Stewart.

Modell, Judith. 1989. Last chance babies: Interpretations of parenthood in an in vitro fertilization program. *Medical Anthropology Quarterly* 3(2): 124–38.

Mohide, P.T. 1990. Maternal-fetal medicine manpower survey. *Journal of Society of Obstetricians and Gynaecologists of Canada* 12: 23–6.

Moore, Lynn. 1989. Judge rules fetus has right to life, won't allow abortion. *The Gazette* (Montreal). 18 July: A1.

Morgan, Lynn. 1989. When does life begin? A cross-cultural perspective on the personhood of fetuses and young children. In *Abortion rights and fetal 'personhood,'* ed. Edd Doerr and James Prescott, 97–114. Long Beach: Centerline Press.

– 1994. 'Imagining the unborn: Technoscience and the ethnoscience in the Ecuadorian Andes.' Paper presented at the annual meeting of the Society for the Social Studies of Science. New Orleans, LA.

– 1996. Fetal relationality in feminist philosophy: An anthropological critique. *Hypatia* 11: 47–70.

- 1997. Imagining the unborn in the Ecuadorian Andes. *Feminist Studies* 23: 323–50.
Morgan, Lynn M., and Meredith Michaels, ed. 1999. *Fetal subjects, feminist positions.* Philadelphia: University of Pennsylvania Press.
Morrison, John C. ed. 1990. Antepartum fetal assessment: an overview. *Obstetrics and Gynecology Clinics of North America* 17(1): 1–16.
Morton, Christine. 1993. Relations in utero: A study of the social experience of pregnancy. Unpublished masters thesis, UCLA Sociology Dept.
Morton, F.L. 1992. *Morgentaler v. Borowski: Abortion, the charter, and the courts.* Toronto: McClelland & Stewart.
Murphy, Robert F. 1990. *The body silent.* New York: W.W. Norton.
Muszynski, Alicja. 1994. Gender inequality and life chances: women's lives and health. In *Women medicine and health,* ed. B. Singh Bolaria and Rosemary Bolaria. 57–72. Halifax: Fernwood.
Myers, Stephen. 1990. The role of the maternal-fetal medicine specialist. In *Assessment and care of the fetus: Physiological, clinical, and medicolegal principles,* ed. Robert Eden and Frank Boehm. 947–50. Norwalk, CT: Appleton and Lange.
National Abortion Federation. 1997. Access to abortion. www.prochoice.org/facts/access.htm.
National Institutes of Health. 1984. The use of diagnostic ultrasound imaging in pregnancy. NIH Consensus Development Conference Statement (6–8 February 1984). *Journal of Nurse-Midwifery* 29(4): 235–9.
Neilson, Jim. 1986. Indications for ultrasonography in obstetrics. *Birth* 13 (special supplement): 11–15.
Neilson, Jim, and Adrian Grant. 1989. Ultrasound in pregnancy. In *Effective care in pregnancy and childbirth,* ed. Iain Chalmers et al. 419–39. Oxford: Oxford University Press.
Neilson, J.P. 1995. Routine ultrasound in early pregnancy. In *Pregnancy and childbirth module* [computer program], ed. M.W. Enkin, M.J. Keine, M.J. Renfrew, et al. Cochrane Database of Systematic Reviews: Review No. 03872, 28 February.
Newman, Karen. 1996. *Fetal positions: Individualism, science, visuality.* Stanford: Stanford University Press.
Newnham, John P., Sharon F. Evans, Con A. Michael, Fiona J. Stanley, and Louis Landau. 1993. Effects of frequent ultrasound during pregnancy: A randomised controlled trial. *The Lancet* 342 (9 October): 887–91.
Nimrod, Carl, and Karen Ash. 1993. Ultrasound in obstetrics. *Journal of the Society of Obstetrics and Gynecology* (May): 418–31.

Nilsson, Lennart. 1990. *A child is born*. New York: Delacorte.

Oakley, Ann. 1986a. *The captured womb: A history of the medical care of pregnant women*. Oxford: Basil Blackwell.

– 1986b. The history of ultrasonography in obstetrics. *Birth* 13 (supplement): 5–10.

Oaks, Laury. 1994. Fetal spirithood and fetal personhood: The cultural construction of abortion in Japan. *Women's Studies International Forum* 17: 511–23.

– 1999. Irish trans/national politics and locating fetuses. In *Fetal Subjects, Feminist Positions*, ed. Lynn M. Morgan and Meredith W. Michaels. 175–198. Philadelphia: University of Pennsylvania Press.

O'Brien, W.D. 1983. Dose dependent effect of ultrasound on fetal weight in mice. *Journal of Ultrasound in Medicine* 2: 1–8.

Ohnuki-Tierney, Emiko. 1994. Brain death and organ transplantation: Cultural bases for medical technology. *Current Anthropology* 35(3): 233–42.

O'Neill, John. 1985. *Five bodies: The shape of modern society*. Ithaca: Cornell University Press.

Oliver, S., L. Rajan, H. Turner, A. Oakley, V. Entwhistle, I. Watt, T.A. Sheldon, and A. Rosser. 1996. Informed choice for users of health services: Views on ultrasonography leaflets of women in early pregnancy, midwives and ultrasonographers. *British Medical Journal* 313 (16 November): 1251–3.

Oppenheimer, Jo. 1990. Childbirth in Ontario: The transition from home to hospital in the early twentieth century. In *Delivering motherhood: Maternal ideologies and practices in the 19th and 20th centuries*, ed. K. Arnup, A. Lévesque, R. Pierson, and M. Brennan. 51–74. New York: Routledge.

Oudshoorn, Nelly. 1994. *Beyond the natural body*. New York: Routledge.

Overall, Christine, ed. 1989. *The future of human reproduction*. Toronto: Women's Press.

Pandolfi, Mariella. 1990. Boundaries inside the body: Women's sufferings in southern peasant Italy. *Culture, Medicine and Psychiatry* 14: 255–74.

Paquin, Gilles. 1989. La Cour Supreme casse l'injonction même si Chantal Daigle s'est déjà fait avorter. *La Presse* (Montréal). 9 aout: A1.

Parker, Ginny. 1999. Japan approves birth control. www.boston.com/dailynews/153/world/Japan_approves_birth_control_p.html.

Pasveer, Bernike. 1989. Knowledge of shadows: The introduction of X-ray images in medicine. *Sociology of Health and Illness* 11: 360–81.

– n.d. The science is that of shadows: X-ray images and tuberculosis, 1900–1930. Unpublished manuscript.

Patel, Vibhuti. 1989. Sex-determination and sex-preselection tests in India: Modern techniques for femicide. *Bulletin of Concerned Asian Scholars* 21: 2–10.

Perreaux, Les, and Chris Wattie. 2001. U.S. crack addict found guilty of homicide in death of her fetus. *National Post*. 18 May: A1, A16.

Persky, Stan. 1988. Introduction. *The Supreme Court of Canada decision on abortion*, ed. Shelagh Day and Stan Persky. 1–23. Vancouver: New Star.

Petchesky, R. 1987. Foetal images: The power of visual culture in the politics of reproduction. In *Reproductive technologies: Gender, motherhood and medicine*, ed. M. Stanworth. 57–80. Minneapolis: University of Minnesota Press.

– 1990. *Abortion and woman's choice: The state, sexuality, and reproductive freedom*, revised edition. Boston: Northeastern University Press.

Philp, Margaret. 1995. Life transformed but pay lags. *The Globe and Mail* 26 August: A6.

Pierson, Ruth Roach, A. Lévesque, and K. Arnup. 1990. Introduction of *Delivering motherhood: Maternal ideologies and practices in the 19th and 20th centuries*, ed. K. Arnup, A. Lévesque, R. Pierson, and M. Brennan. xiii–xxiv. New York: Routledge.

Piontelli, Alessandra. 1992. *From fetus to child: An observational and psychoanalytic study*. New York: Routledge.

Pizzarrello, D.J., A. Vivino, B. Madden, A. Wolsky, A.F. Keegan, and M. Becker. 1978. Effect of pulsed low-power ultrasound in growing tissues 1. Developing mammalian and insect tissue. *Experimental Cell Biology* 46: 179–91.

Plummer, Kate. 2000. From nursing outposts to contemporary midwifery in 20th century Canada. *Journal of Midwifery and Women's Health* 45: 169–75.

Pretorius, Dolores, and Barry S. Mahoney. 1990. The role of obstetrical ultrasound. In *Diagnostic ultrasound of fetal anomalies: Text and atlas*, ed. David Nyberg et al., 1–20. Chicago: Year Book Medical Publishers.

Quéniart, Anne. 1992. Risky business: medical definitions of pregnancy. In *The anatomy of gender*, ed. D. Currie and V. Raoul. 161–74. Ottawa: Carleton University Press.

Rapp, Rayna. 1990. Constructing amniocentesis: Maternal and medical discourses. In *Uncertain terms: Negotiating gender in American Culture*, ed. Faye Ginsburg and Anna Lowenhaupt Tsing. 28–42. Boston: Beacon.

– 1991. Moral pioneers: Women, men, and fetuses on a frontier of reproductive technology. In *Gender at the crossroads of knowledge: Feminist anthropology in the postmodern era*, ed. Micaela de Leonardo. 383–95. Berkeley: University of California Press.

– 1993. Amniocentesis in sociocultural perspective. *Journal of Genetic Counselling* 2: 183–95.

– 1997. Real time fetus: The role of the sonogram in the age of monitored reproduction. In *Cyborgs and citadels: Anthropological interventions into techno-humanism*, ed. Gary Downey, Joe Dumit, and Sharon Traweek. 31–48. Sante Fe, New Mexico: SAR/University of Washington Press.

– 1999. *Testing Women, Testing the Fetus: The Social Impact of Amniocentesis in America*. New York: Routledge.

Reading, Anthony, and David Cox. 1982. The effects of ultrasound examination on maternal anxiety levels. *Journal of Behavioural Medicine* 5: 237–47.

Reading, Anthony, David Cox, and Stuart Campbell. 1988. A controlled, prospective evaluation of the acceptability of ultrasound in prenatal care. *Journal of Psychosomatic Obstetrics and Gynaecology* 8: 191–8.

Reading, Anthony, Stuart Campbell, David Cox, and Caroline Sledmere. 1982. Health beliefs and health care behaviour in pregnancy. *Psychological Medicine* 12: 379–83.

– 1984. Psychological changes over the course of pregnancy: A study of attitudes toward the fetus/neonate. *Health Psychology* 3: 211–21.

Renaud, Marc. 1981. Reform or illusion? An analysis of the Quebec state intervention in health. In *Health and Canadian society*, ed. David Coburn, Carl D'Arcy, Peter New, and George Torrance. 369–92. Toronto: Fitzhenry & Whiteside.

Renaud, Marc, Louise Bouchard, Jocelyn Bisson, Jean-Francois Labadie, Louis Dallaire, and Natalie Kishchuck. 1993. Canadian physicians and prenatal diagnosis: Prudence and ambivalence. In *Current practice of prenatal diagnosis in Canada*. Research studies no. 13. Royal Commission on New Reproductive Technology. 235–507.

Renaud, Marc, Suzanne Doré, Roxane Bernard, and Odile Kremp. 1987. Regard médical et grossesse en Amérique du Nord: L'évolution de l'obstétrique prénatale au 20 siècle. In *Accoucher autrement: Repères historiques, sociaux et culturels de la grossesse et de l'accouchement au Québec*, ed. Francine Saillant et Michel O'Neill. 182–212. Montréal: Éditions Saint-Martin.

Renaud, Marc, et al. 1991. Diagnostic prénatale et choix de société: Le non-dit du développement technologique. *Santé Publique.* 3: 37–48.

Rodwin, Victor G. 1984. *The health planning predicament: France, Quebec, England, and the United States*. Berkeley: University of California Press.

Romanyshyn, Robert D. 1989. *Technology as symptom and dream*. London: Routledge.

Rosaldo, M. 1980. *Knowledge and passion: Ilongot notions of self and social life*. Cambridge: Cambridge University Press.

Rose, M. 1990. Revenge of the cradle. *MacLean's.* 30 May: 12.

Rothman, Barbara Katz. 1986. *The tentative pregnancy: Prenatal diagnosis and the future of motherhood*. New York: Viking Penguin.

– 1989. *Reinventing motherhood: Ideology and technology in a patriarchal society*. New York: W.W. Norton.

Royal Commission on New Reproductive Technologies (RCNRT). 1993. *Proceed with care: Final report of the Royal Commission on new reproductive technologies*, vol. 2. Minister of Supply and Services Canada.

Saari-Kemppainen, A., O. Karjalainen, P. Ylostalo, and O.P. Heinonen. 1990. Ultrasound screening and perinatal mortality: Controlled trial of systematic one-stage screening in pregnancy. *The Lancet* 336: 387–91.

Saetnan, Ann Rudinow. 1996. Ultrasonic discourse: Contested meanings of gender and technology in the Norwegian ultrasound screening debate. *European Journal of Women's Studies* 3(1): 55–75.

– 2000. Thirteen women's narratives of pregnancy, ultrasound, and self. In *Bodies of technology*, ed. A. Rudinow Saetnan, Nelly Oudshoorn, and Marta Kirejcayk, 331–54. Columbus: Ohio State University Press.

Salvesen, K.A., L.S. Bakketeig, S.H. Eik-Nes, Jo.O. Undheim, and O. Okland. 1992. Routine ultrasonography in utero and school performance at age 8–9 years. *The Lancet* 339 (8750) (11 January): 85–9.

Sandelowski, Margarete. 1994a. Separate, but less equal: Fetal ultrasonography and the transformation of expectant mother/fatherhood. *Gender and Society* 8: 230–45.

– 1994b. Channel of desire: Fetal ultrasonography in two use-contexts. *Qualitative Health Research* 4(3) (August): 262–80.

Saunders, R.C. 1998. Legal problems related to obstetrical ultrasound. *Annals of New York Academy of Sciences* 847(11): 220–7.

Savard, Suzanne. 1987. Accouche à l'hôpital: où en sommes-nous aujour'hui? In *Accoucher autrement*, ed. Francine Saillant et Michel O'Neill. 279–93. Montréal: Édition Saint-Martin.

Sawicki, Jana. 1991. *Disciplining Foucault: Feminism, power and the body*. New York: Routledge.

Scarry, Elaine. 1985. *The body in pain*. Oxford: Oxford University Press.

Schacter, Susan. 1982. Working papers on English language institutions in Québec. Montreal: Alliance Québec.

Scheper-Hughes, Nancy, and Margaret Lock. 1987. The mindful body: A prolegomenon to future work in medical anthropology. *Medical Anthropology Quarterly*, n.s. 1: 6–41.

Shafi, M. I., G. Constantine, and D. Rowlands. 1988. Routine one-stage ultrasound screening in pregnancy [letter]. *The Lancet* (1 October): 804.

Shearer, Madeleine. 1984. Revelations: A summary and analysis of the NIH consensus development conference on ultrasound imaging in pregnancy. *Birth* 11: 23–36.

Shrage, Laurie. Forthcoming. From reproductive rights to reproductive Barbies: Post-porn-modernization and abortion. *Feminist Studies* 28(1).

Shweder, Richard, and Edmund Bourne. 1982. Does the concept of the person vary cross-culturally? In *Cultural conceptions of mental health and therapy*, ed. A. Marsella and G. White, 97–137. Dordrecht: D. Reidel.

Silver, Lesley. 1999. Since May 14, 1969 ... Pro-choice Forum. Canadian Abortion Rights Action League. May 1999: 5.

Sobo, Elisa. 1993. Bodies, kin, and flow: Family planning in rural Jamaica. *Medical Anthropology Quarterly* 7: 50–73.

Society of Obstetricians and Gynaecologists of Canada. 1981. Guidelines for the use of ultrasound in obstetrics and gynaecology. *Bulletin of the Society of Obstetricians and Gynaecologists of Canada* 2: 2.

– 1994. Guidelines for the Performance of Ultrasound Examination in Obstetrics and Gynecology. Policy Statement No. 30. October.

– 1997a. Educational objectives for the training of obstetrical and gynaecological sonologists. Clinical Practice Guidelines No. 63. July.

– 1997b. Suggested terminology and expectations for ultrasound examinations used in obstetrics. Clinical Practice Guidelines no. 65. July.

– 1999. Guidelines for the use of ultrasound in obstetrics and gynaecology. Clinical Practice Guidelines no. 78. August.

Spallone, Patricia. 1989. *Beyond conception: The new politics of reproduction*. Granby, MA: Bergin and Garvey.

Sparling, Joyce, John Seeds, and Dale Farran. 1988. The relationship of obstetric ultrasound to parent and infant behaviour. *Obstetrics and Gynaecology* 72: 902–7.

Spiro, Melford. 1993. Is the Western conception of the self 'peculiar' within the context of world cultures? *Ethos* 21: 107–53.

Stabile, Carol. 1992. Shooting the mother: Fetal photography and the politics of disappearance. *Camera Obscura* 28: 178–205.

Stanworth, Michelle, ed. 1987. *Reproductive technologies: Gender, motherhood and medicine*. Minneapolis: University of Minnesota Press.

Stark, C., M. Orleans, A. Haverkamp, and J. Murphy. 1984. Short and long-term risks after exposure to diagnostic ultrasound in utero. *Obstetrics and Gynecology* 63: 194–200.

Statistics Canada. 1992. *Profile of census metropolitan areas and census agglomerations: Part A*. Cat. 93–337. 1991 Census of Canada. Ottawa: Statistics Canada.

– 1997. 1996 census: Mother tongue, home language and knowledge of languages. *The Daily* (2 December).

– 1998. Birth and fertility rates. *The Daily* (8 July) www.statcan.ca/Daily/English/980708/d980708.htm#ART2.

– 1999. Average earnings by sex and work pattern. www.statcan.ca/english/ Pgdb/People/Labour/labor01b.htm.

Stratmeyer, Melvin, and Christopher Christman. 1983. Biological effects of ultrasound. *Women and Health* 7: 65–82.

Strong-Boag, Victoria, and Kathryn McPherson. 1990. The confinement of women: Childbirth and hospitalization in Vancouver, 1919–1939. In *Delivering motherhood: Maternal ideologies and practices in the 19th and 20th centuries*, ed. Katherine Arnup, André Lévesque and Ruth Roach Pierson 75–107. New York: Routledge.

Tarantal, A.F., and A.G. Hendrickx. 1989. Evaluation of the bioeffects of prenatal ultrasound exposure in the Cynomolgus macaque (*Macaca fascicularis*): I. Neonatal/infant observations. *Teratology* 39: 137–47.

Tarantal, A.F., W.D. O'Brien, and A.G. Hendrickx. 1993. Evaluation of the bioeffects of prenatal ultrasound exposure in the Cynomolgus macaque (*Macaca fascicularis*): III. Development and hematologic studies. *Teratology* 47: 159–70.

Taskinen, H., et al. 1990. Effects of ultrasound, shortwaves, and physical exertion on pregnancy outcome in physiotherapists. *Journal of Epidemiology and Community Health* 44: 196–201.

Taylor, Janelle. 1992. The public fetus and the family car: From abortion politics to a Volvo advertisement. *Public Culture* 4: 67–80.

– 1993. Envisioning kinship: Fetal imagery and relatedness. Paper presented at the annual meeting of the American Anthropological Association. Washington, D.C. November.

– 1998. Image of contradiction: Obstetrical ultrasound in American culture. In *Reproducing reproduction*, ed. Sarah Franklin and Helea Ragone. 15–45. Philadelphia: University of Pennsylvania Press.

Teasdale, François, Pierre Sarda, Harry Bard, et Andrée Grignon. 1985. Importance du dépistage échographique anténatal des malformations foetales corrigibles chirurgicalement. *L'Union Médicale du Canada* 114: 498–500.

Teghtsoonian, Katherine. 1996. Promises, promises: 'Choices for women' in Canadian and American child care policy debates. *Feminist Studies* 22: 119–46.

Tew, Marjorie. 1990. *Safer childbirth? A critical history of maternity care*. London: Chapman Hall.

Thobani, Sunera. 1993. From reproduction to mal[e]production: Women and sex selection technology. In *Misconceptions: The social construction of choice and the new reproductive and genetic technologies*, vol. 1. 138–53. Hull, PQ: Voyageur Press.

Thomas, Jo. 1999. Appeals court upholds ban on a type of late abortion. www/nytimes.com/library/national/102799partial-birth.html.

Thompson, Elizabeth. 1990. Three city hospitals risk losing bilingual status: Liberal MNA. *The Gazette* (Montreal). 22 September: A3.

Thompson, Richard C. 1983. The unknowns of ultrasound. *FDA Consumer* (March): 9–11.

Thorpe, Karen, Lisa Harker, Alison Pike, and Neil Marlow. 1993. Women's views of ultrasonography: A comparison of women's experiences of antenatal ultrasound screening with cerebral ultrasound of their newborn infant. *Social Science and Medicine* 36: 311–15.

Tibbetts, Janice. 1997. Supreme court won't recognize rights of fetus. *Times Colonist*. 1 November: A8.

Toi, A. 1990. Update in ultrasound: Fetal diagnosis. *The Canadian Journal of Ob/Gyn.* (December): 125–9.

Trofimenkoff, Susan. 1983. *The dream of nation: A social and intellectual history of Quebec.* Toronto: Gage.

Turner, Bryan. 1985. *The body in society: Explorations in social theory.* New York: Basil Blackwell.

– 1987. *Medical power and social knowledge.* Beverley Hills: Sage.

Turner, Victor. 1969. *The forest of symbols.* Ithaca: Cornell University Press.

United Nations. 1999. Monitoring human development: Enlarging people's choices. www.undp.org/hdro.

United States Department of Health and Human Services, National Institutes of Health. 1984. *Diagnostic ultrasound imaging in pregnancy.* National Institutes of Health Consensus Development Conference Statement 5.

Valverde, Mariana, and Lorna Weir. 1997. Regulating new reproductive and genetic technologies: A feminist view of recent Canadian government initiatives [commentary]. *Feminist Studies* 23(2): 419–23.

Villeneuve, Claude, Catherine Laroche, Abby Lippman, and Myriam Marrache. 1988. Psychological aspects of ultrasound imaging during pregnancy. *Canadian Journal of Psychiatry* 33: 530–5.

Wadhera, Surinder H. 1990. Births and birth rates, Canada, 1988. *Health Reports* 2: 86–8.

Wajcman, Judy. 1991. *Feminism confronts technology.* Cambridge, MA: Polity.

Waldenstrom, Urban, Ove Axelsson, Staffan Nilsson, Gunnar Eklund, Ole Fall, Solveig Lindeberg, and Ylva Sjodin. 1988. Effects of routine one-stage ultrasound screening in pregnancy: A randomised controlled trial. *The Lancet* (10 September): 585–8.

White, D.N. 1990. The conception, birth and childhood of WFUMB and its specialist and continental federations: The first quarter century. *Ultrasound in Medicine and Biology* 16: 333–48.

White, Deena, and Georgiana Beal. 1994. Québec: A Socio-Health Approach to Service Delivery. In *Women, medicine and health*, ed. B. Singh Bolaria and Rosemary Bolaria, 25–38. Halifax: Fernwood.

Whiteford, Linda M. 1995. Political economy, gender, and the social production of health and illness. In *Gender and health: An international perspective*, ed. C. Sargent and C. Brettel. 242–59. Englewood Cliffs, NJ: Prentice Hall.

Wild, J.J., and John M. Reid. 1954. Echographic visualization of lesions of the living intact breast. *Cancer Research* 14: 277–83.

Wilson, Susannah J. 1991. *Women, families and work*. Toronto: McGraw-Hill Ryerson.

Wilson-Smith, Anthony. 1995. Will he or won't he? *Maclean's* 108 (13 November): 14–17.

Woo, Joe. 1998. History of obstetrical ultrasound. www.ob-ultrasound.net/history.html.

– 1999. Obstetrical ultrasound: A comprehensive guide. www.ob-ultrasound.net/joewoo2.html.

Young, Diony. 1982. Obstetrical intervention and technology in the 1980s. *Women and Health* 7(3, 4) [special issue].

Young, Iris. 1984. Pregnant embodiment: Subjectivity and alienation. *Journal of Medicine and Philosophy* 9 (February): 45–62.

Yoxen, Edward. 1987. Seeing with sound: A study of the development of medical images. In *The social construction of technological systems*, ed. E. Bijker Wiebe. 281–303. Cambridge: MIT Press.

Index

abnormality. *See* fetal impairment
abortion: access to, 7–8, 48, 196–7,
 222n14; anti-choice perspectives
 and, 7–8, 17, 48, 197, 203–4, 222n5;
 in Canada, 10, 194, 197, 198; – debate, 48, 195; – funding of, 197;
 – history of, 7; – legal aspects, 48,
 194, 197, 221n10; – policies, 7;
 – Quebec physicians views on, 64–
 5; – variation in access to, 196–7;
 changing social meanings of, 204;
 feminist perspectives on, 17, 202–4;
 ideas about the fetus and, 8, 17, 48;
 in Japan, 9–10; partial birth, 8; in
 the Philippines, 190; Supreme
 Court of Canada decision (1988),
 48–9; United States, 7
amniocentesis, 170, 184; 'anti-
 mother,' 195
authoritative knowledge: post–
 Second World War consolidation
 of, 170; of sonographers, 173;
 women's reactions to, 186

babies: connections to nationhood,
 25; 'baby's first picture,' 22, 23
Barad, Karen, 22–3

Barbie, 204
Bill C-43, 194, 197. *See also* abortion,
 Canada
biomedical discourse: and anxiety,
 182; resistance to, 181; and social
 class, 181; variation in women's
 'commitment' to, 178–81
biopower, 18–20
birth. *See* childbirth
body(ies): anthropological theories
 of, 14–20; biopower and, 18;
 concepts of in Fiji, 17; cultural and
 historical variability of, 14;
 embodied perception and, 15–16;
 fetal (*see* fetal body); North
 American ideals of, 17; symbolic
 meanings, 16; visualization of
 interior (women's), 23
bonding, with the fetus, 67–8, 96,
 184, 217nn8, 9; ambivalence
 toward fetus, 68; between public
 and fetus, 200; facilitation of by
 descriptions of fetal image, 68;
 facilitation of by ultrasound, 68;
 and fetal awareness, 100; following
 fetal loss, 184; measurement of, 68;
 origins in ideology, 67

the ultrasound, 176; importance of regular, 86; institutionalization of, 23; lack of diversity in views, 209; as a marker for passage of pregnancy, 86; medicalization of, 23, 25; portrayal of fetus in, 95–7; and the portrayal of risk, 90–3; pregnancy guides, 25, 71, 88–97, 218n6; pro-choice language and imagery in, 222n5; in Quebec, 61–2; reasons for using, 89; women's different readings of, 179; women's perceptions of, 87. *See also* pregnancy, medicalization of

pregnant women: as echogenic tissue, 171; as maternal environments, 171; surveillance and social control of, 24, 45, 92, 135, 171, 183, 196

prenatal diagnosis, 46, 170, 202; decision to undergo, 207; as fetocentric, 19; as form of control, 62. *See also* amniocentesis; fetal heart monitor; ultrasound

prenatal period, as critical, 25

prescriptive technology, 37, 119

pro-life arguments. *See* abortion, anti-choice perspectives and

Quebec: birthrate in, 62; health care system, 61, 216nn2, 3; ideas about family in, 62; management of pregnancy and birth in, 58, 216n3; medical association's support for ultrasound, 64; medicalization of pregnancy in, 61–3; rise of distinct society, 51; utilization of ultrasound in, 61–3. *See also* ultrasound, Quebec

Queniart, Anne, 90

quickening, 71, 80, 99, 102, 160, 162, 176; comparison to ultrasound, 165–6; privileging embodied knowledge, 166; as a sign of fetal health, 182; technological, 173. *See also* fetal movement

radiologists, stereotypes of, 66

Rapp, Rayna, 178, 187

RCNRT (Royal Commission on New Reproductive Technologies), 41, 64, 127

reproduction: fetocentric view of, 171; meanings of, 62; and technology, 209

reproductive politics, 7, 194, 198. *See also* abortion

reproductive technology, 202

research study: characteristics of pregnancies, 56; education/occupations of, 55–6, 181; ethics, 59; ethnic and linguistic characteristics of, 53; methodology, 56–61, 215n1, 220n6; relationships of, 55; religion of, 53; self-identity of, 55–6; variation in education and occupation, 181; views on abortion, 182; women in, 52–3, 56, 220n6, 211–12

risk, 46, 86, 90–2, 198; to fetus, 90, 179; in Greece, 192–3; as justification for ultrasound, 174–5

Rothman, Barbara Katz, 19, 171

'seeing the baby,' 105–8, 141, 199, 220n4 (ch. 7)

'seeing' as a cultural process, 28–9, 116–17, 123, 191–2

self, 126; definition of, 13; determinants of, 13; multiple, 13. *See also* personhood